GARDENERS' QUESTION TIME

GARDENERS' QUESTION TIME

Ken Ford
Alan Gemmell
Fred Loads
Bill Sowerbutts

Illustrated by Quentin Blake

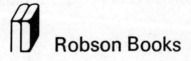 Robson Books

FIRST PUBLISHED IN GREAT BRITAIN IN 1981 BY
ROBSON BOOKS LTD., 28 POLAND STREET,
LONDON W1V 3DB. COPYRIGHT © 1981 KENNETH
FORD, ALAN GEMMELL, FRED LOADS, BILL
SOWERBUTTS

The publishers acknowledge with thanks the co-operation
of the BBC whose earlier booklets on *Gardeners' Question
Time* they have drawn on for this volume.

British Library Cataloguing in Publication Data

Ford, Ken
    Gardeners' question time.
    1. Gardening
    I. Title
    635   SB453

    ISBN 0-86051-111-1

Printed in Great Britain by Redwood Burn Ltd Trowbridge
Phototypesetting by Georgia Origination, Liverpool

CONTENTS

INTRODUCTION

Two o'clock Sunday. And for the last thirty years come hail, rain or shine, Home Service or Radio 4, it's been time for gardening! Not the real hard work of gardening but the more esoteric delights of *Gardeners' Question Time* and a million would-be gardeners, some of them with nothing more than a fly-blown pot plant to justify the title, tune in to listen to three voices persuading, arguing and at times meandering through the unending problems that beset gardeners at every level.

The start of the programme way back in 1947 was a series of happy accidents. A young producer named Robert Stead (later to become Controller of the BBC's North Region) decided that outside broadcasts were the coming thing and that he was going to take gardening to the people. He got in touch with an already established team of gardeners and scientists who had been spreading the gospel of *Dig For Victory* through the war years and the follow-up *Grow Your Own* campaign. He booked the singing room at the Broad Oak Hotel, Ashton-under-Lyne, asked the Smallshaw Gardening Society to provide an audience and he was in business. He decided to call the programme *How Does Your Garden Grow?* subtitled *Gardeners' Question Time* and it went on the air to listeners in the north in April 1947.

The rest is broadcasting history – *How Does Your Garden Grow?* succumbed to the sub-title, the four experts became three and two of those who took part in that very first programme, Fred Loads and Bill Sowerbutts, stayed with it. Professor, then Doctor, Alan Gemmell joined them in 1950, the programme then went out nationally and has done ever since. Bob Stead produced and chaired the proceedings for some time, then there came a succession of chairmen, the best known being Freddy Grisewood and Franklin Engelmann, who between them steered the programme through nearly twenty years.

My first contact with *Gardeners' Question Time* – in the flesh, so to speak – came in 1962; I was appointed Agricultural Talks Producer with the BBC in Leeds and was rather horrified to find that part of the deal was producing this gardening programme. I say horrified as, up to then, my life had been taken up with farming – and everyone knows what sort of gardeners farmers are! My only knowledge of *Gardeners' Question Time* was that it was greatly esteemed by my father who made everyone sit in complete silence while it ran its half-hour course – and that was when I was just a lad!

I first met the team in the lounge of a Harrogate hotel on my way to observe a programme at Northallerton. At that time Franklin Engelmann was nationally known as chairman of *Ask Me Another?*, which I thought was one of the best programmes on BBC television. Not having mixed in these sorts of circles before, I was somewhat apprehensive about this meeting but I needn't have worried; Franklin and the others treated me with kindness and courtesy right from the start. Mind you, I was their new producer and at that time I had little or no idea of the powers vested in this exalted position!

After this somewhat sketchy initiation I was thrown right in at the deep end when the BBC asked me to produce two programmes at Fleet in Hampshire a fortnight later. This put me into something of a tizzy as I hadn't the faintest idea of how to set about producing a radio programme, apart from an hour in the front row of the Northallerton epic. Nothing daunted, I set off on the long haul to Hampshire and tried to give a convincing performance as a hard-bitten, long-suffering old hand. It worked reasonably well and I remember driving home thinking how easy it all was. Perhaps it was just beginner's luck but looking back, over 1,000 programmes later, I now realize it was because of the sheer professionalism of the team and chairman who allowed nothing to stand in the way of their programme – even a rookie producer with a Yorkshire accent.

My first impressions of the *Gardeners' Question Time* team were as usual quite wrong – I saw Franklin Engelmann as a stern, slightly autocratic figure. When I got to know him better I realized he was exactly the opposite. He had a great sense of fun, liked people of all kinds and was a great gossip. His great hate was of pompous, small time officials who, I'm sorry to say, we do meet occasionally on our travels. He was a wonderfully professional broadcaster, a fact I don't think I really appreciated until after his death when I started casting around for a successor.

After much thought I came to the conclusion that I'd have to do it myself. On my first evening as I stood in front of the audience in the Royal Horticultural Society's Hall in Westminster I began to have serious misgivings – but it was a bit late to do anything about it. Here was I a comparative novice as far as broadcasting was concerned, actually proposing to control a gardening programme in front of 350 Fellows of the Royal Horticultural Society; worse still it was different from any programmes we'd done before – it was the programme's twenty-fifth anniversary and 1000th programme. Instead of ordinary people asking the questions we had an all star line-up with Frank Muir, Ted Moult, Esther Rantzen and Alan Melville. To make matters worse, in the front row sat the BBC's Director General and his wife, most of the Board of Governors and the controllers of Radios 1, 2 and 3. I must have been mad! I remember very little of the programme – except that in my imagination I could hear

Franklin right through it.

To me Franklin Engelmann represented the heyday of *Gardeners' Question Time*. I looked upon him as first a friend and secondly as the most professional broadcaster of that era. As regular listeners will know, I chaired the programme for a while after his death. Eventually we settled on Michael Barratt, already familiar to television viewers, to take the chair and he remained there for four and a half years, when I took over permanently.

And what about the others? For a start they'vew all got a great sense of humour – this I am sure is why the programme has lasted all these years. Gardening can be a dry subject, but their humour lifts it on to a different plane – it is so much easier to remember a bit of teaching if it is coupled with a funny story from Alan Gemmell, perhaps a bit of unbelievable folklore from Fred Loads or an unspeakable pronunciation from Bill Sowerbutts.

Bill Sowerbutts is a complex character – a very shrewd businessman, homespun philosopher, golfer of no mean ability and a music lover with a fair touch on the piano. Although on the programme he might sound a bit like the original Lancashire Lad, he plays this up and loves to mispronounce Latin names as part of the act. He likes looking round stately homes and also likes to visit Holland occasionally to see what they are up to in the horitcultural business.

Bill is invaluable on the programme as he knows all the ins and outs of the horticultural business and can quickly tell the rest of us what anything is going to cost – and this can be very useful to counteract some of the expensive flights of fancy by the others.

And what of our professor – Alan Gemmell? He is a man of many parts – JP, chairman of this and that, visiting professor to universities in many countries (although his visits recently have been exclusively to Africa) and a keen golfer. Alan doesn't suffer fools gladly. Having said this, when you get to know him you can appreciate his logical mind, Scottish charm and impish sense of humour which bubbles over. In

22

fact, once or twice we've had to stop recording when this sense of humour has got the better of him and he's collapsed into helpless giggles. One occasion was rather embarrassing as, with tears rolling down his face, he was unable to tell us what was so funny – it turned out to be a lady's hat in the front row.

I think his greatest contribution to the programme is in summing up. His academic training takes over and at the end of each question he inevitably ties up the loose ends. This in itself is worth a good deal and, of course, his explanations on the scientific side of gardening gives a great deal to the programme.

Fred Loads can draw on sixty years of experience of practical gardening at all levels. He has few hobbies, preferring to spend his time looking at other people's gardens. In fact, his whole life is gardening – he has several inventions, all attached to gardening of course, which include a revolutionary instant turf which is now being marketed all over the world. His two interests outside gardening are eating and fruit machines. On one occasion we were in the Isle of Man recording a couple of programmes and he insisted on going to the casino where he'd heard they had the best selection of one-armed bandits in the British Isles. I shall always treasure the memory of Fred's beaming pink face as he stood there practically up to his knees in shillings.

Fred Loads has now retired after more than thirty-three years with *Gardeners' Question Time* and we wish him many more active years in his favourite hobby – gardening, what else? It will never quite be the same without him, but the two new boys, Geoffrey Smith and Clay Jones, bring a new dimension to the programme. Perhaps they'll see us through the next thirty-three years!

K F

I

Soil, Compost and Cultivation

Knowing Your Garden Soil

Knowing your soil is said to be most important in gardening of all kinds. Mr J. C. from the Rutland Horticultural Society would like the Team to give a few hints to someone taking over new land.

The first thing anyone moving into a new garden or on to new land should do is to take a look at the weeds. These are the natural indicators of soil fertility and you can be fairly sure that if weeds will grow well, so will a large number of plants. There may be special conditions which prevent certain species being able to grow, but on the whole, good rich land will grow big fat weeds.

If you have any botanical training you can learn more from the weeds, as the type of weed can give you an indication of the acidity of the soil. For example, if the weeds are mainly docks and sorrel, or maybe poppies, then it is likely that the soil will be acid. If there is a lot of spurrey, groundsel, and chickweed, you can be fairly sure that the soil will be rich and quick-draining. If, on the other hand, the surface of the soil is wet and there is a lot of moss present, then, quite certainly, this soil is deficient in drainage and would be very much drier and warmer if some artificial drains could be introduced or if it were treated with lime.

Before spending any money at all on plants or shrubs, it is therefore a good idea to take a look at the things which are growing. Once you have done this, then it is sound policy to spend a year, or maybe even two years, correcting any of the defects or deficiencies possessed by the soil. After tha, then maybe it is worth spending the money on permanent occupiers of the garden.

It is most important to find out whether you have an acid or alkaline soil and, if you mistrust your reading of this through your natural indicators, then buy a simple soil testing kit. These are relatively cheap and easy to use.

It would take a very long time to specify all the things which one ought to look at, but the most important is quite certainly the amount of compost or humus or manure that you can apply to the soil, because by applying these materials, one encourages the multiplication of earthworms and soil bacteria which add a great deal to the richness of the soil. Compost not only opens the soil up and improves the drainage, but also, especially in a sandy soil, helps to hold a certain amount of moisture.

Another tip which has sometimes helped people taking over new gardens is the very simple one of growing quite a wide range of annuals in different parts of the garden. Because annuals are cheap, they are quite expendable and they can give quite a good indication of the degree of fertility of the soil in various areas. For example, if you put in small annuals you can see in which part of the garden they grow best and you will, therefore, be fairly sure that this part of the garden is the richest. You therefore devote more time to the more impoverished areas.

Paraquat

Mr N. C. of Liskeard asks, 'What is the action of paraquat, and how does it differ from hormone weedkillers? At what temperatures is it more or less effective?'

Paraquat acts through the photosynthetic mechanisms of a plant – in other words, the food manufacturing cells of the leaves. Therefore, it is essential that it goes on to the foliage or other green parts of the weeds.

It differs from hormone weedkillers in that they are selective and some will kill weeds but not grasses, but paraquat kills all green growth on which it is sprayed. A further difference is that paraquat is inactivated almost as soon as it touches the soil, whereas hormone weedkillers will persist in the soil and can accumulate over a number of years. Paraquat is not translocated through the soil to the root system like some weedkillers.

Quality of light and length of day have an effect on paraquat, and it acts much more quickly on a bright day, and should be applied preferably in the morning to get the quickest kill. If applied on a dull day or in winter it is no less effective, but takes longer to kill off the weeds. Warm temperatures have a speeding-up effect too, and in tropical climates, where it is used to clear fruit plantations, its effect is virtually immediate.

A further advantage with paraquat is that if there is a downpour, say, only half an hour after application, it will not wash off as it penetrates into the leaves very quickly indeed.

Treatment for a Sandy Soil

Mrs M. J. H. has great difficulty in growing either flowers or vegetables because her garden soil is very sandy. What treatment can be given to this type of soil?

Sandy soils are notoriously difficult because they are very quick draining and in consequence tend to dry out especially in a dry season. Because of the rapid passage of moisture through the soil, there is also a great tendency for nitrogen to be washed out each winter, so that it becomes necessary to feed with artificial fertilizers containing nitrogen every year. Better still, it is advisable to use a balanced mixed fertilizer. Sandy soils, however, have advantages, for they are easily worked and there is no doubt about it but that they heat up much more quickly in the spring and plants in them are very much less liable to root rots.

It should be clear, therefore, that without a certain amount of treatment, plants will not thrive very well in sandy soils and the treatment basically is the addition of plenty of humus. The purist might say that we cannot apply humus, all we can apply is farmyard manure or compost, and the soil bacteria turns into humus. Whichever point of view you take, it is certainly advisable to apply as much humus or compost as one can, and if there is not enough garden refuse to hand, then some wheat or oat straw may be bought in and composted with one of the so-called 'starting' or 'activating' agents. The addition of a heavy dressing of compost, let's say 28 lb or so to the square yard, will benefit the soil immensely and it will begin to hold moisture and be much more fertile. The compost should not be dug in deeply but is best restricted to the top 3-4 in of soil and when it is well rotted down you will be able to grow even such fussy vegetables as cauliflower or lettuce.

If in this sandy soil flowers are required, then, of course, the amount of compost necessary is very much less and anything up to 7 lb to the square yard would make a considerable difference. The only possible exception to this advice is in the case of onions and leeks and celery which require such a great deal of organic matter in the soil that it becomes rather impractical to try to build a sandy soil up to the necessary level.

Good Soil

Mr M. J. of Maes-Yr-Haf, near Tonypandy, would like a definition of 'good soil'. What are its qualities and is it better than the well known soilless composts?

The question suggests that this refers to soil for potting and up to a few years ago the ideal mixture for this would have been a John Innes peat/soil compost. Nowadays peat/sand composts containing trace elements and slow release nitrogen are available and these are very effective.

The whole gardening scene has changed from the private gardener on an estate where manure, leaf mould and the right sort of sand was readily obtainable, to the mass of people who have to rely almost entirely on what they can buy or what their own small gardens can produce.

One of the big drawbacks to using soil from one's own garden is that nine times out of ten it has been manured and limed and for many pot plants lime is harmful. What might be good soil for vegetables or roses can be completely wrong for many plants normally grown in pots in the greenhouse.

For the true John Innes compost the base should be turf cut from a meadow which hasn't been ploughed for 50 to 100 years, so you can see the problems involved. Shortage of this commodity has meant that even John Innes has been made up from very variable types of soil giving vastly differing results and it is because of this that the soilless composts have been evolved. There are a number of these using various types of peat, sand and clay fractions to which fertilizer is added.

There are still many gardeners who like to use John Innes formula and provided you have access to 100-year-old turf to make up your loam you might like to have a got at making your own. To complicate the issue, true J. I. compost is made with Kettering loam but you might get a reasonable product with a good local loam.

The formula for John Innes seed compost is as follows: Parts by bulk: 2 pts loam, 1 pt peat, 1 pt sand plus 1½ oz of

31

superphosphate and ¾ oz of chalk per bushel.

John Innes potting compost: 7 pts loam, 3 pts peat, 2 pts sand plus ¼ lb of J. I. base fertilizer and ¾ oz of chalk per bushel.

The John Innes base fertilizer can be bought at any good horticultural shop and the chalk should be omitted when used for lime-hating plants such as ericas and azaleas.

And lastly a word of warning about peat – it will absorb a considerable amount of moisture but if it is allowed to dry out it is extremely difficult to wet again.

Artificial Manure

Mr A. R. H. of Barnet would like some advice on the application of artificial fertilizers. He says local gardeners seem to disagree on whether they should be applied as a top dressing or dug in like farmyard manure.

It is always best to apply artificial manures as a top dressing; their big advantage is that they are soluble and when they dissolve they move downwards. If they are dug in they are very soon going to be below the level at which roots will be able to make use of them. There are one or two exceptions to this rule and one of these is application to potatoes. It is generally accepted that an application at the bottom of the drill when planting is beneficial.

As a general rule, two or three light dustings on the surface during the growing season are better than just one heavy application, always taking care that the fertilizer doesn't get on to the foliage.

This has been a controversial point amongst gardeners ever since artificial fertilizers have been invented and many experiments have taken place on fertilizer placement.

For convenience, fertilizers, whether they be compounds or single fertilizers, are divided roughly into two types: quick acting fertilizers such as nitrate or soda and super-phosphate;

and the slow acting fertilizers which are mainly organic.

Base fertilizers, whether they are organic or inorganic, are distributed evenly through the soil either by forking or by rotovating. This is usually done about a fortnight before sowing or planting so that they can start breaking down into components suitable for assimilation by the roots.

Special formulations of slow acting fertilizers used as a base dressing are available and this technique is also applied to the making of new lawns when a pre-seeding fertilizer is applied and worked into the soil about a fortnight before sowing.

Easily soluble, quick acting fertilizers are usually reserved for application to the surface either dry or in solution. In the garden they are usually applied dry, either in the form of a compound containing nitrogen, potash and phosphates mainly for convenience; for specialist subjects such as pot-grown plants and tomatoes, these fertilizers are usually mixed into water and applied as a liquid. These can be supplemented with highly refined chemical formulations applied to the leaves in the form of foliar feed.

The reason for digging manure and compost into the soil is that, if left on the top of the soil, it tends to dry out and will not break down quickly enough. If the weather and worms are depended upon to pull the manure or compost down into the soil it might take two or three years before becoming available to plants.

Well rotted stuff may be worked into the top two or three inches of the soil, but rougher compost or manure should be dug in more deeply, particularly if the soil is 'new'.

Another reason for digging in compost is to encourage the development of deep roots which will help to anchor the plant firmly especially in windy districts. Feeding roots, however, are not usually very deeply buried in the soil and so it is advantageous to most plants and crops to apply a surface mulch of compost which will shade the surface of the soil and so protect it from drying out and damaging these feeding roots. Further, as the question indicates, the food material in the compost will then slowly become available to the plant.

Thus, as in so many gardening problems, by doing both

things one can get the best of both worlds.

New Fungicides

Mrs W. E. R. of Cambridge says that there is now a useful range of insecticides available for garden use but present day fungicides aren't nearly as effective. Are there any new developments in this direction?

For many years the scientists' dream has been the development of systemic fungicides, something that has been lacking in the range of garden chemicals. These are complex organic substances, practically non-poisonous to humans and with a long life in the plant. This is now fact with at least one systemic fungicide on the market based on a chemical called benomyl and it covers a wide range of mildews and blights – most of the fungal diseases that attack plants in fact.

'Systemic' simply means that the product is absorbed into the system of the plant, a fact which makes for ease of application as it doesn't matter whether you cover the plant completely or not when spraying. It has the big advantage too that it lasts for some weeks, cutting out the need for constant applications.

Vermiculite

K. V., a schoolboy from Hingham in Norfolk, asks, 'What is vermiculite and what is it used for?'

Vermiculite is made from mica which is a mineral found in the ground. When mica is heated to a very high temperature it puffs out and becomes rather like a breakfast cereal. It is then called exfoliated mica. As such it is a very light and sterile material as well as being completely clean. It can easily be washed and will suffer no damage. It is, therefore, a very good medium in which to germinate seeds or to root cuttings, for in it there is no danger from pests or diseases. The only real problem raised by using vermiculite is that it is a completely pure medium and therefore contains no food materials whatsoever. Obviously, the way to overcome this difficulty is to germinate the seeds or root the cuttings in vermiculite and assoon as the plants start to grow (and require food materials) to transplant them into an ordinary compost.

Some growers find that vermiculite tends to become acid in use and this problem is overcome by mixing it with an equal quantity of peat in order to obtain a better balance. It must be stressed, however, that many growers use vermiculite on its own without any added mixture of peat to it.

Vermiculite is used for a number of purposes other than growing plants. It is light, heat resistant and nearly sound proof, so it is used extensively in the building trade as an insulator for buildings. When buying vermiculite for use in the greenhouse or garden care must be taken that it is horticultural grade vermiculite that is bought, because the material used for building is exceedingly alkaline and is not at all conducive to plant growth.

Peat Mulch

Mr T. S. T. of Shaldon, Devon, has for the past four years put a 2 in mulch of peat on his rose bed. As the peat is slow to break down there is now a layer which comes too far up each rose bush and which seems to be making the bed sour. What is the remedy?

Peat is often recommended for rose beds but, like anything else, it can do harm if too much is applied. it could be used as a weed smother occasionally, say, every alternate year, but if used for this purpose it is best to use the coarse non-acid peat. The fine horticultural peat should never be used for this purpose as it tends to stop air and rain from getting through.

When applied every year, peat is so slow to break down that it could eventually alter the character of the soil by making it soft and puffy and so unsuitable for roses. Where a thick layer of peat has been used, it is best to remove some of it and to top dress with a complete rose fertilizer containing phosphates, potash and nitrogen and fork it in *very* lightly.

A much better mulch for roses would be straw or seaweed compost or even old mushroom bed compost. Such composts would rot down much more quickly than peat and, what is more important, they contain a considerable quantity of plant food.

Herbicides Hardening the Ground

Mr T. M. of Darwen, Lancashire, recalls reading some time ago that herbicides make the ground hard. If this is the case, how does one go about getting water and fertilizers to penetrate the soil, or is it just as porous even though it is hard?

If soil is left bare and exposed to the elements it does one of two things: it either blows away and one gets soil erosion, or else it forms a relatively hard crust. The purpose of weed-killers and herbicides is to kill vegetation and by doing this the ground is, of course, left bare and under these situations one would naturally expect it to become hard. So the first part of the answer is that it is not the herbicides which make the ground hard, but rather the absence of vegetation and cultivation.

The second part of the question concerns how water and fertilizer get into the soil. Although the ground may seem hard to us, there are certainly a large number of small cracks and crevices in the ground into which rain water will soak and, in so doing, will carry down fertilizers and any food materials which one may apply. It must also be remembered that where there is a crust on the soil there is no doubt that the amount of water lost from the soil is going to be considerably reduced, and thus the necessity for watering could almost be eliminated. Experiments have shown that where weedkillers are used to keep weeds down, beneath roses and shrubs and raspberries and so on, then feeding is more successful, probably because there is no weed competition for the nutrients. The subjects do not seem to suffer at all from what used to be thought the disadvantage of growing in a soil with a hard surface. A corollary of this is that where herbicides are used under shrubs, it is largely a waste of time and energy to cultivate the soil, as all one does under these conditions is to bring seeds of the various weeds to the surface where they will germinate and grow, and the whole process will have to be repeated. It is much better to leave the soil alone once the weeds have been killed, to let the weeds decay naturally and there will be very little need to repeat the process.

Couch Grass

Mrs H. R. of Hutton Rudby in Yorkshire has a problem with couch grass, wicks, twitch, wickens, call it what you will. She would like to know whether there is any good way of eradicating this pest other than by removing every piece and burning.

This is a very difficult weed to get rid of as any small fragments of roots left in the soil will start to grow. This means it is nearly impossible to get rid of it by forking, picking out and burning. There is now a successful chemical treatment for couch grass and several preparations are available, based on a substance called dalapon. This is best applied in the winter, when nothing else is growing and should eliminate the weed after two winter applications.

Another way is to spray the affected area in spring with a paraquat weedkiller, or if you don't like using chemicals it can effectively be smothered out by applying a thick layer of lawn mowings.

Couch grass is a bigger problem if it is amongst plants in, say, a herbaceous border or rockery. Chemical treatment becomes impossible as both dalapon and paraquat would kill the plants as well as the weeds. It might be possible to apply paraquat between subjects using an accurate sprayer or a weeder bar on a watering can, but this wouldn't really be very successful as the shoots are usually entwined in those of the plants you wish to keep. In a case like this it's a case of laboriously digging out every root. If a bed is badly affected it is probably better to take the plants out and put them somewhere else for a year or two and get the bed really cleaned up before bringing them back.

Another of the things one must be careful with when there is couch grass in the garden is not to get it into the compost heap otherwise it grows there and if you spread your compost about then in fact you will be spreading this weed. It is also wise, when you buy plants or shrubs from a nursery, to take very great care to remove any bits of root or rhizome which might belong to couch grass from any soil adhering to the plants. Many a person has introduced this pest into his garden simply by buying a dirty stock from a nursery or even being given it by a 'friend'.

A Replacement for DDT

Mrs A. A. of Morpeth asks, 'As DDT is no longer obtainable, can the Team say what can be used with safety in its place?'

DDT has been banned for use by the amateur gardener for three reasons: (a) because it persists for a very long time in the soil, (b) because it does not break down in the human body and (c) it is a broad spectrum insecticide and kills all insects, even the friendly ones.

These are the disadvantages that have to be overcome by a

new chemical, and it looks as though a substance named carburyl will meet these requirements. It kills nearly all the insects that DDT kills, including, unfortunately, honey bees. Like DDT it isn't effective against greenfly or against the raspberry beetle.

It is also completely non-poisonous – about one-tenth as poisonous as DDT; it doesn't have a long life and breaks down in the soil in about two weeks, so won't eventually be washed into rivers and oceans, as has happened with DDT and some of the other persistent insecticides. This also means that if fruit or vegetables treated with carburyl are eaten, there's no risk attached to it as it is quickly broken down in the body.

So the thing to look for is an insecticide containing this substance carburyl. It won't be sold under this name, but under various brands, and somewhere on the pack it will tell you that it contains carburyl. Use it like DDT, not when pollinating insects are around.

Nettles

Mr A. S. of London has cleared a piece of waste land to make a garden. It was infested with nettles which are still growing, and he'd like to know how long he can expect the seeds to keep germinating.

Nettles always follow civilization, usually where there has been heavy manuring or perhaps on the site of an old rubbish heap, where vegetable matter has made the soil rich. In this case, it's probably the underground stolons and not seed that is making new growth. If this is the annual stinging nettle, it is reasonably easy to get rid of by using a total weedkiller: paraquat, or nitrate of soda on the young growths is very effective. If it is the perennial nettle, then it is necessary to use a hormone-type weedkiller. There are several preparations on the market specifically formulated to deal with this nettle.

The treatment necessary depends on what sort of crops are

to be grown in the garden, if it is to be put down as a lawn, then there is no problem, as frequent mowing will kill out the nettles in about a year. It wouldn't be wise to plant herbaceous subjects or shrubs until this land has been cleaned up and probably a crop of potatoes for a year or two would be the best way of cleaning it.

Horticultural Gypsum

Mr M. S. of Swansea wants to know whether horticultural gypsum used on heavy soil would leave a residue that might be harmful to any vegetable, particularly potatoes, planted the following year?

Well, of course, gypsum is a recognized treatment for lightening heavy soils and is the basis of many of the soil conditioners on the market these days. If horticultural gypsum alone is used it should be applied at the rate of 6 oz to the sq yd and this should be done during the winter months.

One thing that should be remembered is that it will cause a quicker breakdown of fertilizers and subsequent applications should be heavier to take this into account.

Applications of gypsum shouldn't have any effect on vegetables. It is neutral and if used on acid soils will not raise the pH value which means it also won't correct acidity. It may safely be used on soil for lime-hating plants such as azaleas and rhododendrons.

The real answer to this question is that it is quite safe to apply gypsum on the vegetable garden and in fact it is claimed that it is instrumental in reducing potato scab and it may actually increase the flavour of vegetables due to its sulphur content.

Hormone Weedkillers

Mr J. A. of Heald Green in Cheshire likes to compost his lawn mowings but would like the Team's advice about using these after applications of hormone weedkillers. Will they do any harm and if so how long must he wait before the lawn mowings can be composted again?

The types of hormone weedkillers used on lawns for the control of broad leaved weeds can be reckoned to persist in the grass mowings for at least three months. This means that lawn mowings straight from the collecting box certainly should not be thrown on to flower beds as a mulch.

Preferably for the first two or three cuts after applying the hormone, the clippings should be composted separately and used for digging into the vegetable garden rather than putting into a general compost heap which eventually may find its way on to the flower borders. Certainly it is best to play safe and work on a figure of three months. Really the only risks are when the clippings are used as a mulch immediately or may be composted and used in the herbaceous border later – a slight trace of hormone can have disastrous effects there. There is little risk if used around shrubs or roses and, if it is dug into the soil of a vegetable garden, the chemicals very soon break down.

Having said all that, if you have any doubts apply the three-month rule rigidly and you need have no worries.

Bindweed

Mr J. R. of Tadcaster asks, 'Is there really any way of eradicating bindweed from the garden other than by sheer hard work?'

This is the large-flowered convolvulus and indicates a certain amount of neglect in a garden if it is present in flower beds, etc., as the roots should always be removed when digging. However, it is difficult to get rid of it completely and it is usually found climbing up fences, hedges, poles, etc. There is a smaller variety, the lesser bindweed, which can be an even bigger nuisance.

In fact both types of bindweed can be fairly easily eradicated these days by using one of the hormone weed-killers based on 2.4-D, 2.4.5-T or MCPA. Many people say they have tried these on bindweed and they haven't worked. This is because they tend to apply them at too great a strength. The young growth of bindweed is very tender and easily killed by a strong dose of hormones so the technique is to apply it at about half the recommended strength so that it will be absorbed by the plant and passed down to the roots, which then burst and the plant dies. If the hormone solution is applied at too great a strength, the leaves die before the substances are absorbed and the plant quickly puts out new growths.

Fred Loads's technique (which he swears by) is to allow the bindweed to make growths 3 to 4 ft long, to unwind them and dip the leaves in this weak hormone solution which he carries around in a dish or bucket. When this is done correctly the leaves should gradually yellow and take about three weeks to disappear. If they die off more quickly than this then the treatment is most likely to be a failure.

Compost Heaps

Miss E. O. D. of Chelmsford would like to know how to make a compost heap correctly.

Compost is produced by the action of soil bacteria on organic matter such as straw or garden refuse, and for the necessary chemical changes to take place oxygen and a certain amount of moisture are necessary. The manufacture of the compost is greatly assisted by the presence of nitrogen and this is usually added in the form of sulphate of ammonia or calcium cyanamide.

The compost heap should be built on soil, not concrete, and to keep it tidy four stakes should be driven in to form a square or oblong surrounded with coarse mesh wire netting. Start off with a 2 to 3 in layer of soil and 2 to 3 in layer of straw or garden refuse, followed by a sprinkling of the nitrogenous material and so on until the heap is built up. To save carting soil from another part of the garden, it may be taken from around the compost enclosure and so at the same time a drainage channel around the heap will be formed. Never use woody refuse or diseased material, and don't make the heap too big or air will not be able to get through to the centre to help decomposition. If the heap is too dry, decomposition will be slowed down and watering may be needed during dry spells, but the inclusion of green materials such as cabbage leaves will help to avoid dryness. Conversely in wet districts it may be necessary to put a shelter over the heap. This could simply be a layer of heavy soil patted down with the back of a spade.

Hoof and Horn Meal

Mr G. M. D. of Sanderstead, Surrey, wonders how much hoof and horn should be used in the garden. Is he right in thinking that it is equivalent to bone meal plus some organic matter?

Hoof and horn meal contains a much higher percentage of nitrogen (12-14%) than bone meal (about 4%) which is primarily phosphatic with only a small percentage of nitrogen. Hoof and horn is quite a rich food and is slow acting, so that it is a very good material to mix into a potting compost where it will become available to the plant over a long period. It is also a valuable ingredient in a lawn fertilizer because it supplies nitrogen to keep the grasses in good condition in June, July and August when quite often they start losing colour.

Hoof and horn is not a good fertilizer for fast growing vegetable crops like lettuce or cabbage as it is too slow acting, sulphate of ammonia or nitrate of soda being better for growing crops.

Farmyard Manure

Mr H. D. B. of Swindon has been told that the best thing for the garden is stable or farmyard manure and yet these have a much lower manurial value in terms of NPK than fish meal, poultry droppings, bone meal or National Growmore. Will the Team please explain?

The answer to this is that in order to have a good rich soil a number of things are required. Nitrogen, phosphorus, and potash (NPK) are essential but there are other requirements like organic compounds which help to bind the soil particles into crumbs, as they are called, and these are available in abundance in farmyard manure. Thus farmyard manure improves the drainage, the tilth, and the aeration of the soil as well as providing a certain amount of NPK. Fish meal and the other substances mentioned are not so good at supplying these additional things although they do supply NPK. The real value of farmyard manure, therefore, is not solely what it contributes to the soil but also what it does to the soil.

There is a safety value also in using farmyard manure or well made compost, for trace element deficiencies seldom occur where the land is well manured. For instance boron deficiency does not occur in celery, nor boron or manganese deficiencies in cauliflowers. So what is needed for optimum growth is both the farmyard manure or compost and then additional fertilizers during the growing season.

Usually, well made compost is equal to farmyard manure but compost is only as good as the materials put into it. If materials are used which have little value, the compost also will be of little value and that is why straw is recommended as the best basis for compost in order to arrive at the nearest approximation to farmyard manure.

At the Agricultural Research Stations, prolonged experiments have been carried out with a number of different natural manures and surprisingly good results have been obtained by using sawdust, which has considerably improved the structure of the soil. It is not recommended that sawdust should be used indiscriminately all over the garden, but if organic materials are really scarce, a heavy sprinkling of sawdust as a mulch will do a lot of good, plus the fertilizers applied during the growing season.

Sequestrenes and Limestone

Mrs M. S. who lives in Ramsbury, Wiltshire, writes, 'I have read glowing accounts of the use of sequestrenes on limey soils. As this is of considerable interest to gardeners in this area, I wonder if any of the Team have had personal experience of their use? Also, if it is necessary to water the garden after their use, would it be necessary to use rainwater instead of the local water?'

In a limestone area, such as Ramsbury, there is very often a shortage of iron in the soil, and the idea of these sequestrene compounds is to put iron into the soil in such a form that the lime will not tie it up, and the iron will be available to the plants.

Subjects which suffer particularly from iron deficiency when growing in an alkaline soil are azaleas and rhododendrons, and these certainly benefit from the use of sequestrene Fe, as also do fruit trees, shrubs, gooseberries, blackcurrants, and raspberries. It is fairly expensive but is applied only sparingly and it may last for two years although an annual application is advised in limestone areas. For big trees use 2 oz per tree, but on roses, hydrangeas, and the like, use ½ oz per plant. The best time to put it on is in late winter or early spring so that it can be well washed in. It can be used again in summer-time providing there is plenty of moisture available. Sequestrenes are chemicals so composed that they do not react with lime and even if limey water is used it will not make any difference.

These chemicals should not be used on every apple tree or rhododendron in all parts of the country, but only if the leaves of the trees or bushes are going yellow at a time of year when they should normally be green. Leaves can be expected to go slightly yellow in August, but in spring and summer the leaves should be green, and it is only if they are yellow then that sequestrenes are indicated.

The use of sequestrenes will not mean that in districts like Ramsbury, azaleas and rhododendrons will grow really luxuriantly but they will be helped considerably.

Sterilizing Soil

'Why and how does one sterilize soil?' asked Miss E. M. C.

Soil sterilization is carried out for a variety of reasons but the ultimate purpose is to secure a soil which is free of diseases, insect pests and weed seeds. This means that so-called 'sterile' soil is not quite the same as a sterile dressing in a hospital, for the latter must also be free of bacteria whereas sterile soil usually contains many bacteria which are beneficial to plants. A better, and more correct term, would be 'partially sterilized' soil, for if all bacterial life were removed from a soil it would be inert and not very well able to support plant life.

Commercial growers often use steam to heat the soil to around 212° F. This is a temperature which kills all harmful pests and diseases but does not kill all the beneficial bacteria. Among the bacteria which are not killed are those which can transfer nitrogen from the air to the soil and, as a result, steam sterilized soil is rich in nitrogen consequently needing the addition of phosphates and potash to balance it up. It is not usually practicable for an amateur to steam his soil, but electrical sterilizers are available which are very effective. Small quantities of soil for sowing seedlings can be baked in an oven or saturated with boiling water, but it is important that the temperature is not allowed to get too high, or the humus in the soil may be consumed, with detrimental results.

Various chemicals can be used to sterilize soil, too, such as formaldehyde, cresylic acid and metham-sodium, and the manufacturers' recommendations should be closely followed. Attention must be drawn to the difficulty experienced by the amateur in sterilizing soil chemically for it is often very difficult to ensure that the chemical agent reaches all parts of the soil and if this is not done thoroughly then reinfection will occur very quickly.

Nitrification

Mrs O. O. has been told that nitrification is the process by which nitrate is formed in the soil. How is the process brought about?

Nitrates are formed in the soil from nearly any substance which contains nitrogen. In gardening many such substances are used, for example, dried blood, bone meal, farmyard manure, sewage, sulphate of ammonia and so on. All these contain nitrogen but it is essential to realize that the nitrogen is usually incorporated in highly complicated chemicals such as proteins or amino acids which plants cannot use. The only nitrogen freely available to plants must be in the form of nitrates, and so most of the nitrogen which is added to soils in any form must be acted on by bacteria first.

An example can make this clear. Dried blood contains nitrogen in the form of protein. When the blood is put into the soil it is used by many bacteria and fungi as a source of food and incorporated into their bodies. When the bacterium

47

dies, it, in its turn, is used by other bacteria for food and eventually after passing through a long chain of micro-organisms the nitrogen will appear in the form of ammonia. There then follows a kind of competition between two groups of bacteria – one group, the nitrifying bacteria, converting the ammonia to nitrates, and the other group, the de-nitrifying bacteria, converting it to nitrogen and returning it to the atmosphere.

It is, therefore, clearly to the advantage of the gardener to encourage the nitrate-forming bacteria in the soil. This can be done in many ways – for example, by making certain that there is always a good supply of humus in the soil, for bacteria use the humus to help make the nitrates. A good supply of air is also essential, for nitrates contain oxygen and this is usually obtained from the atmosphere. A water-logged soil or a tight, wet compost heap will slow down or prevent the formation of nitrates.

II
Lawns

Conditions for the Best Lawns

Mr G. G. wants to know what conditions should be created in a soil to make the best lawn. Is it true that the soil should be slightly acid and that lime dressings are harmful?

Good drainage is essential, so prepare the soil and put in a drainage system first. This does not necessarily mean elaborate tile drains as sometimes all that is necessary is to break up the subsoil with a fork. A layer of coarse clinker or rubble will certainly ensure that the drainage is adequate. If the lawn is well drained it will stay desirably acid but, in order to ensure that this is maintained, spike the turf every autumn and then top-dress with fairly coarse sand. Ideally the lawn should then be brushed to sweep the sand into the holes and so prevent a badly draining surface mat of grass from being formed.

Position is the next consideration and, if possible, the area should be open to the sun for moss will be troublesome if there is considerable shade.

After a year or so, depending on the quality of the soil, an organic feed such as fine peat mixed with sand and a turf

51

fertilizer will help. Use one part of peat to two parts of sand and 2 to 3 ozs of fertilizer, and apply at the rate of 2 lb to the sq yd brushed evenly into the grasses. Additionally it is sometimes wise to mix about a quarter of an ounce of the finest grass seed with the dressing.

Lime and basic slag encourage clover and coarse grasses and so should not be used on a lawn, but a correctly balanced fertilizer or sulphate of ammonia will maintain acidity. If the lawn is uneven do not roll to make it flat but level it up by means of the organic dressing or even by using sand alone.

Always start any feeding early in the year, say the beginning of March, for this is when the finer grasses start to grow; feed later and it is more than likely that the coarser grasses will get the benefit.

Starting a Lawn

From Kimberworth in South Yorkshire, Mr C. W. L.'s question follows on naturally. In making a lawn on a new estate, would you advocate the use of the minimum of first class grass seed or the maximum of an inferior seed, where the emphasis is on the ornamental rather than the hard wearing?

A really good lawn cannot be made by using inferior lawn grass seed containing ryegrass however much is used but, if the lawn is going to be subjected to heavy wear, then a seed mixture containing 10% short seeded ryegrass is best. For good ornamental turf, first class rye-free lawn seed should be used, consisting of a mixture of 70% Chewings' fescue and 30% browntop, 1 o only per sq yd being needed; in practice, it is almost as cheap to use the best seed. When purchasing lawn seed it is not always possible or desirable to obtain the varieties separately, but make sure that the seed is stated to be 'ryegrass free' and it will probably then contain Chewings' fescue and browntop, perhaps with one or two more fine varieties, but no ryegrass.

The finest grasses are slow to establish and unless you are willing to weed the very young lawn to get the coarse grasses out, they may eventually take over. The real secret of producing first class turf is in looking after it during the first six months so that the fine grasses have a chance to become established.

There is a lot of emphasis today on the use of hormone sprays for killing weeds in turf, but these should not be used during the first six months after sowing or the grass will yellow and, in some cases, die. You can, however, buy special formulations for use on newly sown lawns – look out for these if weeds come early.

Moss in a Lawn

Mr J. H. W. lives in Conway and his cri-de-cœur *is, 'I am troubled with patches of moss on my lawns, which have spread considerably during the past year. I've given the usual treatment – proprietary fertilizers, weedkiller and occasional doses of sulphate of ammonia to eradicate clover. The lawns are spiked three times a year and the lawn rake applied at intervals. Can the Team advise me whether this raking spreads moss spores and whether my treatment is the correct one?'*

It should always be recognized that moss on a lawn is a sign that something is wrong with the method of treatment and so any attempts to eradicate the moss, without removing the conditions which encourage it, can only have a very short-term effect. If a lawn is badly drained, e.g. on a clay soil or in deep shade, then moss will almost certainly invade it. If it is uneven so that the tops of ridges are 'skimmed' bare by the mower moss will get in, and finally if the lawn is so badly cared for and underfed that the coarse grasses oust the fine ones, then almost inevitably moss will gain entry.

53

Aeration of lawns by spiking is a step in the right direction towards controlling moss but once the spike holes have been made it is important to brush into them something such as a mixture of one third peat, one third soil and one third ¼ in charcoal or coarse sand, which will keep these miniature drainage holes open.

A Substitute for Grass in the Shade

Is there any substitute for grass which Mr J. M. can grow on the north side of the house in a place shaded by large trees?

Seeds of the grass, Poa nemoralis, could be sown for it will grow in quite dense shade but will not form a thick mat of grasses, and within two or three years the lawn might be taken over by moss, which whilst looking quite attractive can be dangerous to run or walk on.

After cultivation and the application of hydrated lime there are one or two plants worth considering to cover the area such as ajuga (bugle), bergenia, pulmonaria (lung-wort), funkia, Geranium pratense, and vinca (periwinkle). These are all tolerant of shade and will colonize the area quite effectively but again are hardly suitable if children are going to use it as a playground.

Clippings Left on a Lawn

Mr S. E. P. of Harrow Weald is able to cut his lawn two or three times each week. Is it wise or unwise to use the grass box?

The use of a grass box is desirable really for two reasons. The first of these is that without the grass box there is a great danger that annual meadow grass which seeds very freely will simply be spread all over the lawn in the clippings if they are left lying there. These seeds will then germinate and could eventually replace the finer grasses completely. The second reason for using a grass box is, of course, a lot of clippings left lying on the surface can look very unsightly, and in a wet season these clippings can become so sodden and matted that they will actually clog up the surface and deprive the roots of the grass of air. On the other hand, one ought to realize that a lawn on a sandy soil can benefit by leaving the clippings occasionally on the surface. These clippings will rot down and eventually form a certain amount of humus which may help the sandy soil to retain moisture during very dry periods.

Floral Lawns

Mrs H. L. P. of Sidcup, Kent, has heard of a floral lawn and would like to know how to prepare the ground and what plants to put in. She understands that this would require no mowing.

In 'floral lawns', many subjects such as camomile, thyme, purple clover, penny royal, and saxifrage are used, but all need some attention and, strangely enough, the main trouble is keeping them free from grass and other weeds, particularly while they are getting established. Such lawns should be clipped at least once a year. They are really only desirable as ornamental lawns, as most of them will get up to about 4 in high and seem to be damp most of the time. Thyme is the slowest to spread and cover the ground but it is also the lowest growing and so looks very compact and like a carpet. A purple clover lawn looks beautiful when in flower but it is difficult to walk on, for when the leaves are wet either with rain or dew it can be very slippery. To establish a floral lawn the ground should be well prepared and drained as for an ordinary grass lawn. It is best to sow seed of the desired species in a nursery bed in spring and then to transplant seedlings to the prepared area. An alternative method is to seed the lawn directly but many 'floral lawn' species are slow to germinate and the area can become covered with weeds which may choke out the desired seedlings.

No matter what method is chosen careful hand weeding is essential until the surface forms a tight sward.

It is perhaps worth experimenting with a small area, but often these labour-saving lawns turn out to be more troublesome than an ordinary grass lawn.

Combined Lawn Dressings

Mr J. A. R. of Prestbury, near Cheltenham, has dressed his lawn in March each year for four successive years with a combined selective weedkiller and lawn fertilizer, but has found that the weeds have returned within a few weeks. Can the Team suggest a more effective way of dealing with the weeds and improving the grasses?

The idea of a combined/fertilizer selective weedkiller is a good one but, in fact, it is better in theory than in practice. Selective weedkillers are most active when the weeds are growing quickly, but in early spring the weeds are more or less dormant and, in consequence, the weedkiller does not act to the best advantage. Certainly, March is a good time to apply a nitrogenous fertilizer to grass but it will not be able to crowd out the weeds very effectively unless the weeds have been weakened by weedkiller, so the net result is rather less beneficial than one would have expected.

It is very much more satisfactory to apply the nitrogenous fertilizer in the spring as a separate dressing. This will encourage the grasses to grow and they will develop a good root and a good leaf system. The weeds will normally start developing later and in May and June, when they are flourishing, the weedkiller should be applied. At that time of year the weeds will be killed and the grass growing well will be able to recolonize the vacant spaces left by the weeds.

In this way most of the weeds will be killed but a few may

escape and it might be advisable to have a second application of the weedkiller towards the end of July. It is always a good plan to follow an application of weedkiller after an interval of about two weeks by a light application of a quick acting nitrogenous fertilizer, such as sulphate of ammonia, because this immediately encourages the grass to expand into the bare soil where the weed originally was.

Winter Management of Lawns

Tips on lawn management during the winter are needed by Mr K. H. of Cwmbran, particularly on very heavy soil.

Because of the heavy soil, the lawn will probably lie wet and moss will flourish, so the first thing to do is to improve the drainage by means of a hollow-tine fork. This will not be easy work because of the nature of the soil but is certainly worth the effort. The tining should be done in the autumn or early spring, followed by a dressing of coarse sand and granulated charcoal brushed into the holes so that they remain open and allow excess water to drain away. Do not feed the lawn in autumn, but after hollow tining again in spring, about the first week in March, apply a spring fertilizer which has been bulked with sand, and brush this into the core holes.

Continue mowing through the autumn and any mild spells in winter when reasonably dry weather permits. Many people put their lawn mower away in early November, which is a mistake as growth can continue right up to Christmas in milder districts.

It is a mistake to attempt to do too much on the lawn during the winter as any heavy equipment will certainly compact the surface of the soil and may damage the grass. It is also useless to try to control weeds or to eliminate moss during this wet heavy period, and so it is by far the wisest procedure to try to improve the drainage.

Coarse Grass in Lawns

In winter there seems to be an increase in the coarse grasses and moss on Mr L. C. T.'s lawn. What can he do about this to get the lawn into good shape for the summer?

The apparent increase in the amount of coarse grass and moss on a lawn during the winter is a well known phenomenon and is due to a number of causes. The most important of these is the fact that during the winter the coarse grasses will continue to grow whilst a number of the fine grasses, especially the fescues, will hardly grow at all. Sometimes the fescues will suffer from what is usually called winter burn, which browns off the tips of the grass and reduces its vigour. Under these conditions it looks as if the lawn is coming increasingly under the influence of coarser grasses but when the spring comes, if cutting is resumed regularly again, the amount of coarse grass will then be seen to diminish.

Other steps can also be taken to ensure that the lawn comes into good shape in the summer. For example, during the winter at some time one should pay attention to the drainage and be sure that there is no water lying where it might eventually flood out the grass. With an established lawn, feeding at the right time is important because one wishes to encourage the growth of the fine grasses and not the coarse ones. Most of the fine grasses start growing in late February or early March and it is about this time that the first feed should be given to the lawn. This can take the form of a top dressing of 7 lb of sand with about 2 lb of fine peat per sq yd, and to this should be added a spring lawn fertilizer at the rate of 2 oz per sq yd. If the lawn has been spiked in the autumn the sand will work its way into the holes left in the lawn, the drainage will be improved, and the fertilizer will easily get to the roots of the fine grasses and encourage their growth. If a lot of moss has appeared then mercurized lawn sand can be used later in the year, say, in early June.

Another very important factor in controlling coarse grass is the quality of the mowing machine. Good mowers should have a large number of blades and they should be used by frequently mowing the lawn in different directions, using the grass box. The use of the grass box will collect any grass seed which comes mainly from the coarser grasses and so will once again tend to reduce grasses such as annual meadow grass, but will encourage the finer ones such as the fescues and the bents.

Control of Fusarium

Mr T. H. G. who is a green-keeper in the Isle of Man, wants to know the best way to control fusarium patch and other brown patch diseases in lawns.

Many people get worried when they see brown patches appearing on their lawn and think that of necessity the lawn must be diseased. This is not so, for there are many causes other than disease which can produce these disfiguring patches. For example, detergent drippings from washing can kill local areas, as also can scald produced by the urine of sheep or dogs. These latter marks can be fairly easily distinguished for although brown in the centre they generally tend to have a bright green edge which results from the ammonia or the nitrogen present in the urine.

The real lawn diseases caused by fusarium and other fungi produce smaller patches to begin with which are dark brown in colour, gradually becoming lighter brown as the grass dies. These small patches (sometimes called dollar spots) tend to fuse and by their fusion they may produce much bigger patches. They do not generally occur all the year round and they are most frequent in the spring or in late autumn. During the summer the grass is usually too dry for fusarium patch to develop.

The methods of control are many and various, but one of the simplest is to use mercurized lawn sand in exactly the same way as if the lawn were being treated to kill moss. One disadvantage of this is that it tends to scorch the grass and at the same time contains nitrogen which can lead to a very lush growth of the grass which may be soft and therefore may succumb easily to further attacks of fusarium. There are, however, a number of proprietary compounds on the market which are specific against this disease, which although they contain mercury do not contain nitrogen and therefore reduce the chances of further attack.

It is very well established that the disease is generally at its most frequent in the late autumn and on grass which is growing quickly and well. If these two possibilities are combined it should be seen that grass fed in the late autumn will be much more likely to succumb to fusarium patch than grass which is only growing very slowly. All these patch diseases in lawns very often follow too high feeding and it is for this reason that it is much better to feed grass a little at a time but often, in order to avoid any very vigorous surges of growth.

Rough Grass

Miss R. M. S. of Basingstoke has just moved house and has inherited a large area less like a lawn than a rough field, with large tufts of coarse grass which just lie down under the mower. She is in despair and asks if the Team can help.

In the end it is always better to improve an already existing lawn than to try to lay down a completely new one. In this case the listener has an area rather like a rough field but, were she to try to clear it and returf or even reseed, she would find that the problem of keeping down weed grasses would be almost insoluble.

The best solution, therefore, is to get a rotary mower. The action of this mower is such that any coarse grass is cut, and although one cannot get very close to the surface one can cut sufficiently close to kill out the coarse grasses. As a consequence of this a reasonable sward can be obtained within a few months. Later the turf can be made still finer by using an ordinary cylinder mower and remembering to mow in various directions to get still closer cuts of any coarse grasses which have tended to lie down. The lawn can be levelled up by filling in depressions with either compost or with sand and, if the lawn is well fed, and maybe treated with selective weedkiller if that is necessary, a level area of turf will result. This may not be an abolutely first class lawn, but it will certainly be as good as 99% of the lawns in Britain.

Rolling a Lawn

> *Mr J. A. D. of Loughborough says that in many of their programmes the Team tell listeners that a roller should never be used on a lawn. Surely there are some occasions when this could be beneficial.*

This tradition of cut and roll probably orginated hundreds of years ago when the only way of cutting was with a scythe or sickle and so the lawn became soft and spongy. With the introduction of mowing machines with a roller this need diminished as, although the machine would be relatively light, the whole weight is carried on the roller, giving substantial ground pressure.

In the last few years the situation has changed again: the development of rotary mowers, and more recently still the hovercraft-type lawnmower, has meant that the roller attachment has been dispensed with and we are again getting spongy, soft lawns; so, given this, an occasional rolling will do no harm at all. This would be best done in early spring after the winter rains and before mowing starts.

Although our British lawns are some of the best in the world, many of them suffer from bad drainage and regular rolling only aggravates this condition. The idea of a light rolling in spring also is a good one after a long, hard, frosty winter when bits of the lawn have lifted with the action of the frost.

Of course the last word on this subject could well come from those people who say that using a roller in the autumn kills the larvae of the daddy-long-legs (crane fly) in the lawn. This is a doubtful procedure and the application of an appropriate insecticide such as chlordane would be a great deal more effective.

Mowing the Lawn in Winter

Mrs E. A. of Aldershot says it is common practice for amateur gardeners to stop cutting lawns about the middle of October. Why is it that golf greens, which are amongst the finest lawns, are cut throughout the winter whenever the weather permits? In view of this, are gardeners just being lazy when they tuck their mowers away at the first sign of frost?

'When weather permits' is the important phrase in this question. Most gardeners do stop mowing lawns earlier than they need to do, and given the right weather conditions, there's no reason why grass shouldn't be topped during the winter. It's a matter of using common sense and not mowing when a lawn is too wet or when frost is present, and never cutting very short.

Having said this, it should be pointed out that golf greens are usually better drained and cared for than the average lawn. They are looked after by professionals, who can choose the correct time to mow, and are not limited to weekends only, like the amateur gardener. Another important aspect is that their mowing machines are well maintained, and consequently are better able to do a good job under the more difficult conditions that prevail in the winter months.

Lawn Mowings as a Mulch

Mr C. B. of Great Barrow would like some advice on lawn mowings and fresh grass cuttings. Could he use them fresh as a mulch?

There are differing opinions on this subject. Many people like to use fresh lawn mowings as a weed smother on flower beds and in fact this can be quite effective. A thick layer of grass like this can be used to kill out bad infestations of couch grass, bishop weed, etc., but there are many reservations.

For one thing, great care must be taken never to use mowings taken from a lawn after an application of hormone weedkiller, as this could well kill off most herbaceous plants in the border.

The spread of weed seeds is another drawback to mulching with fresh lawn mowings. From July onwards some of the grasses will be seeding and of course these seeds will germinate in the rose beds, herbaceous borders or wherever the mulch has been applied. Although beds look nice for a few days after application, the grass soon dies and looks unsightly. So taking all these things into consideration, it isn't a practice to be recommended.

Fairy Rings

Mrs G. of Whitehaven says she has two fairy rings on her lawn, in fact she's had them for a few years now and the novelty has worn off somewhat so she'd like to get rid of them. How should she go about it?

Well, the so-called fairy rings are of much more prosaic origin than the name implies. They are rings of darker green grass in lawns and are caused by certain fungi such as the champignon, marasmius oreades and some 59 other fungi.

These rings tend to spread outwards annually and sometimes the effect is of an arc, not a full circle. After rain in summer and autumn toadstools develop at the edge making the arc or circle more definite still. Inside the circle the soil is impoverished but at the ring, the death of the fungus tissues increases the available plant food and the grass grows stronger. The fungus is partly parasitic on the grass and just outside the ring of darker green the grass is lighter and poorer. The ring grows outwards to the untouched grass year by year and increases in size.

Having explained just what fairy rings are, what can the questioner do to get rid of them? Well, basic slag applied at 4 oz per sq yd will effect a cure but to prevent a recurrence, the turf should be hollow tined forked, dressed with a mercurized turf fungicide or sulphate of iron solution (2½%) or of potassium permanganate (1%).

Buying a Lawn Mower

Mrs M. E. of Cheltenham says that she has a rather large lawn, nearly half an acre, and her old motor mower has got beyond repair. She went to see about a new one but found such a bewildering array of machines that she couldn't decide what she wanted. She must get a machine before next spring and could the Team help her to make the best choice?

The best advice to anyone in this position is to ask a disinterested but knowledgeable person to do this for her, certainly before she pays over the money, and to try out several machines to see if she can handle them satisfactorily. For an area of this size, a power-driven model is essential as distinct from one which has to be pushed yet the cutting blade is driven by a motor. An area this size is too large for an electrically operated machine because of the length of trailing wire.

A rotary mower is preferable as, if the lawn is cut twice a

week during the time that the grass is actively growing, it would not be necessary to collect the grass mowings.

There are rotary mowers available now which are easily adjustable, can be fitted with a collecting box if necessary, and have a roller attachment on the back so that you get the striped effect which is caused by the roller and which is heavy enough to consolidate the soil without overdoing it.

Many people make heavy weather of a mowing machine and cultivator because they try to do work which should be done by the engine and the clutch. The rotary machines which work on a cushion of air and have no wheels or rollers do an excellent job but usually have no provision for grass collection.

A cylinder machine with a grass box will give a better finish than a rotary machine, but it must be remembered that during the season an awful lot of grass must be carted away and this type of mower is best used when the grass is dry, whereas the rotary mower can be used when the grass is very wet and the hovercraft type can be used when the soil is soaking.

To summarize, get a knowledgeable person – not the salesman for a particular firm – to advise you, but above all insist on a demonstration to see if you can handle the machine.

III
Trees

Non-flowering Almond

A flowering almond in Miss S. H.'s garden at Charlton Kings, near Cheltenham, is eight years old and has never flowered fully, only bearing one or two flowers each year. It is in clay soil and each year Miss H. has given it bone meal and compost, which does not seem to have made any difference.

The first thing is to stop applying bone meal, but continue the compost dressings. The tree should be securely staked to prevent windrock, which is most important, and it will settle down and arrive at a flowering rhythm. Possibly a dressing of lime would help, unless it is a limestone area.

Flowering almonds are quite often planted in a herbaceous border with stuff growing all around them, and they do not like this sort of competition.

It usually happens that the first year after planting an almond will flower quite well, which puzzles many gardeners, and the same thing can happen with rhododendrons, and then perhaps no flowers for years. This is because the nurseryman knows how to get these subjects to bud up – by keeping them 'on the move' from one position to another. This is not feasible in an ordinary garden, for when the tree is planted it is put in its permanent position.

Pruning a Misshapen Weeping Willow

Mr B. B. of Newton-le-Willows in Lancashire wants to know if he can prune a lop-sided weeping willow tree. He would need to cut off a main branch approximately 1 in in diameter. This tree grows beside a garage.

Often when willows are planted near a building they do grow lop-sided and this is what's happened in this case. It should be stressed that great care must be taken when planting such a tree as they grow very quickly and plenty of space must be given. As well as reaching a great size there is the problem of the root spread undermining walls and these trees should never be planted less than 25 ft from any building.

However, the problem of an asymmetrical main branch can arise occasionally and has in this case. This would be difficult to tie down and train, so it should be taken off with a pruning saw, flush with the tree trunk. This would best be done in the autumn and the wound should immediately be painted with some anti-canker paint.

Growing Christmas Trees

Mrs P. of Ramsgreave in Lancashire says that some Christmas trees are sold with good roots. Will they grow if they are planted out in the garden after the festive season?

This is a difficult question to answer as a great deal depends on how long the tree was dug up before it was sold. It if had been freshly dug there is a possibility it would survive the 12-15 days it was in the house but it is unlikely. Usually it has to endure anything up to 75° F in the house and unless it was sprayed with a plastic transplanting spray its needles will be dropping all over the place.

If the effort is made to preserve the young tree, then it must be potted up in a drained pot using good soil, but it must not be hung with electric lights or candles as this will dry the foliage out excessively and damage the terminal buds from which the new growths will spring.

Furthermore, it should not be stood in a dark corner and, if it is hoped and expected that this young tree will grow, then it must be treated as a living plant. It is no good treating it as an inanimate thing for a fortnight and then expecting it to revert to an actively growing tree.

Killing a Tree Stump

Mr G. B. of Porthcawl would like to know the most effective way of killing a tree stump. His particular problem is the stump of a flowering cherry which keeps on sending up growths.

This is quite difficult as these trees have a large supply of food in the base and roots will keep on sending up suckers as long as this food lasts. The fact is that more often than not, they are budded on to a wild cherry which will throw up suckers from the roots, particularly if they have been damaged in cultivation. Even when the actual stump is removed, these suckers may appear a considerable distance away, being provided with nourishment by an extensive root system, and this can go on for many years. These suckers must be treated as though they were small weed trees, by killing them off with a brushwood killer based on 245-T.

An alternative method of killing tree stumps is to drill a few holes in the top about 5 in deep and pour in some sodium chlorate mixed with water. The holes should then be plugged up with clay and the solution will be absorbed by the tree, eventually killing it.

Another quite effective method is to clear away the soil at the base of the stump, exposing the roots, then peel off the bark down to the roots and apply a solution of equal parts brushwood killer/paraffin. This can be painted on with a brush.

There are now specially formulated products on the market for killing tree stumps but the above suggestions are much cheaper. Of course it should be remembered that a tree stump can be made into an attractive feature if say honeysuckle or clematis is planted at the base and allowed to climb over it. It is always as well to remember this when felling a tree and leave the stump from 3 to 6 ft high. Even if you change your mind afterwards and decide to remove it, you will find it much easier to handle than a short stump, as if you loosen the soil around the roots, attach a rope to the top and get three or four people to give you a pull, the leverage given by the long stump will allow it to be pulled out easily.

Having said all this, it ought to be pointed out that a rotting stump in a garden can be a source of a fungi infestation which may pass on to all your other trees and shrubs – worst of all it could be the bootlace fungus (*Armillaria*) which is a real killer.

The Spindle Tree

Mr M. P. of Calne in Wiltshire has bought a spindle tree but now hears that they harbour blackfly in the winter. He asks whether it would be possible to get rid of these by spraying while they are hibernating.

The spindle tree (Euonymus europaeus) is an attractive subject bearing a profusion of red berries in the autumn. It does harbour blackfly but it would be difficult to kill these off in winter as they don't overwinter as insects but as eggs. A DNOC wash would be the best remedy but it would have to be sprayed on very carefully and it's unlikely that it would give a 100% kill. In addition, spray and water the bush in April with a systemic insecticide which will take care of the flies as they hatch out and start to feed.

Pink Hawthorn from Cuttings

Mr J. A. of Surrey has tried to grow pink hawthorn from cuttings without success. Some of his cuttings have made bushes 6 ft high but have never produced flowers. Why?

There is no good reason why these cuttings shouldn't produce flowers eventually. It may be that the questioner hasn't waited long enough – at 6 ft high they would be about five years old and it could take longer before the trees would produce flowers.

In the trade the pink or red thorn is generally grafted on to a common thorn root stock as this is much more vigorous and will enable it to flower much earlier. Mr A. would have got a better shaped tree if he had kept the stem clean up to about 6 ft although this wouldn't have made it flower any earlier.

Ironically, the richer the soil the longer it will take to flower. Shape by taking the centre out to make the tree goblet shape. This allows in air and sunshine to ripen up the wood.

Do not feed.

The Tulip Tree

Mrs V. J. of Cardigan has often read about tulip trees although she's never seen one. She says they sound very attractive – are they as attractive as they sound and would they grow in Cardigan?

The tulip tree, or more correctly Liriodendron, belongs to the magnolia family. It has curiously shaped three-lobed leaves which turn a clear yellow in the autumn and in fertile soil is a

73

very fast growing tree indeed. Although fast growing, it may take anything from fifteen to twenty years before flowering and is really a timber tree.

There are several varieties including tulipifera which is the North American tulip tree, Aureo-marginatum which has golden-edged leaves and Fastigiatum which has a tall, erect growing form, ideal for the smaller garden. Incidentally this was one of the earliest introductions from North America and is known to have been cultivated here since 1688. To give some idea of its size, one has been recorded growing at Waltham Abbey that is 100 ft high and has a girth of 9 ft. To answer this listener's question – it would probably grow well enough in Cardigan but as she has probably gathered by now it is more a tree for the park than a home garden.

Pruning a Cedar

Mr G. L. of Slinfold in Sussex has a cedar of Lebanon which is about 12 years old and 12 ft high. It is in a rather bad position and he would like to know whether it is possible to prune off some of the lower branches without causing any permanent damage?

This is the old problem of a large tree in the wrong place and anyone with ideas of planting trees should be very careful to get the right sort. Forest trees should never be planted in the average sized garden, they may be all right for a few years, but they will eventually create problems of shade, blockage of drains or even damage to houses and buildings.

It would be possible to take some of the lower branches off this cedar but it would spoil the rather beautiful shape which is its chief attraction. The branches should be taken off flush to the trunk and the wound painted with an anti-canker paint. The operation should be done in late autumn – there would be some bleeding of sap and the anti-canker paint should not be applied until this has stopped.

74

Conifers Dying

'Conifers in their natural habitat seem to withstand the bitterest weather conditions,' says Mr J. D. K. of Snitterfield, in Warwickshire. So can the Team suggest any reason why his conifers – cupressus, spruce, Austrian pine – have either died or make poor growth where they are exposed to the east and north yet thrive when in a sheltered position?

Conifers in their natural habitats do seem to be able to withstand very severe weather conditions, but it must be remembered that in nature they are growing in forests or at least in large clumps, and in consequence each tree is protecting every other tree. In our gardens we tend to plant them singly, so they are exposed to cold drying winds which can actually kill the foliage by desiccation and not by actual coldness.

Another reason why many conifers die is that in the winter in industrial districts there is a very heavy deposit of atmospheric pollution materials coming down on the leaves, and conifers are notoriously susceptible to this kind of damage. Thus one finds that in areas where conifers are exposed to cold drying winds from the east and the north, they tend to die easily. Furthermore, in industrial areas of heavy atmospheric pollution they also die very easily, and it ought finally to be said that they should always be planted, if they are going to be planted singly, where they derive a certain amount of shelter and not where they are fully exposed.

There is reason for this, other than the actual cold, for many of them, especially the cupressus, are rather shallow rooting trees and if they are sheltered a little bit they are unlikely to suffer from windrock which can so easily bring about their death. It is also good policy to give an annual mulch of well rotted leaves or compost over the root spread of most conifers, as this helps to simulate their natural environmental conditions.

Propagating Flowering Cherry

Mr R. F. a member of the Peel Gardeners' Association, would like to propagate a double pink flowering cherry. He asks if this is possible and, if so, how is it done?

Most double pink flowering cherries are sterile and it is impossible to propagate them from seed. The method is, therefore, to propagate them by cuttings, and short cuttings taken maybe in June should be struck. It is well known, however, that in most varieties of double pink flowering cherry the production of roots is very limited, and cuttings on their own roots very rarely grow into substantial or reasonable trees. For this reason most highly ornamental cherries are either grafted or budded on to a common cherry rootstock.

The process of budding or grafting is a rather complicated one, and before embarking on it it is a very good idea to get a good book on the subject and study it carefully. A rootstock of the common cherry should then be bought, planted in the garden and grown on for two years until it has become well established. The double cherry that it is desired to propagate should then be grafted on to it using the special type of grafting wax which can be bought from any horticultural sundriesman. On the whole, it is rather a tricky job and it would be less trouble to buy the variety already grafted, but, on the other hand, there is a great deal of pleasure to be got from doing a job with this degree of difficulty.

Laburnums in Limey Soil

Being new to gardening, Mrs I. of Kington Langley, planted a laburnum in limey soil ten years ago. The tree blossoms beautifully each year but is very stunted. Is there any treatment which will encourage growth or is the lime impossible to combat?

The answer to this question is not obvious as laburnums are very tolerant indeed of soil of nearly any type and one would have expected this laburnum in a limestone soil to do very well. One point, however, about limestone soils, which may be important in this case, is that they tend to be shallow, as they often lie over rock which is near the surface. Under these conditions there may be shortages of either iron or boron, and dressings of sequestrenes or borax might help the tree considerably. The other practice which can be followed with advantage is top-dressing the tree with heavy dressings of any organic material at all. On limestone soil there is usually a very quick turnover of humus and, in consequence, the soil can become impoverished, and heavy dressings of compost will help to counteract this tendency.

Another consequence of a shallow limestone soil is that the tree may be susceptible to windrock if it is in an exposed position. This windrock would break roots and would certainly cause stunting. To overcome this, secure staking seems to be indicated, or else the removal of the tree to a less exposed position.

Pruning a Gingko

Mrs D. B. asks how and when she should prune a gingko tree to get it to branch.

Gingko biloba is a fascinating tree which is sometimes known as the Chinese temple or maidenhair tree. It gets the first name because it was held sacred and preserved in the temple gardens of China and so far has never been found actually growing in the wild. At one time it grew in Britain and it has been found in fossil beds in Yorkshire and on the Isle of Mull off the coast of Scotland. There is probably no other tree which is so worthy of the name of a 'living fossil'.

In appearance it grows on a single stem and branches at the top only. The leaves are fairly large, with two distinct lobes. It is a member of a unique family and is best cultivated in a relatively rich soil. In gingko, the male and female reproductive structures are borne on separate trees, and in Britain most of the trees in cultivation are males and, therefore, one very rarely sees the seeds of gingko. This may be just as well because the seeds contain an oil to which a large number of people are allergic, and this can be rather dangerous.

In common with most of the gymnosperms, gingko should not be pruned at all. It is best left to its natural shape which is very simple but pleasant. If, however, it is getting too big, it could be lightly trimmed but any severe pruning would certainly harm the tree and detract a great deal from its pleasant appearance.

Pruning Japonicas

Miss M. A. H. of Kettering has a japonica in her garden that makes a lot of new growth each year, but does not flower very well. She prunes it back to the old wood immediately after flowering. Is this wrong?

This tree has a number of different names. At one time it used to be called japonica, as Miss H. says; commonly it is known as a quince; it was then known as cydonia, but is now given the rather tongue-twisting name of chaenomeles. It is really a member of the apple family and should be pruned in exactly the same way as one prunes an apple. This tree usually flowers in the relatively early spring, and then after flowering it produces a lot of vigorous growth. If all this growth is left on, then undoubtedly the wood will not ripen up and flower buds will not be produced. The ideal way to treat it is to cut the new wood in early August to within one or two leaves of where the new branches arise. The questioner has probably been pruning her tree rather too early and by delaying until August it is hoped that once again she will induce it to flower.

Pruning Lilac

Mrs D. G. of Wakefield, in Yorkshire, has a lilac tree which is so huge that she has to go upstairs to see the flowers and she would like some advice on reducing its height.

This is a fairly common problem and in many cases trees and shrubs are bound to grow on and on, just because the owners do not know how to shorten them. The position is eventually reached when really drastic action is called for. Lilacs can be pruned but it should be realized that if heavy pruning has to be done, one may have to wait two or three years before flowers are produced again.

In this case, some really hard pruning needs to be done in order to reduce its size. The best time to prune lilacs is in early April, for then the weather is relatively mild and growth will shortly be beginning. At that time it should be cut back to about 3 ft and, as so often happens in these cases, Mrs G. may find that there are a large number of strong growths coming out of the ground. These should be reduced to a maximum of about fifteen and the ones which should be eliminated are those in the centre.

A consequence of this hard pruning will be vigorous new growth, which should be still further reduced making sure that the shoots which are left are well positioned, both as regards showing the plant off to best advantage and as regards casting shade on other parts of the garden nearby. A further consequence of this pruning might be an increase in suckering from the roots, and any suckers which may appear should be traced right back to their origin and torn off. The reason for this is that most varieties of lilac are grafted on to a common lilac rootstock. The suckers would therefore be of common lilac and would not be half so pleasant as the new more brightly coloured varieties.

IV
Shrubs and Hedges

Treating Azaleas

Mrs L. planted eleven Japanese azaleas in manured acid soil in autumn two years ago. The first year, they all flowered well, but this year during the winter all the leaves dropped off. At the moment only one has leaves and flowers, five have leaves only, and the other five seem to be completely dead.

When the azaleas were planted the buds would have been formed in the nursery, and unless they received a severe check either by drought or hard frost, they would certainly flower in the first year. If the summer following planting was very wet, the wood would not ripen and form flower buds to flower the second year, and if the wet summer was followed by a severe winter, the frost would 'burn up' the azaleas killing the soft green growth. Their lack of establishment would also contribute to this.

The incorporation of manure at the bottom of planting holes is not helpful, for as it rots down it collapses and may cause the plant to move suddenly in the soil, tearing roots and doing damage. It would have been better to mix peat in with

83

the soil and to top-dress with peat.

Many varieties of Japanese azaleas are tender and are more difficult to establish than the mollis or sinensis varieties. If the weather becomes severe it is often wise to protect the more tender azaleas with bracken or straw in January and February to break the worst of the frost.

Remember also that you can never mulch azaleas too heavily, so mulch them twice a year with peat or leafmould, once in April and again in September. This conserves moisture and provides the shallow root system with the food and shelter it needs.

Diseases of Lilacs

Advice on lilac bushes, please, for Miss D. who lives in Shoreham-by-Sea. Her lilac bushes have died right down, though there was little sign of blight or pests on the leaves or bark. Would the garden being waterlogged the previous winter account for this, and is it any use trying with new bushes?

Where ground has become waterlogged and has stayed that way for a considerable length of time all the soil air is used up and displaced, and no more can enter below the surface. In consequence, the roots of plants usually die and this may be the reason why Miss D.'s lilac bushes have died down. If this is the case, then there would be very little useful purpose served by replanting in the same position until some method had been devised for draining that particular area of ground.

In many cases, however, lilacs which have been long established may be killed by a fungus which attacks the roots. This is known as the 'boot lace' fungus, and if attacked plants are dug up, these fungal growths, looking rather like boot laces, can easily be seen around the roots of the plants. This soil, therefore, should certainly never be used again for growing lilacs or a large number of other plants, and once

84

boot lace fungus has appeared it is advisable to take all valuable bushes out and try to save them by transplanting.

Another fairly common cause of sudden death, especially in coastal areas, is drift, either of salt water from the sea, or of hormone weedkillers from neighbouring farms or even from a lawn, and any one of these causes may be the reason for this questioner's lack of success.

Pieris Forestii

Mrs M. W. of Watford was given a very small Pieris forestii which she thinks is marvellous and she'd like to know whether it is possible to take cuttings from it successfully.

The pieris family are attractive ornamental evergreen shrubs with panicles of white, urn-shaped flowers appearing in March to May. Forestii has the added attraction of fiery red young foliage in the spring. They like an acid soil, preferably peat or humus enriched and a well-sheltered position with light shade.

There is no reason why one shouldn't take cuttings from this shrub: side shoots taken with a good heel will do best and these should be taken in July-August. They will need to be put into a cold frame or under a handlight or if these aren't available they will do quite well in a small pot, placed in a plastic bag which should then be closed and hung in a light position.

Pieris, which is known also as the lily of the valley bush, can be grown easily from seed and these can be sown outdoors in April but probably the most sure way of propagating is by layers. These are quite easy to do – just peg down one or two of the lower shoots in the soil underneath the bush, making a small notch at the point where they enter the ground, and cover the same point with some damp compost. When the layer has rooted, cut it off and pot up.

Lime-hating Shrubs

Mr E. A. P. of Northampton has a small shrub border planted with several lime-hating subjects such as camellias, magnolia, pieris, etc. They are planted in peat and leaf mould and he wants to know whether this will have sufficient feed value when the shrubs become established? The natural soil is slightly alkali.

As the natural soil is limey these shrubs will need constant dressings of leaf mould and peat. They may need more than this when better established and National Growmore would be ideal.

Having said that, the conditions are hardly ideal for these lime-hating shrubs and there could be yellowing of the leaves particularly in the case of magnolia. They might just survive if top dressed regularly with acid material as they are all fairly shallow rooting but it may be necessary to give them chelated iron sequestrene which is a fairly expensive business.

The perversity of human nature is such that people will try to grow subjects that are entirely unsuitable for their growing conditions and if they would only accept the old maxim 'horses for courses' life would be much simpler.

Pruning Forsythia

Two years ago Miss M. was advised to cut down her forsythias to within 1 ft of the ground. This she did, but they have never bloomed since, although they bloomed profusely before cutting. Why should this be?

This is not the correct treatment for forsythias if you want them to flower well. When they are cut back severely an imbalance is created between root system and top growth, and there is a consequent adjustment which leads to the production of a lot of top growth, but no flowers. Once severe pruning has been carried out there is nothing that can be done, except to let the shrub grow until it arrives at the necessary balance between root system and top growth, when it will once more flower regularly. Do not attempt root pruning, and do not give any fertilizers of any kind.

It is not necessary to prune forsythias each year and indeed the only pruning carried out should be to reduce the size of the shrub, say, when it is encroaching on to a path, or is getting out of shape. Even then prune as little as possible, only cutting out old, discoloured wood just after flowering time. If pruning is necessary, this, as in the case of nearly all spring flowering shrubs, should be done immediately after flowering.

Pruning Erica Darleyensis

A listener from Cumberland says her Erica darleyensis has 'gone funny' after heavy pruning. Is the damage permanent or will the plant recover?

Erica darleyensis is quite a tall, deep pink variety of heath that flowers in winter. It should be cut back in April when it is growing vigorously so that it will then break and send out new growths to flower the following year. After cutting back, it is good policy to apply a top dressing of peat/sand/compost to encourage this new growth. A well established plant should not be pruned back very hard or really old wood is cut into which does not easily make new growths, and those that are produced are often spindly and yellow for two or three years afterwards.

It is probable that the plant in question has been damaged by the heavy pruning. Given reasonable conditions, the erica should certainly recover, but if the conditions are not ideal and if the 'funniness' continues for more than two years, the plant should be scrapped and replaced with a similar variety.

Hydrangeas Turning Pale

A border of bright red hydrangeas in Mrs E. M. C.'s garden in Beverley attracts much admiration. They are not special varieties, just cuttings taken from house plants. Unfortunately two or three have become pale pink which spoils the whole effect. Should these be taken up?

The flowers of Hydrangea hortensis change colour fairly frequently and this seemingly is caused by chemicals in the soil. What chemicals are responsible for the change is not known but gardeners can influence the change in one direction, by using aluminium sulphate in November. If this substance is applied to the soil at the rate of about 1 lb to a large plant and then hoed in, the colour of blue hydrangeas will be very much intensified and pale pink ones will tend to become blue. Alternatively, the aluminium sulphate can be mixed with compost at the rate of about 2½ lb of crystals to 1 cwt of soil, and if this mixture is then sprinkled around the plant an intensity of the blueing will occur.

Unfortunately, this is not the problem posed by the question, because the question really seeks to find the reverse to this. Here our ignorance is really displayed, because although we know how to make blue hydrangeas bluer, so far we are not very certain how to make red hydrangeas redder. Many people have suggested that the addition of flowers of sulphur to the soil and hoeing it in at the rate of about ¼ lb to a large plant will effect a change, but opinions are varied on this and it is only with hesitation that we mention this at all.

If having made these chemical additions to the soil, the pale pink hydrangeas remain pale pink, then it is probably wisest to take cuttings from the deep red plants and replace the pale ones with them. Mrs C. should not, however, be too impatient of result because, once again, for reasons which we know nothing about at all, plants which produce red flowers one year may produce pink ones the next, and then revert to the original red colour, all without anything at all being done by the cultivator.

Growing Heather in Alkaline Soil

Mr J. E. T. has a new garden but the land has been used as a lime pit. How should he prepare the ground for growing heathers?

To plant heathers on a limey soil is really going against nature, although some varieties, such as the Erica carnea group, will grow in slightly alkaline soil. However, as lime hardly ever moves upwards in the soil, it is possible to grow heathers under alkaline conditions by making raised beds, edging them with stones and filling in with peat, leafmould, sand and suitable top-soil. The stone edging could be made attractive by having plants tumbling over. Another idea for growing heathers is in stone troughs, which should be filled with acid soil. In this particular case, scrape away as much lime as possible before doing anything else.

Another possibility is to treat special areas of the soil with iron sequestrenes. These are substances which do not react chemically with the lime in the soil and, as a result, the iron which they contain is available to be used by plants. Many of the lime-hating plants, such as rhododendrons, heathers, azaleas, etc., are in this category because they suffer from iron deficiency and die in a lime soil, but when sequestrenes are added, the plants obtain the iron and so will do very well.

These substances are, however, rather expensive, and are best used on prized specimens rather than as a general garden treatment. On the whole, gardeners should work with nature and not against it, and in an alkaline soil grow the types of plant which like these conditions.

Evergreens for Floral Art

Mrs H. G. from Rochester would like to know the best evergreens for all the year round use in floral art, preferably some that are easy to cultivate.

There is an increasing interest in floral art. Here are some evergreens that can be cut without any real damage. Pernettya with its lovely variously coloured berries, and pittosporum with leaves shaped something like privet but more widely spaced, are not too difficult to grow and can be cut quite heavily. Skimmia, laurel, symphoricarpus, kerria, euonymus, cornus, spiraea, pieris and, providing you live near the coast, tamarisk, are very attractive and will thrive on cutting.

Many of the berberis family are very attractive, such as B. darwinii which has lovely berries during the winter, B. sargentii and B. wilsonii. Berberis bealii and mahonia are ideal for spring decorations. Useful species of the cotoneaster family, easy to grow, are frigida, adpressa and macrophylla. Others would include the fire thorn family (berry bearing again), and the winter flowering subjects like chimonanthus (winter sweet) and winter jasmine, and hollies such as the variegated, and silver or golden.

Cupressus foliage is very lovely and graceful, but with this family any cutting must be done very carefully, for if cut too hard the trees may suffer. Another reason for being discriminating in trimming cupressus is that they do not regrow too well and the shape can soon be spoiled.

For early material for floral decoration, branches of such flowering subjects as ribes (flowering currant), prunus, forsythia, quince and even lilac may be forced into flower in water and warmth indoors.

Growing Broom

Mrs M. S. of Liverpool asks about growing broom in her garden. As she has only a passing acquaintance with this attractive shrub she'd like to know more about it before taking the plunge and buying one or two.

Broom or cytisus is a hardy deciduous subject growing to approximately 7 ft, giving white, pink, yellow or crimson flowers from April to July. The common broom, cytisus scoparius, is well known to most gardeners, having whippy green stems and flowering in May or June. Typically bright yellow, numerous varieties can be obtained ranging in colour from cream to crimson.

The Moroccan broom, cytisus battandieri, is a very different sort of shrub – it has long flexible stems, silvery leaves and an upstanding cluster of yellow flowers in June or July. The flowers have a very pleasant pineapple-like perfume and it can be grown as an open branched shrub up to 8 ft high or if preferred, trained against a wall or trellis.

All the cytisus like well drained soils but they aren't too fussy and will grow in most soils. They need sun and as a rule aren't very long lived, seven to ten years being about all you can expect from them. Although they may well survive much longer, they tend to get leggy with flowers near the top. This can't be corrected by pruning as they should never be cut back into the old hard wood. The only pruning that should be done is very lightly as soon as the flowers have faded.

All brooms are easily grown from seed but seedlings of garden varieties and hybrids may vary considerably so these are usually propagated by summer cuttings.

Non-flowering Forsythia

Mr R. C. of Carnwarick in Cornwall has several forsythias which have reverted and aren't flowering. Can anything be done to bring back the flowers?

It is unlikely that this *is* reversion, as reversion is a kind of abortion. The most likely cause of this non-flowering is pruning at the wrong time or perhaps the trees are in the wrong position. Forsythias need to be in full sun and any pruning should be done immediately after flowering.

It is necessary to know the difference between flower buds and leaf buds. If you look at the tree in, say, February, the whippy branches that were last year's growth can be picked out. The old wood in the centre should be cut out and these whippy branches which should bear abundant flower buds should just be headed back.

Generally speaking, unless the bush has outgrown its position and needs pruning, the less that is done to it the better and the cutting of sprays for house decoration will be all that is needed.

Cutting back Hydrangea Paniculata

Mrs B. of London, N.W.2, is uncertain about how far back she should cut her Hydrangea paniculata.

Hydrangea paniculata must not be confused with the florists' hydrangea which is Hydrangea macrophylla and is grown as a greenhouse or house plant or in gardens by the sea, as a small shrub. Hydrangea paniculata is a small tree or shrub, but it may reach 30 ft high, although in Britain it is usually much smaller. It should be pruned by cutting back established plants to about 1 ft from the ground in late winter or early spring. This treatment will ensure that the new growths will be well clothed with foliage and will carry bigger panicles of flowers. If really showy flower-heads are wanted then they should be reduced in number as the season progresses.

Fastening Shrubs to Walls

*Mrs J. of Croydon wants to know an effective way
of fastening branches of trees or shrubs to a wall
without piercing the wall with nails.*

This is a perennial problem and one which has no immediate
and permanent answer. It is certain that the best way to go
about this business of having trees or shrubs close to a wall is
to erect a wooden trellis on battens, standing about 6 in clear
from the wall, and to train the climbers along this trellis. This
method has very many advantages, for it allows the plant a
good chance to spread its roots, and it also allows air to
circulate freely between the trellis and the wall. This free
circulation of air will reduce the chance of mildew, will reduce
the chance of insect damage and will give all the leaves a
chance to develop well since light will be coming from both
sides and not only from the side away from the wall. Another
advantage of this method is that it helps to protect the wall
and one does not need to drive nails into it with the
consequent small holes and the chance of water getting in and
freezing and breaking the brick.

The difficulty with this method is that wooden trellis is not
everlasting and begins eventually to rot and has to be
replaced. It is exceedingly troublesome to replace a trellis,
especially if you have plants climbing up it and then they
have to be taken down carefully in such a way that they can
be re-tied in position when the new trellis has been erected.

An alternative is, however, available and this is wire coated
with plastic material. This is almost everlasting and it can, in
fact, be attached to a wall very easily or could even be
attached to a trellis. If attached to a trellis the wire network
could maybe be held up in position by posts when the
wooden trellis has to be replaced.

The post idea can, of course, be used in other ways; if two
posts are sunk at an appropriate distance apart, about a foot
away from the wall, the plastic-coated wire trellis can be
stretched between them and used there as a material on which

to climb.

If only a few nails are necessary, no great harm will be done and it is best to recommend that the minimum number of nails is used, and wire, either plain or coated with plastic, is stretched between them. In these cases, it is useful to use nails with lead heads which can be bent around the branches of climbers, but in a high wind these tend to break off and so these too have a disadvantage.

It can be seen, therefore, that this problem is not an easy one and it is added to the strictly horticultural problem that against a wall is an area where plant food materials are very quickly depleted from the soil. So climbers and any plants on trellises or against walls should be fed liberally and regularly and a top-dressing of compost be given each autumn in order to keep the soil in good shape.

Starting a Hedge

Mr B. of Warrington has just moved into a new house and asks the Team what hedging subject they would recommend for his district.

In some industrial districts green oval-leaved privet is often the only subject that will make a satisfactory hedge, and, as with all hedging subjects, initial soil preparation is important. See that the drainage is adequate, incorporate plenty of compost into the planting position, and a little bone meal also could be used with advantage. It must be recognized that unless the rootsystem is fed it will wander away from nutrients and so impoverish surrounding soil. The roots can be kept at home by feeding them occasionally and so the depletion of the food supply of many borders can be avoided.

With all hedging subjects it pays to plant fairly small young stuff, say about 2 ft 6 in preferably in November. Tip them back on planting by a quarter, and then in mid-March cut back to 12 in. This will ensure that all new growth is thrown from the bottom and in a couple of seasons or so a good hedge, 3 ft high or so, should result.

In polluted districts golden privet is rather unattractive and will not stand the conditions as well as green privet.

Other more attractive hedging subjects which will do quite well in difficult conditions include Cotoneaster simonsii and Berberis stenophylla. And if you want to produce a really impenetrable hedge, then plant Berberis sargentii, or mix quick thorn with green privet at the rate of 2 green privet to 1 quick thorn.

Bamboo as a Windbreak

Mrs J. H. of Camelford, in Cornwall, would like to grow bamboos as a windbreak and would like the Team to suggest a small-leaved variety that would not be too invasive.

In many areas bamboos of any variety will become invasive – having accepted that, it should be pointed out that they aren't very good as a windbreak as the varieties that will stand up to wind aren't very attractive and will become very tattered until they establish themselves enough to protect the lee side.

Although we refer to them as bamboo they are arundinaria and they come in all sorts of shapes and sizes – dwarf, golden, striped canes, striped leaves, etc. They can be grown in tubs if desired and a few good varieties are aurecoma (yellow), graminea (narrow-leaved and growing 6 ft high) and Bambusa virginica.

All bamboos are gross feeders and the soil should be well prepared, well dug and plenty of leaf mould and manure dug into it.

Not all varieties are hardy even in Cornwall but giganteo and niteola will thrive in all but the coldest areas.

Most are moisture loving or require a deep rich soil. The edge of a stream or pond suits them admirably.

Trimming a Beech Hedge

Mr H. M. of Sheffield wants to know the best time of the year to trim an established beech hedge.

Generally speaking, beech hedges should be trimmed twice a year. Neither of these trimmings should be carried out in the early part of the year and, in fact, the first is best done about the beginning of July. At this time the hedge will look a little bit ragged, but this trimming can tidy it up and carry it through the summer, until the beginning of September. Once again, the hedge should be trimmed, and the reason for the second trimming in September is to give the hedge long enough to grow fresh leaves which will enable it to be clothed nicely and neatly for the winter ahead.

Stopping Cupressus Leaders

Mr K. wants to know the best time of year, spring or autumn, to stop leaders in a Cupressus macrocarpa hedge? Also, which is the correct tool to use for trimming afterwards – shears, secateurs or a billhook?

Cupressus macrocarpa is a very strongly growing tree and it can be used quite well as a specimen tree in a largish garden. It can, however, be a very useful hedging subject also, but one has to be careful to keep it cut back or else it may easily get away. Its main drawback as a hedging subject is that it is rather sensitive to cold winds and the exposed side of the hedge may suffer from frost burn.

Cutting the hedge should be done in the month of April. The reason for this is that cupressus grows most in the spring and if the leader is cut back in April there is plenty of time for new growth to be produced before the next year. It could then be trimmed to shape in July and this will also help to thicken it up.

One very important point about this job is that it is inadvisable to let the cupressus grow tall and then cut it back too far, because this method usually results in the base of the hedge being thin or bare. It is best to cut the leader out at a relatively early date before the hedge has reached the desired height, and then keep the secondary growths in check by trimming with shears in July.

Feeding a Privet Hedge

Mr F. B. of Sheringham, Norfolk, wants to know what fertilizer to give a well established privet hedge; he gave it a dressing of bone meal two years ago, since when it has been kept free of weeds, but has not been fed in any way.

A privet hedge will survive and grow under the worst conditions but, whilst this is so, it is certainly true that it will grow even better if well fed. Probably the easiest and most economical feed is last year's tomato or chrysanthemum soil. This is very often thrown out and since it contains a considerable quantity of food material it should be used in the garden, and a privet hedge is as good as place as any. Such soil can be applied as a top dressing in the spring, every third year or so, but if you do not have any of this material, then bone meal is very good or you may use a compound fertilizer about every third year.

One of the problems with privet is the difficulty that gardeners have in keeping the roots at home. It is a fairly gross feeder and, unless there is sufficient food material in the immediate vicinity of the hedge, the roots will spread quite widely through the garden and they may impoverish nearby soil. This is the reason why beds of herbaceous subjects or even perennials near a privet hedge are often rather small and undernourished, for they cannot compete with the privet when it comes to obtaining food materials. Thus, whenever a hedge is being planted, it is always very good advice to dig in plenty of organic matter as this will ensure not only that the roots will stay at home, but also that there will be a supply of food to keep the privet from starving other nearby plants.

Conifers as a Sound Barrier

Mr J. G. K. of Sudbury, Middlesex, is a member of the Management Committee responsible for the care of a block of forty flats. It has been suggested that conifers should be planted in the gardens to break up the noise of the traffic on a nearby main road. Cupressus lawsonii has been suggested. Would the Team comment on this?

Many of the different varieties of cupressus would make a good sound barrier. Before making any decision it is as well to find out the ultimate heights of the different varieties and also take into consideration the fact that they will create shade problems for any flowerbeds, etc., that may be planned nearby.

Initially the trees should be planted close together to obtain a fairly immediate screen. They can be thinned out later to approximately 6 ft apart. This distance would vary depending on the type of trees chosen. To get a better visual effect, alternate planting of green and golden varieties could be made: aurea would make a nice contrast to lawsonii.

If a decision hasn't already been made there are other subjects that would make a more effective sound barrier than cupressus. Birch or any twiggy tree is very useful in this respect, and if it suits the surroundings, bamboo is the best of all.

The information at our disposal doesn't tell us the height of the block of forty flats, and this is a very important thing when one is considering sound barriers. The reason for this is that it is very simple to produce a barrier which will keep out the sound from the lower floor or even the second floor simply by using any of the subjects mentioned already. On the other hand, if these flats are high-rise flats, maybe eight or nine storeys high, then very few trees are of any value at all in this connection, because if one plants tall trees they will automatically shade the lower flats, and if one plants small trees, then they will be of little value as a sound barrier. The problem then is really quite unresolvable in absolute terms and the best that can be suggested is to take into account the height of the flats, and then try to plant a barrier at a sufficient distance from the flats so that the shadow on a summer evening will not be too dense in any of the rooms.

Dwarf Conifers in Pots

Miss M. of Cuckfield has four dwarf conifers in pots on her roof garden. They are four years old and only 15 in high. She would like to plant them out in the garden, but wants to know whether they should be sunk in their pots in order to keep them dwarf?

It just depends whether they are dwarf varieties, or whether they have just been dwarfed by keeping them in a tight pot. Some of the dwarf varieties grow at the rate of only ¼ in per year, and even if they are planted out in the garden they will still only grow at this rate.

If there is any doubt about the type of these conifers, it would be best to play safe and plant them in their pots, which should have the rims just proud of the ground. If they are dwarf varieties they will stay small, if they are ordinary conifers grown tight, they will stay dwarf for ten years or so, until the roots burst the pots.

Topiary

Miss M. N. of Stockport in Cheshire would like to know the best way to reshape long neglected bushes, also how to set about shaping a new bush. She adds, what type of shrub is best suited to this work and could box or privet be used?

The art of topiary is very ancient and it takes its name from two Latin words which mean ornamental gardening. It was developed to a very high art by the Romans from the first century onwards and many of the villas of the Roman aristocrats in the country were highly decorated with shrubs cut into shapes of animals, of letters, of statues and of many other things. In Britain it became popular in the sixteenth and seventeenth centuries and although it never, in fact, reached the stage of being a craze it is still carried out in many places. Very careful interesting work can be seen in a large number of cottage gardens.

The best plants to use for topiary are undoubtedly box and yew since these are evergreens with very small green leaves all the year round, so that at every season the work looks complete and attractive. Nowadays, people use privet and this is not a bad subject, although the work which can be done on it can never reach the quality of the yew or the box.

Since the shrubs are intended to be there for many years it is a very good idea to plant them in well manured deeply dug ground. They should not be clipped at planting, but you start the shaping treatment the following autumn preferably in August or September. As a general rule, it is wisest to have some kind of shape in your mind which has a broader base than a top. The reason is that unless this is done sometimes people produce shapes which are eventually top heavy which puts a very great strain on the roots of the trees, as well as looking rather unnatural and untidy. It is always best to start with new shrubs, but if you want to start with long neglected bushes then the first thing you have to do is to cut them right back to the very old wood. This old wood will have very little or no foliage, so will have to be well fed and started into growth again, maybe for two or three years, and only when it is growing strongly will you be able to make any decent job of topiary work on it.

There is much more to topiary than meets the eye, and if you examine some of the more elaborate shapes closely you will find very often branches and twigs either tied together to form the tail of a bird or spread out to form a wing; they may have a wire frame inserted into them in order to be sure that the correct shape is reached, and all in all, it is not a very natural way of treating plants.

You should reckon that the first three years of pruning will be spent trying to get the general shape of the object you are trying to depict. Thereafter you can start putting in finer details and clipping to produce dense growth so that the whole thing is solid looking.

Once the final form has been reached all that is needed is a regular clipping over usually in August or September. This clipping should help to keep the twigs well covered with leaves so that a solid looking form is produced.

V
Climbers

Pruning Wistaria

Can the Team tell Mr E. W. of Tibshelf,
Derbyshire, the best time to prune a wistaria?

Wistarias grow very slowly and, for the first seven to ten years, little or no pruning should be necessary. In the early years it is best, therefore, to concentrate on shaping the framework of the plant over the trellis or wherever it is being trained; remove any laterals that are ill-positioned, and try to position the main stems, in order that later the racemes of flowers will hang clear of the trellis and their beauty can be seen.

When the wistaria is about seven years old serious pruning can start. This means pruning the lateral growth back to about two leaves, and the spurs so left will ripen up and probably flower the following year.

The timing of any pruning should be immediately after the flowering season, which will vary according to district.

Growing Clematis

Mrs G. a member of the Soham Village College Gardening Club, has a clematis, one of the blue Jackmanii types but she does not know which variety. What are the best conditions in which to grow it?

Clematis is often described as a plant which likes to have its feet in the shade and its head in the sun. For this reason it likes a position of full sun with a cool root run. Its natural habitat is usually a woodland where it will climb up trees into the sun whilst the base of the plant is in the shade. The best way, therefore, to grow clematis is to try to recapture the situation and, when planting, especially if the soil is dry and sandy, plenty of humus must be incorporated into it, either in the form of well rotted compost or farmyard manure. To this a little lime can be added to the surface and, in order to keep the root run cool, a stone flag should be placed over the root. If stone flags are not available, it is a very good idea to feed the clematis very heavily with compost or manure each year, giving an annual dressing of some 3-4 in.This not only provides food for the plant, but also tends to conserve moisture and to provide shade and keep the root cool.

Newly planted clematis should be cut back, but if an established one has got to the stage where all the flowers are borne at the top of the plant, one can also cut back old bushes. The result of this will be that shoots will rise from the bottom of the old plant and they can be induced to flower and the flowers kept nearer ground level.

Some of the varieties of clematis such as Jackmanii flower in August and September and, if so, they should be pruned in the early spring. Many other varieties of clematis flower in the early spring and when this takes place, pruning should be carried out immediately after flowering time. In each case, the purpose of pruning is to allow a sufficient time interval for flower buds to be formed before the next flowering season.

Controlling a Russian Vine

Mr R. A. P., in moving house, has inherited a very vigorous growing Russian vine in an open verandah. How can he keep it in check?

This was not a very happy choice for a position because of the very vigorous growth of this vine, whose proper name is Polygonum baldschuanicum. It is ideal for covering unsightly buildings, away from the house, but on a verandah a better choice would have been a variety of clematis or honeysuckle, or one of the jasmines, which are much more attractive and easier to contain.

In the mass, the flowers of the Russian vine are quite attractive so, if it is retained, it will be necessary to prune it twice a year. The easiest way to do this is to cut it back with ordinary garden shears, which won't kill it, but will keep it to a reasonable size.

Anyone interested in covering an oil-storage tank or a tool-shed would find Polygonum baldschuanicum useful because of its very vigour, but it should be planted with discretion as it can get out of hand and prove a troublesome nuisance.

Chimonanthus Fragrans

A seven-year-old Chimonanthus fragrans (winter sweet) has not yet flowered. It is growing on a west wall, is fed on liquid horse manure, and the roots covered with leafmould. What can Mrs D. McD. of Hockley, in Essex, do to encourage it to flower?

Winter sweet is usually a very floriferous shrub and the most obvious answer to this particular question is that the plant is not flowering because it is suffering from 'an insufficiency of neglect'. Undoubtedly, shrubs grown againsta wall or against a house very often are starved, but in this case it seems as if

107

the opposite effect has been produced, by applying horse manure and leafmould. Leafmould can still be applied for the next few years, but the questioner should certainly stop feeding the plant and let it embark on a period of starvation. This very often encourages shy flowering plants to come into flower.

If any long lateral branches are produced, these should be cut back and July is a good time to do this. Under normal conditions where the plant is doing well, it is best to prune in early March and, at the same time, weak and overcrowded shoots should also be removed. If, after two or three years of this type of treatment, flowering is still not being induced, then it very often pays to tie some of the longer lateral branches downwards so that their tips are below the horizontal. This process has been shown to work with climbing roses and it seems to encourage them to produce flowering buds rather than leaf buds. It should, however, be unnecessary for winter sweet as, given a chance, it should flower without any difficulty.

Tropaeolum Speciosum

Mr F. J. of Arnside in Westmorland has tried to grow Tropaeolum speciosum at the foot of a yew hedge three times without any success. In view of this, could the Team tell him whether it requires some special treatment?

Tropaeolum speciosum is commonly called the flame flower, the flame nasturtium, or the scotch creeper. It is a most beautiful creeping climbing plant which grows very well, especially in the north and west of Britain. It forms a delightful covering for a wall and gets up to 15 ft or more under the most favourable conditions. When it is in flower it has bright orange-red fluted flowers which are most attractive and the whole front of a house can be coloured absolutely crimson by this plant.

In order to grow well, the plant requires a certain amount of shade and more important, the soil should be very rich in humus. In fact a peaty soil is very good for it, as the plant also dislikes lime. Thus, to grow it best, one digs a lot of humus into the soil, one makes sure there is no lime present and one keeps the lower part of the stem and the roots shaded.

Tropaeolum can be propagated by seeds which can be sown any time in the early spring, or since it spreads underground by long creeping rhizomes, these can be cut off and planted about 9 in deep when they will very quickly start sending up shoots. This division of the rhizomes is best done in March.

This listener's problem is really not his inability to grow the flame nasturtium, but the fact that he is trying to grow it at the foot of a yew hedge. Yew is well known as a plant which seems to poison the soil in its immediate vicinity for other plants, and if you look under a yew tree or by a yew hedge you will find very, very little growing there indeed. I think therefore that he will do much better to grow his tropaeolum somewhere else for after three attempts at the foot of a yew hedge he should have learnt the lesson by this time.

Some tropaeolums produce tubers and indeed some of these tubers can be boiled and eaten. Usually the best use for them is as a means of propagating the plant and such beautiful varieties as T. tuberosum or T. tricolorum fall into this category.

VI
Fruit

Varieties of Apple

Mrs Q.'s apple trees have had to be cut down because of the building of an arterial road. What varieties should she plant, bearing in mind the speed of fruiting, and the weight of the crop?

Where speed of fruiting is important, it is not so much the variety of apple grown which is the important thing, but the type of stock on which is was grafted. There are a number of stocks easily divisible into two groups: dwarfing stock, on which fruit will be borne in as little as three to four years, or standard stock which might take seven years and maybe more before fruit is produced. There are other differences between the two types of stock; the dwarf stock, although it comes into flower sooner, has a shorter life and the fruit may only be produced for about twenty years. The tree is also very much smaller. On standards, the fruit may be produced for fifty years and sometimes even more and, of course, the tree is very much taller. Thus, in choosing the type of stock, the size of the garden should be considered as well as the speed of fruiting.

Apples grown on a cordon system will also come into fruit

very quickly and they should bear edible apples by the end of three years, and if space in the garden is limited a family apple tree is a good idea, as up to five varieties of apple may be grafted on one rootstock and still occupy the space of one tree.

The question of varieties is almost an embarrassment of riches. In choosing varieties a number of things must be taken into account of which probably the most important is the time of flowering. In the north of the country, where late frosts occur, early flowering apple trees are always at a disadvantage as the blossom tends to get frosted, and so late flowering varieties are preferable. Another point which must be remembered is the fact that some apples will not bear fruit on their own but require to have a pollinator present, and before anyone embarks on the planting of apple trees, they ought to be sure that they have the correct varieties to make a crop certain. Having considered these points, probably the best two dessert apples for good districts are Laxton's Fortune, which is not very long keeping but is very good eating indeed until November, and Cox's Orange Pippin which is a very long-keeping apple and can be eaten until March. Of the cookers, Lane's Prince Albert is a very good one, and Edward VII is an apple of very high flavour and rather late flowering so it is not very liable to damage by late frosts.

Ground Elder and Nettles in an Orchard

In his small orchard in Devon, Colonel S. W. J. is troubled with ground elder and nettles, but he doesn't want to use a poisonous weedkiller as it might affect the trees. What can he do?

Ground elder and nettles are difficult to eradicate. There are several ways to tackle the problem, and one is by continually chopping off the heads of the weeds until you exhaust them, or become exhausted yourself. An easier way would be to use a rotary mower, cutting down to about 2 in or so, and eventually the weeds will mow out, and grass walks will be left between the trees. It might be that the orchard is planted up with daffodils or other bulbs, and in this event the mowing could not commence until the bulb foliage had died down.

Where bare ground is not objected to, it is very possible to use some of the weedkillers which are based on tarry acids. The spray should be directed on to the weeds, and it should only be used below trees which are reasonably well established, and which have a fairly thick wood stem. It is best to take considerable care to keep these tar acid sprays off the foliage of the trees, and in consequence, they can be used most effectively in the early part of the year before the foliage of the fruit trees has come on. This method, however, may prove expensive in a large area and should certainly only be used under established fruit trees or bushes. The new weed-killers based on the chemical glyphosate will kill ground elder and nettles but will also kill the grass and other vegetation. Applied carefully they would not harm the fruit trees.

Spraying Apple Trees

A question that bothers several listeners with small apple orchards is summed up by Mr W. S. R. of Muswell Hill, London. 'Could the Team please give a spraying programme for a few apple trees? They are Cox's Orange Pippins which are infected with woolly aphis and American blight.'

It is difficult to give a comprehensive spraying programme, but here is the sort of programme an amateur gardener might follow. For American blight, which is a disease carried by woolly aphis, spray the trees at the green bud stage; that is when they are just beginning to show a touch of green. This can be done using a BHC, lindane, derris or malathion solution and it can be repeated at the pink bud stage when the flowers are just beginning to show. If there are still signs of

115

the disease during the growing season spray again with any of the foregoing, and repeat as frequently as necessary, say every three weeks, which will prevent the disease from spreading. These sprays are also effective against red spider. In winter actual areas of woolly aphides can be treated either by painting with neat tar oil, paraffin or turpentine, and the whole tree should be sprayed with tar oil wash whilst fully dormant. As Cox's is a sulphur-shy variety, none of the sprays should contain sulphur, and it is advisable at all times to read the manufacturers' instructions carefully on this and matters of dilution.

Storing Apples

Mrs R. V. of Bristol would like some hints on storing apples. She says she has plenty of room but results are never very good, the apples becoming wizened very quickly. They are laid on a wooden floor in an outside building.

The first important point is to decide whether the apples are worth keeping for a start and this depends a great deal on the variety and their condition. For example, it's not worthwhile storing a variety like Beauty of Bath (these should be eaten directly off the tree) but varieties like Lane's Prince Albert or Bramley Seedling will keep until the following April.

Apples in store are very easily tainted and will pick up even the smell of resin from a pinewood bench or the scent of soap if it has been scrubbed so this means you have to be very careful not to use paper or wood wool as these cantaint. A cool frost-proof room or cellar is ideal; the light should be subdued, so if it is a room with windows, they should be darkened. For preference store in a single layer, stalk side down with about ½–in between each fruit. However, immediately after picking they can be stored for a short while in a conical pile, preferably on an earth floor and covered with straw.

At all times the apples must be handled carefully to prevent bruising – don't drop them into the basket when picking as the bruises will quickly develop in store and contaminate the others around. In fact they should be examined at frequent intervals and any fruit showing signs of rottenness taken out and thrown away.

If indoor storage space isn't available you can clamp your apples like potatoes and if properly done they will keep this way until the following spring. To do this, select a dry part of the garden either near a hedge or a wall, cover an area big enough with 6 in of straw and place the apples in a conical pile on this. Make sure that the stalk of the apple above does not press into the one beneath. Cover the pile when completed with another 6 in of dry straw and then cover the whole thing with about 3 in of soil. This should be taken out of a trench around the heap and will help with drainage – if very heavy frosts persist it may be necessary to add an extra layer of soil during the winter.

Cracked Conference Pears

Miss C. A. of the Lindfield Horticultural Society says that for the first time in twenty years, her Conference pears when quite small developed cracks. These have since filled up, but the pears are small. Could this trouble have been prevented, or is it due to a very dry spell of weather? The tree was given a small amount of farmyard manure in the spring and no other feed since.

From the description of the symptoms, it would seem as if there is no pest or disease present, otherwise one would have expected either the cracks to increase in size or any insects which are present to show themselves. Because of this, the cause could by physiological and it could very well be due to the spell of dry weather mentioned in the question. An element in the trouble must also be the lack of feeding.

Conference is a self-fertile variety of pear and because of this is inclined to set a heavy crop. This puts a considerable strain on the tree and so, in years when a very heavy set of fruit has been obtained, the number of pears left to mature should be reduced, leaving say onepear to every three inches of branch. Those pears which were left would then grow to a reasonable size and be of good quality, but before they could do so they would require to be well fed. This is best done by applying a heavy dressing of farmyard manure in the spring which will improve the soil, and then to supply a complete fertilizer at flowering time. Although it is not usual to give pears nitrogen, in the case of trees which have been starved, it is often good policy to apply sulphate of ammonia at about 4 oz per sq yd to trees at the time of petal fall or when the fruit is swelling. This has a very palliative action that will help to produce larger fruit in the year in which it is applied. In succeeding years, complete fertilizers can be given, otherwise the soil will become rather unbalanced.

Pear Tree Midge

Miss H. B. has two pear trees which produce an abundance of blossom but, if the fruit sets, much of it is infested with pear midge, so that many of the affected fruits become misshapen and drop to the ground. What is the best treatment for this?

Pear midge is becoming increasingly common in this country and this listener accurately describes the symptoms. The midge is, as its name implies, a tiny insect scientifically called *Contarinia pyrivora*. It attacks the pear tree at the time when the flowers are open and the insects will lay eggs in the middle of the flowers. The flowers will set fruit, the fruit will gradually develop and the grubs of the insect will then emerge and eat out the centre of the fruit. This means that the fruit will then become misshapen and, of course, fall to the ground. If such fallen pears are cut open, it will be seen that the centre is hollow and blackened and it is usually easy to find many of the little white insect larvae eating away.

It is essential, therefore, if you wish to control this pest, to remember that it is the *flower* that is attacked and not the fruit, and so any protective measure must be taken at flowering time. It is, of course, unwise to spray plants, especially fruit trees, when the flowers are open as this may affect pollination, and so in this case sprays should be applied immediately before the flowers open, at the stage which is usually called the 'white bud stage', i.e. when the tips of the petals are just showing through the flower buds. There are many sprays which can be used for this and BHC is very effective.

It is also a wise plan to carry out a certain number of hygienic measures. For example, a winter spray with a DNOC wash will often help to control the pest and, since fallen fruit lies on the ground and may act as a source of infection, it often pays to spray the ground also, in the autumn or in the winter, with a winter wash. Many farmers, of course, allow animals to eat the fallen pears as this also reduces the number of over-wintering larvae within the pears, and in many cases the soil may, in fact, be cultivated and dug over in order to bury the pears which have fallen from the tree the previous year.

Small Conference Pears

Of three kinds of pears in a small orchard, at 900 ft above sea-level, Conference trees (five years old) have set fruit, but after reaching the size of a walnut the pears do not grow any more. The other two varieties of pears do bear quite well, says Mr E. R. G. of Abertillery.

The situation of the orchard, at about 900 ft above sea-level, could well have a lot to do with the poor behaviour of the Conference pear, as this is a rather fussy variety. At this altitude the trees will be subjected to cold winds fairly late in the season. But there is still time for the Conference pear trees to settle down as they are only five years old, and one very important point is that they should be well staked against high winds.

If grass is allowed to grow around the bole of the trees it should be kept cut; or preferably the area immediately around the bole should be cleaned and kept free from weeds, otherwise competition from the grasses may result in a shortage of nitrogen, which can delay young fruit trees becoming established.

Additionally there may be fertilization problems as insect flight is often limited in high winds and possibly the varieties of pears may be incompatible, although Conference is self-fertile and requires no pollinator. It would be wise to check if, in fact, the other varieties are compatible, and it is always good policy to make sure on this point when buying fruit trees.

Peach Leaf Curl

Can the Team tell Mr C. L. O. of Stevenage the reason why a five-year-old fan-trained peach tree has not yet flowered? Each year it starts off well with plenty of foliage, but about the end of May the leaves start to curl and discolour.

The tree in question is almost certainly suffering from an attack of a disease usually known as peach leaf curl, which is caused by a fungus named *Taphrina deformans*. This disease causes the leaves to curl tightly and take on what is sometimes called a 'fisted' appearance. Later on these leaves usually turn reddish or reddish-orange on the upper surface. As the disease progresses the leaves get more and more tightly curled up until eventually they fall off. The fallen leaves will then stay on the ground all winter and can act as a fresh source of infection for the tree the following year. Obviously, then, it is good practice to collect any infected leaves which fall off and to burn them, because by doing so one reduces the initial infection the following year.

The fallen leaves are not, of course, the only source of infection, because some of the fungus will stay on the young twigs and even on the wall or trellis if one is dealing with a fan-trained tree. It is, therefore, important to spray the wall or trellis and the tree during the dormant season, that is the winter, with a good fungicide, such as Bordeaux mixture. The tree itself should be sprayed early in the season just before the buds burst, either with lime sulphur or copper fungicide, and this spray when applied should kill any infective spores which might have gained access to the tree from outside sources.

Although peach leaf curl does not kill the tree, it is a very debilitating disease and if the attacks occur every year the tree gradually becomes weaker and weaker and bears very poor crops of fruit or none at all. Eventually, the tree may succumb although usually by this time effective counter-measures have been taken and fungicidal sprays applied.

Growing Apricots

Mr J. M. of Burton Lazars in Leicestershire has an apricot tree 17 years old and planted on the end of a greenhouse facing south-east. The last five years it has had quite a lot of foliage but no fruit. Could the Team advise on feeding and pruning?

If left to its own devices an apricot, like most other trees, would form a head but in most areas of Britain they need some form of protection, so they are either grown on walls in sheltered gardens or trained on wires or are under glass. This means that they must have a special form of training which is known as 'fan training' where all the branches are kept on the one plane.

As this tree seems to have been left severely alone, what has probably happened is that all the new growth is forming on

121

the ends of the older branches and consequently is not ripening and forming fruit buds. This means some drastic pruning to encourage new growth and this isn't a good idea with such things as apricots, peaches and cherries, etc., as the wood tends to exude gum. Bearing this in mind, the best time to do any pruning is in July when the risk of gumming, as it is called, is considerably less.

Ideally the new thin growths should be tied to wires spaced 6 to 9 in apart and the unwanted new growth removed when small with the thumb-nail – pinching back to about one leaf, tying in with raffia only the straightest and best growths with roughly a hand width space between them. No other plants such as tomatoes should be planted in the vicinity of the roots and the root system should be lightly pricked with a fork, thoroughly watered and kept wet. Give a good dressing of a complete fertilizer such as National Growmore, water this well in and cover the root area with half-rotted manure or compost. The following year give a dressing of crushed limestone at the rate of approximately ½ lb for each sq yd of root run.

It should be remembered that the pruning of trained trees like this isn't just a once only operation but wood should be selected or discarded according to need, right through the growing season.

So far as pests and diseases are concerned the apricot is susceptible to green fly, red spider and peach leaf curl. For the former, forceful spraying with a hosepipe or syringe is as good a control as any and for peach leaf curl, spraying with a good fungicide should start in February and continue throughout the growing season. If the tree is trained against a wall, spray the wall thoroughly as well.

Growing Trees from Fruit Stones

Mr A. S. of Huddersfield wants to know if small trees can be grown from plum and prune stones and, if so, how and when should they be sown, and how long do they take to grow?

Many people derive much pleasure from growing trees from seeds of orange, date, peach, plum, prune, grape, etc. and, so long as the fruit has not been cooked, there is very little that is difficult in producing these trees. Usually such seeds can be planted at any time of year in a light, open soil, with a fair amount of humus and in the case of stone fruits such as peaches, plum or prunes, a dusting of lime is beneficial.

The seeds may take a long time to germinate and so the pots should be kept moist in any out-of-the-way place until growth begins. The young plants should be kept in full light and given a light liquid feed once every two weeks.

It is advisable not to expect too much in the way of crop for a number of reasons. For example, in many cases the variety does not breed true, e.g. plum or apples, or the climate may not be hot or sunny enough, e.g. oranges and dates. Again it may take a long time (ten years) for the tree to reach fruit-bearing age. So although Mr S. will enjoy *growing* his fruit it is unlikely that he will enjoy *eating* it.

Plum Pollination

Mr W. C. of Sandown on the Isle of Wight recently planted a President Plum, a Cambridge Gage and an Old Gage. He would like to know whether these will pollinate one another?

This isn't a particularly good choice as the Cambridge Gage is a late flowering variety, President mid-season and the Old Gage early. There may be some overlap of blossom but it is unlikely and the solution might be to plant a Victoria Plum nearby as this has a long flowering season. The President is completely self-sterile, the Cambridge Gage partially sterile and the Old Gage is self-sterile. When buying fruit trees it is essential to make sure they are compatible and that they will flower at the same time.

Lime is essential for all stone fruits so when you buy your trees, mix crushed limestone into the soil in which you are to

123

plant them, taking in an area which will ultimately accommodate the mature tree. If you want to dress a tree already established, apply about ½ lb of crushed limestone to the sq yd around it.

Returning to the newly planted tree, always stake securely so that there can be no root damage before it becomes well established. This may mean keeping the stake in for several years so make sure it is a good thick one. Always be careful to avoid root damage by cultivation, never fork, hoe or dig deeply around stone-fruited trees as this can cause suckering which goes on for ever. Plums suffer badly from aphis infestation which causes their leaves to roll and curl so that it can't make the best use of its foliage, so spray early and regularly with a good insecticide.

And one last thought – plums often take up to 15 years before they come into full bearing so in addition to all the advice above – have plenty of patience.

Silver Leaf on Plum Trees

Mr G. P. of Belfast has what has been diagnosed as silver leaf on his plum trees and would like to know if there is anything he can do to cure this.

Silver leaf is a fungus disease caused by *Stereum purpureum*, the spores of which gain entry to trees through wounds or lesions and grow under the bark, causing the foliage to appear glazed and silvery, hence the popular name given to it.

It affects apples, pears, cherries, peaches, plums, other stone fruit trees, poplars and other ornamentals. Treatment must of necessity be rather drastic as the fungus does not develop until the attacked branches die when scales of purple, overlapping fungus scales break through the bark.

For a start all the dead wood should be cut away and burnt, preferably before mid-July. Then you should apply a heavy dressing of a balanced manure to the roots, e.g. a compound fertilizer mixed with rotted manure or compost. There is another school of thought that advocates slitting of the bark of the tree in May or early June, on the north side of the main branches and stem, in single joining cuts to ground level.

Pruning cuts should be treated with a tree paint and none of the silvered branches should be removed for a year until the success or otherwise of your treatment can be assessed. If you have failed then, as Bill Sowerbutts often says, 'Nothing makes a better, more sweet-smelling fire than a bit of pear or apple wood.' Perhaps Mr P. will be able to fill us in on the pyrotechnic qualities of plum trees!

Plum Trees not Fruiting

Mrs E. D. of Conway has two plum trees which never bear any fruit. One is a Victoria and one is a monarch, and they are about eight years old. Can the Team give a reason for this?

Victoria is a mid-season flowering plum and monarch is an early flowering variety, but, as both are self-fertile, there should be no pollination troubles.

There could be several causes, possible frost damage at flowering time, although in an area like Conway this is not likely to happen every season. It could help if some protection from frost was given, say by draping 1 in fish netting over the branches. Or when frost is predicted, to spray the open flowers late at night lightly with clear water, and the ice, strange though it seems, would form a protective covering.

A further suggestion is to dress the soil around the root spread once every three years with lime at about 4 oz per sq yd.

But seeing that these trees are (for plums) not yet fully established, they will almost certainly, in a few years' time, arrive at a balance between root development and top growth and fruit regularly.

Suckers from Fruit Trees

Mr J. F. W. of Leeds asks whether there is anything that will stop suckers from growing at the base of fruit trees.

Any tree or shrub, including roses which have been budded or grafted on to a root stock of a different type, is capable of throwing up suckers. In most cases trees are grafted on to a stock (this is the portion in the ground) because this has a more vigorous root system than the variety. This means that the root system collects food with its numerous roots and is literally bursting with energy and vigour and will throw up suckers from dormant root buds at the slightest provocation.

Suckers should not be confused with side growths which often appear at the base of old fruit trees and are themselves of the variety of the tree – if they originate from below the graft then they belong to the stock. Once they have started it is almost impossible to control them except by chopping off or spraying with a total weedkiller such as paraquat. The latter must be done when they are only a few inches high as if they are allowed to become woody, only the leaves will die.

The real answer is to avoid hoeing, digging or cultivating around the roots of the bush or tree as every nick on the root will produce a sucker. If you have a weed problem use either the paraquat or simazine weedkillers to take care of it and eventually replace the old trees with new varieties which won't sucker.

Grease-banding Fruit Trees

Mrs J. S. of Lancaster would like the Team to explain what is meant by grease-banding fruit trees and why it is done.

This is an old and well tried method of insect control and consists of a greased paper band placed around the trunk of the tree about 3 ft from the ground. The idea is to stop insects crawling up and down the trunk and the grease is usually put in position at the end of the summer, remaining there until the following spring or early summer. A great many insects can be trapped like this, woolly aphis creeping downwards to over-winter on the roots, wingless female moths going up the tree, etc.

The particular pests for which the grease-band is used as a barrier are the larvae of the Winter moth, the mottled Humber moth and the Vapourer moth. The females of these are wingless and hence only capable of reaching the branch of the tree by crawling up the trunk. Once these females reach the branches they commence to deposit their eggs in the crevices of the bark or around the base of the dormant buds. These eggs hatch out to produce tiny caterpillars in the spring which attack the leaves, blossoms and young fruits and if the infestation is severe, will entirely defoliate the trees. When these caterpillars are gorged they spin a thread and lower themselves to the ground where they change into pupae, staying there until early autumn when they hatch out and climb up.

Proprietary brands of grease-bands are available and are about 8 in wide, they should be placed around the trunk about 3 ft from the ground or in the case of dwarf trees, around the short main stem and the base of the branches. They should be firmly secured with twine and, if used on old trees, some of the rough bark and mosses should be removed otherwise the insects will be able to crawl underneath the sticky band. Some special greases can be obtained which can be applied directly to the tree but ordinary types of banding grease should not be used in this way as they can damage the tree.

Examine the bands frequently as leaves or twigs may stick to them, making a bridge over which the insects can crawl in safety, and keep the bands in good order until April – this will ensure you trap the other moths which make their appearance at this time of the year.

Preparing Ground for Soft Fruit Trees

What are the most important points that Mr P. S. D. should note when preparing the ground for the planting of soft fruit trees?

Choice of site is important – make sure it is open and sunny and well drained, and it would be beneficial also if the trees could be planted so that they are sheltered from north and east winds. A good rich soil is needed with plenty of manure or compost in the top 6 in because soft fruits are mostly surface rooters and unless the soil will hold a considerable amount of moisture, the maximum yield will not be obtained. In preparing the soil some bone meal should be added, and for redcurrants and gooseberries charcoal is invaluable. For blackcurrants some hoof and horn meal will help to produce heavy crops over a long period.

Equally important is the choice of varieties – do not choose commercial varieties, which often have tough skins and are not very tasty. Some suggestions for flavour and quality are – Laxton's Giant blackcurrant, Keepsake gooseberry (this variety produces its foliage very early and protects the flowers from frost), Red Lake redcurrant, White Versailles whitecurrant, Lloyd George raspberry.

Plant in early November so that the trees get well established and, once they have settled down, remember that blackcurrants are particularly gross feeders and like a lot of nitrogen in the form of sulphate of ammonia or dried blood, whilst gooseberries need regular supplies of potash.

The blackcurrants and raspberries should be cut down to almost ground level the first year, and should not be allowed to bear a crop.

Pruning Blackcurrants

Mr S. J. F. says that one is usually advised to prune blackcurrants immediately after they have fruited. Doesn't the plant need the leaves on those branches to build up new growth, and would it not be better to delay the pruning until autumn?

Blackcurrants are grown on a 'stool', that is, a large number of growths which arise directly from the soil and the object of this hard pruning is to encourage these new growths to come from the base as they will bear the following year's fruit. If the growths are not pruned, the existing branches will continue to grow but they will only grow a limited distance and be 6 or 9 in long, and in consequence they will bear much less fruit than the new growths which would be 4 or 5 ft long. It is important to time this pruning correctly, for if one waits until the autumn the new shoots coming from the ground have not time to form and ripen up sufficiently to bear the next year's crop.

A new technique adopted by commercial growers is to cut down the whole of the bush to 6 in when the fruit is ripe, and the currants are harvested mechanically. The branches are then burned, so destroying any pests or diseases harboured there. This method means that the blackcurrants only fruit every other year, but it could be adopted by the amateur with, say, a dozen trees, cutting half of them down one year, and the other half the next year.

Pruning Raspberry Canes

Mr E. A. S. asks if established raspberry canes should be pruned. If so, how much and when?

When raspberries have finished fruiting, it is good policy to cut out the wood which has borne fruit, thus leaving the new young wood which the plant has produced in June and July.

129

This young wood will develop throughout the autumn and bear the crop the following year. To leave all this wood is sometimes very unwise and therefore two practices are often followed. Firstly, the number of canes per plant is reduced to about six as this allows those canes which are left to ripen well and give them plenty of space. Secondly, it is advantageous to tip back the season's growth by a few inches, enough to leave the cane about 3 ft 6 in high. This seems a rather silly thing to do but the reason is very simple, for raspberries keep growing nearly all the year and in consequence the tips of the shoots never become tough but always stay soft and succulent. As a result of this, they are very likely to be killed off by frosts and a die-back can start which may kill the whole cane unless it is prevented. By tipping back the season's growth in the autumn this problem is completely avoided.

This advice does not apply to new raspberry canes. These are better planted in the autumn and then cut down to within a foot of the ground in early March. This will encourage new wood to be produced and it may bear some fruit late in the season; however, it will certainly bear fruit the following year when the routine described above can then be followed.

Controlling Fruiting in Raspberries

How to treat raspberries so that they will fruit later in the season is what Mrs M. C. of Ramsgate wants to know.

This can be done in two ways, both connected with pruning, and most varieties of raspberries will respond satisfactorily. One method is not to prune the raspberries at the normal time, which is after fruiting, but to prune say in March, cutting the new growth back to 2 ft. This will delay fruiting by three weeks or a month. Another simple way is to treat the raspberries as herbaceous plants and to cut them back hard in the autumn, right down to 4 or 5 in from ground level. They will then make new growth which will flower and fruit much later in the season. If only half the raspberries are so treated then you can have both early and late crops.

Varietal control of fruiting season is perhaps the best way of spreading the cropping. If you plant an early such as Lloyd George, a mid-season like Malling Enterprise, and a late such as Norfolk Giant, fruit can be picked from June to November.

Cordon Gooseberries

Mr G. B. of Norwich took some cuttings from gooseberry bushes last autumn. They have done well and he'd like to grow them as cordons. Could the Team give some hints on how to do this?

Rooted cuttings should be planted out in their permanent positions at leaf fall, approximately October/November. For a single cordon, remove all the growths except one; this will come out sideways and should be taken up as high as needed. It will be necessary to tie it to a cane to do this and when it gets to the desired height it will have to be topped. It will then begin to produce side growths and looks rather like a walking-stick with little spurs.

These little spurs – the lateral growths – should be allowed to grow to the desired length and afterwards consistently pruned back to that length in early spring. They need plenty of support, of course, and, if you live north of the Trent and have space on a north facing wall, then that's the right place for a cordon.

Non-fruiting of Gooseberries

Mr L. H. W. of Manchester writes, 'I have had many flowers on my gooseberry bushes in recent years but the flowers or the tiny fruit drop off. How can I avoid it in the future?'

131

There could be several reasons for this – poor root action, mildew, insects or bird damage, the latter being prevalent following a hard winter. The best means of protecting bushes from bird damage is the use in winter of the nylon-thread web, which when draped over the bushes may look rather ghostly, but is most effective. If you look closely, mildew can be seen as a whitish film on the surface of the small fruits and a karathane fungicide would control this. Spray the bushes when in early flower with derris to control sawfly caterpillar, and in March each year give a tomato fertilizer at 3 oz per sq yd. Good tomato fertilizers are rich in potash and gooseberries have a high potash requirement.

The Gooseberry Sawfly

Mr E. G. D. wants to protect his gooseberries from attacks by the gooseberry sawfly, and asks how subsequent attacks can be countered.

The gooseberry sawfly (*Pteronidea ribesii*) is on the wing in April and May laying eggs on the undersurface of gooseberry leaves. From these eggs the caterpillars, with a black head and a green and black spotted body, emerge in May. They feed voraciously on the gooseberry foliage and may completely strip the bush except for the mid-rib and the main veins. When the caterpillars are fully grown, they spin a fine silken thread and lower themselves to the soil where they pupate in readiness for next year.

The first attack on the sawfly ought, therefore, to be in the winter when the trees are dormant. If the soil below the bushes is then sprayed with a tar oil wash, the initial infection will be much reduced.

However, if this has not been done and an attack of gooseberry sawfly is expected, then the bush must be protected by dusting or spraying, just as the leaf buds are breaking, with derris. Three or four applications may be necessary during the growing season, but do not use these insecticides when the gooseberries are in flower, or pollinating insects may be harmed.

Bushes that have suffered from an attack will become debilitated, and will need a good mulch of manure, and additionally most gooseberries need 1½ to 2 oz sulphate of potash around the root-spread each year.

Pruning Cultivated Blackberry

Mr A.P. would like to know how and when to prune a cultivated blackberry bush.

The cultivated blackberry should be pruned rather like a raspberry: that is, immediately after the fruit has been gathered, say about the first week in October. In general the growths which have fruited should be cut out. There is one variation from raspberry pruning, however, for if the blackberry is growing very vigorously it does not pay to remove all the fruited wood or the remaining canes may grow too lush. In such cases, therefore, some of the old wood should be left.

In northern areas and in exposed gardens, if too much thinning is done, the wind will blow right through the bush, and pollination and so fruit set may be poor. In nature wild blackberries are often underneath a hedge or in a quarry where they are protected from winds and, more often than not, on these there is a good set of berries. Also in these positions the bushes are producing surface roots in leafmould, so remember to use lots of humus.

Propagating Mulberry and Medlar

'How does one propagate a mulberry and a medlar tree?' asks Sir W. C. A.

Mulberry trees can be propagated by seed. The seed should be washed from the ripe fruits and thoroughly dried. It should be sown in March under glass or else in May in the open air. The seed will grow relatively easily, but they are very slow indeed in reaching maturity, and one might wait many years before any fruit were obtained. Because of this the practice is to take cuttings or layers. Cuttings are taken in the usual way by choosing young wood, one year old, and inserting it in a good open compost where it will root fairly quickly. The most popular method, however, of propagating mulberries is to take a branch, maybe 2–3 in thick, and insert it as deeply as possible into the ground. It will act rather like some fence posts do if they are cut green and they will eventually root and by this method one obtains trees which will fruit quite early. Another common means of propagation of mulberries is to layer them in the spring or the autumn and any of the usual methods of layering can be applied.

The medlar, on the other hand, is a very much more difficult proposition, as it has to be grafted either by a cleft graft in April or budded a little later in the year, usually June. Unless one has considerable experience of grafting on to stock such as hawthorn or quince, then the best advice would be to buy a medlar and not to try to propagate it. The best varieties of medlar are Dutch and Nottingham and they have very good fruit of a rich flavour.

Growing Grapes for Wine-making

Mrs D. of Whitkirk, Yorkshire, is an amateur wine-maker and would like to know whether suitable vines could be grown in the Leeds area?

There are reasonably successful vineyards in certain parts of the north, and of course the Romans grew grapes extensively all over England. The main factor is having the right kind of soil conditions, and ideally you need thin soil on a south-facing slope. These are the sort of conditions you will find in the vineyards of the recognized wine-making areas of Europe.

Thin soil is important as, if you grow vines in deep, rich soil, all you get is a big growth of foliage and very small grapes. Additionally the vine growths are stunted by being planted very close together.

Variety is, of course, very important, and for growing conditions in Britain some of the best are Black Cluster, Royal Muscardine, Turner's Black, Dutch Sweetheart and one called Brandt.

Don't forget that you will need a considerable quantity of grapes to make it worthwhile, and if you are unable to pick the desirable thin, dry soil, then tread or roll the ground very thoroughly and disturb it as little as possible, controlling weeds by spraying with paraquat or similar weedkillers. Make arrangements to train the vines on wires, 2 ft 6 in – 3 ft apart, with 4 ft between the rows.

Ornamental Gourds

Mrs A. E. B. grew ornamental gourds last year for the first time with wonderful results. Will the seed she has saved from these bear fruit?

The quick answer to this question is that undoubtedly seed saved from ornamental gourds will grow into plants which in turn will bear fruit. The reason for this is that the gourd, unlike the cucumber, has to be fertilized before it will bear fruit, and as a result the seeds are almost certain to be viable. Cross-pollination, however, occurs fairly frequently and a certain amount of genetic segregation might also take place, and, in consequence, one cannot be certain that the new plants will be identical to the parents. Nevertheless, it is worth pursuing this practice of planting seeds because the resulting gourds could still be very attractive.

Gourd seeds have a hard coat and it is often very difficult indeed to start them germinating. This is sometimes done by giving them a light rub with sandpaper or even by nicking the seed with a sharp knife. Gardeners used to hasten the germination process by keeping the seeds in their mouths for a few hours before sowing and by doing this the digestive juices in the mouth helped to soften out and decay the hard coat.

The seed should be sown in 3–in peat pots, one to a pot, and they should not be allowed to lie flat in the soil but should be set on their edge. This is a wise precaution because if they are sown flat, one of the seedling leaves may get trapped under the seed and uneven growth will result. In extreme cases where the seedling leaf could not get free the plant might, in fact, die.

Sawdust as a Top-dressing

Mr H. R. H. says there is a large quantity of sawdust to be had locally. Does the Team recommend top-dressing shrubs and soft fruit bushes with sawdust to eliminate weeds and also adding humus to the soil? If so, what would they point out as the most important aspect of top-dressing?

For a long time there has been a great prejudice against sawdust in the garden, but the results of extensive experimental work have shown that sawdust was found to be very good and beech sawdust best of all. Avoid all sawdust from wood that has been chemically treated, say with boron, creosote, or against dry rot, and use only fresh raw sawdust cut from the trees.

Sawdust should not be applied too thickly, otherwise air movement down into the soil and to the roots is stopped. A thin layer applied fairly frequently is the best technique. This will act as a weed smother and, when weeds eventually do come through the surface, the sawdust can be lightly hoed and another layer applied.

When used in this way in a mixed shrubbery it may be that some types of shrubs will like it and some won't. If any particular subjects are not looking too happy under this treatment, then the layer of sawdust should be drawn away with the hoe, and a boost feed of nitrogen such as sulphate of ammonia or dried blood should be given to the plants. Extra nitrogen may be necessary in any case after the prolonged use of sawdust mulches.

VII
Vegetables

Unusual Vegetables

Mr R. B. of Levington, in Suffolk, would like to grow vegetables that are out of the ordinary run. Have the team any suggestions for some unusual vegetables that deserve to be more widely grown?

People are a little more adventurous than they used to be and this is reflected in the vegetable catalogues. There are many improved vegetables, too, and one of these is a tomato called Small Fry. These grow in huge bunches up to 3½ lb in weight and each tomato is about the size of a small golf ball. Two other good new varieties of tomato are Sugar Plum, another small sweet-flavoured type, and one called the Fruit Tomato.

A new sweet corn which can be grown successfully in any district is named North Star and an old vegetable coming back into favour is the huge winter radish. Although it's a big vegetable, it slices and cooks nicely.

Two variations on well known themes are Little Gem cos lettuce which only grows 6 in high and has an attractive nutty flavour and the old January King cabbage which isn't widely grown these days, but has the best flavour of them all.

For the gardener who wants the best of two worlds – a

Dutch runner bean Floret. This grows about 2 ft high and as well as providing a well flavoured bean, makes a nice bedding plant with its prolific, highly scented flowers.

Salsify is known as the vegetable oyster on account of its very, very attractive flavour. It does best in a rich soil well manured for a previous crop. The seed is sown in April in shallow drills about 12 in apart and, once the seedlings are through, they should be thinned to 8 in apart. Salsify requires a long growing season and is ready for use in early November when the roots can be lifted and stored in boxes of sand. To retain the flavour the roots should be scraped before cooking and then boiled until tender and served with white sauce. The best variety is Giant Island Mammoth.

Mercury, or Good King Henry, is a wild plant which used to be grown in cottage gardens in the Middle Ages. If the seed is sown in shallow drills in April the seedlings can be transplanted when they are large enough to handle and they should be spaced at intervals of 12 in. Once the plants have reached a reasonable size by the end of May, the young shoots can be cut off and boiled. If the young shoots are served with butter they taste rather like asparagus. Growth can also be helped by earthing up the young shoots which helps to increase their tenderness. Established plants can be mulched in the autumn and they will begin to make new growth early in the following year so that, in fact, Good King Henry is a perennial vegetable which is a very welcome addition to the garden.

Growing Peppers and Aubergines

Mrs E. D. of Burton Lazars would like to grow peppers and aubergines in an unheated greenhouse. Could this be done successfully and, if so, how many plants would she need to produce a reasonable crop?

South of the Trent this would be possible but further north it would be difficult to get the seeds started off early enough. They need roughly the same sort of treatment as tomatoes, and the same sort of soil can be used for the seedlings. Seeds should be sown in a half pot in March. If you can get the use of a warm greenhouse so much the better, otherwise you should keep the pots in a warm light window to get them off to a good start.

Pot them up singly in 3 in pots and advance them as the plants grow, finishing in 6 in or 7 in pots. When the plants get to 6 in high the tops should be pinched out to make them bush.

The aubergines should have 6–8 fruits to a plant and the peppers rather more, so for the average-sized family half a dozen plants should be sufficient.

When it is seen that some of the flowers have set, the plants may be fed with liquid fertilizer giving weak doses about every ten days.

They are liable to the same pests as tomatoes, which include greenfly, red spider and whitefly. Thorough syringing particularly on the undersides of the leaves, or even turning the hosepipe on them in a fine spray will do much towards keeping down pests.

If they need support, tie to a cane.

Growing Endives

Mr J. B. of London grows endives but they don't blanch to professional standards. He uses cloches which are placed in position when the plants are dry, then places a container (such as that used for ring culture of tomatoes) over them with a stone on top.

Endives are often confused with chicory – in fact many dictionaries define them as being the same. They are of the same family, though, and both are extremely bitter unless well blanched. As the endive is a useful addition to the salad bowl and can be produced for eating most of the year round it might encourage a few more people to grow them if we look at its cultivation.

A medium to light sandy soil is best – it is nearly impossible to grow endives in a heavy soil as it has to stand well into the rainy season and will rot off. The soil should be rich in humus and seeds should be sown in drills in the spring; they should be sown about ½ in deep with the drills 15 in apart. Thin out the resultant seedlings to 6–8 in apart.

Attention during the growing season consists mainly of hoeing to keep the weeds down; watch out for slugs and make sure the drills don't dry out. Blanching must be commenced immediately the plants are full grown and they must be cut as soon as the blanching is complete otherwise the heart will quickly rot. The most likely reason for Mr B.'s failure is the light finding its way between the container and the stone – even the smallest chink of light will spoil the endive but on the other hand, air circulation has to be maintained to avoid fungus diseases.

It is fairly easy to have endives ready for Christmas but difficult for say January or February as the plants aren't hardy: they will stand a light frost only and in most districts of Britain they ought to be covered with cloches from September onwards.

Outdoor Tomatoes

Mr A. K. of Leicester would like to grow outdoor tomatoes. How should he prepare the soil and what varieties does the Team recommend?

The tomato is a tropical plant and grows naturally in very sunny, warm conditions. Therefore unless it is grown under glass its cultivation in this country must remain something of a gamble. Whether you are going to grow your tomatoes under glass or outdoors, the method of raising the plants remains the same.

144

Generally speaking, it is best to buy in plants making sure they have been hardened off before delivery. If you can raise you own under warm conditions, sow the seed thinly and prick off when the first seed leaves have developed. For preference pot up into 3 in pots in John Innes No. 1 compost. After about six weeks they must be hardened off to withstand the lower temperature outside.

Any good garden soil will suit tomatoes provided it has been well manured and cultivated but preferably they shouldn't be following potatoes. Where possible give your plants the shelter of a wall but not a boarded fence as draughts will blow through this.

If planted in the open garden, plant two rows 2 ft 6 in apart; drive a strong post in the middle of the two rows at each end and stretch a wire tightly between the two and grow your plants up canes or strings to the wire. This means that your tomatoes will hang inside a sort of tent or canopy of leaves giving them protection from cold winds. Unless the season is very dry they will require little watering. Make a trench about a foot away from the plants and water into this to avoid chilling the roots.

If, as recommended, you have planted in a fertile soil, little feed will be required except an occasional watering with sulphate of potash and superphosphate dissolved in water at the rate of a heaped dessertspoonful of each in a 2-gallon can of water. Avoid using nitrogenous fertilizers as this tends to make the leaves and fruit too large.

A few general hints which may be useful: fluctuating temperatures upset young plants more than anything else and, if only the sun is to be relied upon for warmth, then try to give the protection of a cloche or failing that make a temporary shelter by using three canes and push over these a clear plastic bag.

Don't buy plants of an unknown variety, don't buy from boxes and never buy plants that have been standing in cold draughts such as outside a shop or from an open market. Order your plants early, tell your supplier what you want them for and when you will want to collect them which should be early May but somewhat dependent on where you live. Some good varieties raised particularly for outdoor growing are Outdoor Girl, First in the Field, Amateur, and Primabel.

Tread the soil firmly before planting otherwise the fruits will tend to be coarse and corrugated – there is seldom any trouble with setting of tomatoes grown outside. And above all, don't be greedy – stop the plants at one leaf beyond the fourth truss and remove all side shoots during the growing season.

Feeding Tomatoes

Mr W. W. of Stockport asks if sheep droppings mixed with cow dung provide a good food for tomatoes as a substitute for horse manure? Last year his tomatoes did very well until three trusses were reached, and then they withered just when they were in full flower. Also, should he take them out of the cardboard pots before putting them in the ground?

Sheep droppings and cow manure are reasonably good for tomatoes, but they are not a complete food. Whilst improving the physical condition of the soil they supply mainly nitrogen and it is necessary to feed tomatoes additionally with potash and phosphates.

The failure of the tomato plants after reaching three trusses has nothing to do with the method of feeding, but could indicate that something had gone wrong with the root system, caused either by lack of feeding, particularly nitrogen deficiency, or perhaps the use uf unsterilized soil in the making up of the compost, so that some pest such as root eelworm was present. It is preferable, therefore, that sterilized loam be used in the potting compost.

Another important point is to ensure that the soil is warm at planting time (warm being not less than 56° F). If the plants

146

arrive before the soil has warmed up, stand them in the greenhouse and don't put them in cold soil for this could lead to them collapsing later.

Whether the cardboard pot should be removed before planting is optional, as it will rot away anyhow. However, the safest plan is to take them out of paper or cardboard pots, but if the plants are in peat pots, then plant the lot.

Vegetables in a Flower Garden

Mrs D. C. of Topsham in Devon says that the cost of vegetables is making many people think of growing their own. Can the Team tell her how she can incorporate vegetables in her flower garden to look reasonably tidy and help her budget?

Growing vegetables and salads amongst flowers is an ideal way to provide a regular supply and the two are by no means incompatible. Obviously the bulk won't be as great as could be obtained from rows across a vegetable plot but successional sowing can provide a regular contribution ample for a small household.

Many vegetables are quite ornamental – one can think of things like Swiss chards, beetroot, carrots, ornamental kale and coloured cabbage which can hold their own in flowerbeds. Then, of course, there is the foliage of the asparagus and globe artichoke which can add to the charm of the herbaceous border. Chives can make a very attractive edging as can the tiny golden Tom Thumb lettuces which measure only a few inches across but have a very solid heart and make excellent eating.

Plan your border carefully leaving litle island sites and in most cases the seed can be sown direct, as one would sow clumps of annuals in a herbaceous border. In the case of asparagus, put in three, five or seven roots depending on the size of the garden, cut a few and then allow the rest to grow up to provide an ornamental foliage. This is quite attractive and is also required to build up the crowns for the following season.

The tall silvery-leaved artichokes are most decorative at the back of a border and carrots can be sown amongst petunias or antirrhinums, just putting in a few seeds and extending the spacing of the flowering plants to accommodate them. Perennial onions are very unobtrusive and provide a constant source of young onions right through the year. Egyptian or tree onions, sage or parsley never look amiss in a border and if you give this matter a little thought there's no reason why you shouldn't work out your own permutation which can look most attractive and help with the housekeeping.

A Disappearing Mint Bed

What could be the cause of a mint bed, established five years ago in Mr C. C.'s garden, fading away and disappearing?

In this country mint is very liable to attack by a fungus known as mint rust and, scientifically, *Puccinia menthae*. This disease is easily recognized as it forms orange coloured pustules on the stems and on the under sides of the leaves. Very often these leaves or stems may be deformed and twisted into rather strange contortions, but the eventual effect of the disease is that the plant is weakened and gradually fades away and disappears.

Puccinia menthae is very difficult to control as it often attacks the underground rhizomes or runners of the mint, and there it is fairly well protected against anything the gardener can do. Where the attack is persistent, a number of palliative measures can be adopted. For example, if the mint is growing in very good soil, it can often survive the disease and yield a crop, and in order to provide these conditions a dressing of good rich compost, maybe 2 in thick, in early March would prevent the disease being very serious.

Another method of attack is to wait until the foliage has

died down in the autumn and then to cover the mint bed with straw and set it alight. The fire will kill off most of the fungal spores which are above the ground and may effect a certain amount of kill on the rust on the underground rhizomes. It is not, however, a certain cure, but is very often better than nothing.

Commercially, mint rust is controlled by immersing the dormant runners in a hot water bath. The treatment is very exact and for the amateur it is almost certainly out of the question.

Thinning Asparagus

Mrs B. D., who lives in Llandudno Junction, has a small asparagus bed which has produced quite a good crop for the last two years, but recently some of the shoots have been rather thin. What must she do to improve it, and when should she cut back the fern which is now rather untidy?

There are several things that will cause asparagus to go thin – over-cutting, cutting too late in the season (cutting should stop at the end of June), insufficient moisture at the roots and low fertility.

A heavy top-dressing of well rotted compost or strawy farmyard manure each November will conserve moisture and provide plant foods for the asparagus; then in early spring a closed handful of salt to the sq yd should be given, which will also help to counteract dryness at the roots.

About August, the female plants will be flowering and producing small red berries, so to reduce overcrowding, take out some of the female plants, leaving the male ones which are more desirable as they produce fatter, more edible growths. The grass or tops produced by the remaining plants should be cut down in November.

Growing Parsley

Mr J. L. P., a member of the Pennard Garden Society near Swansea, is moderately successful with general crops, but has no luck with parsley. It is sown in early April, then thinned out, but turns yellow when only a few inches high.

It is very difficult to diagnose accurately what has happened to this parsley crop. It is most likely that it has been attacked by a fungal root rot caused by species of *Pythium* which will very often kill parsley whilst still young if the soil is wet. Another common cause of death of parsley is carrot root fly which will also attack the young plants, killing them off, and to make the confusion even worse, grey aphids will also attack the roots. Without actually seeing the plants, therefore, it is impossible to decide which of these causes has brought about the present trouble, but some general advice may be useful. For example, when sowing parsley many growers dust along the drill with BHC insecticide; this will prevent attack by carrot root fly and grey aphids, and so the parsley may get over the very young and delicate stage. When sowing it is also advisable to choose a moderately shady position and to make the soil very firm as this also tends to prevent the pests getting down to attack the roots.

It is a very long established practice before sowing parsley seed to pour a kettle of boiling water along the drill. Some gardeners even go so far as to sow the parsley seed and then pour a kettle of boiling water along the drill. This, of course, helps to sterilize the soil in the immediate area and allows the parsley to germinate and grow away without any weed competition. The boiling water may also assist the parsley to germinate rather more quickly and not lie in the soil so long.

If only a little parsley is desired for the house, undoubtedly the safest way to grow it is to sow it in a greenhouse or in a cold frame and just grow it as a pot plant. The leaves are fairly attractive and a few can always be picked off and put into soups or on new potatoes without any difficulty at all.

This method can be extended by growing the parsley in the cold frame, pricking it off into peat pots, and transplanting it later without any root disturbance at all.

Sowing Lettuce

Mr J. R. A. asks, 'Would the Team advise sowing lettuce in rows and then thinning, in preference to sowing in a seed bed and then planting out, as invariably transplanted lettuce run to seed, especially in hot weather?'

Early in the season, say in April or May, it is good practice to sow one drill or part of a drill thinly, then from that drill thin out enough to plant another row. The lettuce left undisturbed will mature more quickly than those that have been transplanted and a successional crop results.

Later on in June or July this is doubtful practice, but outside sowing can be continued by using small peat pots or lettuce tubes. Sow two or three seeds per pot, thin out to the strongest seedling, and they can be transplanted without any check by leaving them in the pot or tube. Water both the plants and the soil beforehand, and plant them a little proud, that is with the rim of the peat pot 1 in above soil level, so that the foliage is not touching the surrounding soil.

Remember that lettuce like a soil very rich in humus and a heavy liming before planting is beneficial and will also help to keep slugs away.

Early Lettuce

J. C., who lives in Lincolnshire, wants to grow some early lettuce under polythene cloches and has a greenhouse to start the seedlings off. What varieties would the Team recommend, and what would be the earliest date to sow the seed?

151

Sowing should be delayed until the end of January when the days are just beginning to lengthen, and the seedlings should be transferred into peat pots. They should be planted out about the first week in March on a rich, well prepared bed where the cloches have been in position for at least a month to warm up the soil. Treated in this way, varieties of lettuce such as Blackpool or May Princess would be mature about the beginning of May.

To get an earlier crop, similar varieties could be transplanted into a cold frame in mid-February, and these would mature around the third week in April.

Self-blanching Celery

Last season, for the first time, Mr F. P. of Whaley Bridge grew the self-blanching type of celery from seed sown in early March and planted out in May. The celery grew all right but, when nearly ready for pulling, each plant started going to seed. Mr P. asks why this should happen.

The cause of celery going to seed is always a check of some kind. A check can be brought about in many ways, but one of the most important is by sowing the seed too early. This does not apply in the present instance, for sowing in early March and planting out in May is absolutely right for self-blanching celery and for any other kind of celery as well. One must, therefore, look for another cause for the check, and this could be dryness, celery fly attack, or a shortage of organic matter in the soil. The listener will be able to decide which of these three apply, but for anyone who is hoping to grow celery these are the points which must be noted. The bed should be prepared early and must contain plenty of humus and about 4 oz of bonemeal per sq yd. The bonemeal is very important as celery grows best where there is an ample supply of this material. If self-blanching celery is being grown this should be in a block rather than in a single drill, and a useful way of doing this is to arrange the celery in six rows each of six plants, the plants being 9 in apart. This amount of space helps to draw the plants up and does, in fact, help the flavour.

Self-blanching celery, however, is not of the highest quality and it would be much better to grow a blanching type such as Bibby's Defiance. Lately, American types of celery have appeared on the market. These are green and as such are not very well received by us in this country, but they are very much better flavoured than they appear and a good variety of this type is Tall Utah. The advantage of this green American celery is that it does not need any blanching at all, but it should be grown in exactly the same way as our English celery, that is, in a rich soil containing plenty of organic matter.

Wood Ash on Onions

Writing from Llanbedrog, Miss S. A. H. says, 'Each year I cover the plot for my onion sets with a good half-inch of wood ash, the very fine white powder, and I notice that weed seeds are very slow to germinate. Is this due to the wood ash? Does the wood ash also retard the growth of the onion sets?'

Fine wood ash would certainly act as a weed smother amd might keep out the light needed by a number of weed seeds before they will germinate. In addition, wood ash contains considerable quantities of potash which, when applied to many seeds, will act chemically as a germination inhibitor.

Very fine wood ash is of some value in areas where the soil is sandy, but it is best worked into the soil some three or four weeks before any sowing or planting, or growth may be slowed up. If it is used in quantity it might produce an excess of potash in the soil and dried blood could be used to supply the nitrogen to counteract this.

Many crops, such as fruit trees and especially gooseberries,

153

are avid for potash, and wood ash can be usefully applied to them.

In preference, however, gardeners should use the chunky coarse pieces of wood ash rather than the fine powder, for these larger pieces have a mechanical effect on the soil, helping to improve drainage.

White Mould on Onions

From Mr H. of Southend a question about onions. 'Could the Team please tell me how to get rid of a white mould on onions? This is known locally as mouldy nose.'

White mould, or white nose, in onions is caused by a fungus whose technical name is *Sclerotium cepivorum*. The disease shows itself firstly as a yellowing of the leaves, and when the bulbs are lifted they may be seen to have slightly browned and, perhaps, rotten leaves. Later on the bulb may become covered with a white fluffy growth of the fungus and in this white fluffy material, small pinhead-sized black bodies are formed. These small black bodies are the way in which the fungus over-winters in the soil in the absence of the host plant, the onion. The black bodies are called sclerotia, are extremely long lived and are very difficult to kill, so that really once this fungus gains entry to a garden probably the only solution to the problem is to stop growing onions on that part of the garden for several years. The disease will also attack leeks and shallots, but you can safely grow brassicas, peas and beans and all other crops in affected areas, as they will not be harmed at all by the fungus.

The difficulty about growing onions is that they require a very rich soil with plenty of humus. In consequence, once the fertility in a certain part of the garden has been built up to this high level, growers are reluctant to move their onions to another part of the garden, and so rotation tends not to be practised. This gives any sort of disease a chance to become prevalent and so, although diseases of onions are relatively uncommon, when they do occur they are very, very difficult to eliminate.

Transplanting Onions

Mrs D. M. B. of Bewdley would like to know whether it is better to transplant onions into pots or boxes for show purposes.

There is no doubt that they should be grown in pots for this purpose – the roots are emitted from a basal plate and as they are monocotyledons they don't have branching roots like a tomato for example and care must be taken not to break these very fine roots. For preference they should be in peat pots or soil blocks. This means that they haven't to be knocked out of the pot when planted out.

It is important that both onions and leeks be transplanted either to 3 in pots, soil blocks or pricked out in boxes in a light compost such as John Innes No. 1 and spaced at 2 in apart. See that there is no lumpy material in the seed pan or box as the first roots go straight down and, if these become anchored in pebbly coarse material such as is often placed there for drainage, this long root is broken off and the plant starts off with a handicap.

Seeds should be sown in December or January in gentle heat, 60° F is about right to get them started off well. Sow the seeds thinly so that they can be easily and carefully lifted with a pointed label. The time to do this is when the second needle-like growth comes up straight; the first shoot will be U-shaped with the root at one end and the old seed coat attached to the tip of the green growth, which will eventually pull out of the soil. This is what is known as the knee and if the soil is very dry and loose, the seed coat will remain attached to this first seed leaf, very much to its detriment.

As soon as this first seed leaf has pulled itself out of the soil, another erect, needle-like leaf will form by its side and when this is about 1 in high, the seedling should then be transferred. By this time the plant will have about three roots made and should grow away without any check.

Now for exhibition onions, they should be transferred to a 4½ in pot as soon as the roots touch the side of the 3 in pot and kept in this until the stem is about as thick as a pencil. If you are going to win any prizes with your onions you've got to learn how to select those which are most likely to produce the largest bulbs and this can be done very early in its life. During February or early March, pick out those with the greatest number of leaves because the more leaves, the bigger the bulb.

Onion Eelworm

Can the Team advise Mr T. E. B. on the time that should elapse before onions are cultivated on land where they have been extensively attacked by onion eelworm? No other plants, such as broad beans, parsnips, rhubarb or strawberries have been planted on the site.

The onion eelworm is sometimes known as the stem or bulb eelworm. Scientifically it is called *Anguillulina dipsaci* and is one of the most widespread and serious of the stem and bulb nematodes. Its symptoms are fairly easy to distinguish. Usually the young plant becomes swollen or misshapen at the base, and as the plant grows older the leaves do not elongate at the normal rate. On the other hand, the leaves tend to become distorted, shortened and thickened, and the actual onion bulb swells irregularly. The foliage may become wilted and yellow and, on many occasions, a soft rot may gain entrance to the centre of the bulb itself, rendering it absolutely useless.

No really good control for this soil-borne parasite is known. There are one or two chemical soil sterilizing agents which may be used in small areas of soil, but they are expensive, their use is slightly dangerous, and considerable intervals of time have to elapse between treatment and replanting. The best method is to adopt a system of crop rotation which will omit onions from the affected soil for about five years. The onion eelworm is not very wide-ranging in the plants it will attack and it is perfectly safe to grow such subjects as beans, potatoes, peas, strawberries, etc., in soil containing the parasite. There is, however, a certain amount of evidence that the onion eelworm will also attack leeks and narcissi, chives, and shallots, and so it is worth avoiding using these crops in the rotation.

Growing Show Leeks

How to grow show leeks, and how to control the amount of stem to be blanched, is what puzzles Mr A. B. of Kielder, Northumberland.

In growing show leeks an important point is to obtain the right variety, and a good strain of variety, such as Finney's Monarch. Sow in January in heat, plant out early, and cloche the plants to get some early growth; later soil up to the leeks, or use drainage tiles and peat for blanching. The most successful exhibitors of leeks grow them, not from seed, but from 'pods', and this particularly applies in the north-east where the pitman's pot leek is widely grown.

Leeks demand land that has been very heavily manured and is very rich, and for feeding there is nothing better than potash nitrate and an occasional pinch of good tomato fertilizer.

Rotation of Crops

Mr J. J. asks, 'In my plot last year I had potatoes, then leeks, then Brussels. This year I shall follow the potatoes with Brussels, the leeks with potatoes, the Brussels with leeks. I have moved them around like this for years. Will the Team please comment and advise on rotation of crops?'

Plant rotations are necessary where it seems as if the same crop is going to be grown in the same soil for a number of years in succession, because, under these conditions, three things can happen. Firstly, there can be a build up of pests and diseases of that particular crop in the soil. Secondly, the soil can become exhausted of the particular food materials which that specific crop demands. And, thirdly, the roots will only penetrate the soil to a given depth, and so one tends to get a rather dead layer of soil below the roots.

A good rotation, therefore, avoids all these dangers and a yardstick which the questioner should apply now is how well his crops have been succeeding. Of the three crops he mentions, leeks like new manure, and it would be as well to follow the leeks with the brassicas, followed eventually in the third year by the potatoes. If slugs are troublesome, however, the potatoes should come immediately after the leeks, between the leeks and the brassicas.

It is rather strange that he seems to have forgotten all about peas and beans, and it might be advisable to introduce these into his rotation. Peas and beans have a particular virtue, that they add nitrogen to the soil and so benefit the brassicas which might follow them. A reasonable rotation would then be, first year, roots, i.e. potatoes, second year, pods, i.e. peas and beans, third year, leaves, i.e. leeks or Brussels sprouts, and in this way the families would not be mixed. If he divides his garden into three parts he could then work this rather simple rotation, but it might be worth while mentioning that he could make the rotation more effective if on some years he plants his three crops across the garden instead of along the garden. This would mean that the rows in some years would run at right-angles to the rows in other years, and this helps to mix the soil and make the rotation more effective.

Planting Potatoes

Mr F. E. D. wonders if we attach too much importance to the depth that a potato should be planted? For example, is there anything to be gained, or lost, by planting deep to save hoeing up?

This depends on the soil. With a very light soil you can plant deeply, say 5 to 6 in, because the ridging up will collapse with the weather. On very heavy soil which will stay cold and wet it is a disadvantage to plant deeply as the plant will take a long time to get to the surface. So under these conditions it is better to plant shallowly 4 to 5 in and to ridge up after the plants are through. Many gardeners tend to plant too deeply in the belief that, as it will take longer for the tops to get through, they will stand less chance of getting frosted. Some have a wrong idea as to where the new tubers are formed on a potato: they form on the stem, and there is nothing to be gained by planting too deeply.

A modern technique is to lay the tubers on the surface of the soil, cover them with black polythene, make crossed slits for the foliage to come through, and do nothing more about them. There is also the lazy bed method, where the potatoes are placed on the surface of the soil and the soil is drawn lightly over them. This is quite a good method in very wet districts and where the soil is very heavy.

Cutting Potato Tubers

Mr F. B. a retired gardener in Kimberworth, finds that these days a bag of seed potatoes when purchased often contains a considerable proportion of large tubers. Would the Team give some guidance on how to cut and treat large tubers before planting?

Although some varieties of seed potatoes do cut satisfactorily, on the whole it pays to plant the large tuber rather than to cut it, but if cutting is decided on, it should be made lengthways in order to ensure that each portion carries some sound eyes. The cut surfaces should be left to dry and callus over for a few days before planting.

Perhaps the most satisfactory solution is to grow those varieties of potatoes that do not produce big tubers and leave alone those such as Majestic, Home Guard, and Arran Pilot which do. First earlies producing small tubers include Epicure, Duke of York, and Sharpe's Express, all three varieties of high quality and flavour which will never need cutting. Small tubered main crop varieties include Golden Wonder, Kerr's Pink, and Bishop, none of them heavy croppers but of quite excellent flavour.

The difficulty with Golden Wonder is that nearly all the stocks of this variety have virus disease, so you must get stock seed. This is why it is called golden – because the leaves are infected with the virus in most cases and look rather yellowish.

Eelworm in Potatoes

Is there a variety of potato immune from eelworm, asks Mrs L.

Scientifically potato root eelworm is a nematode called *Heterodera rostochiensis*. It attacks the roots of the potato plant by burrowing into them and so damaging the water-conducting tissues of the plant. This results in damage to the leaves which in turn prematurely yellow and fall off giving the plant a 'feather duster' appearance, and, of course, the loss of leaves means that the crop of tubers is very much reduced. In a dry year, when water is critical, there may be no crop at all.

The eelworm can last in the soil for many years in the form of a small brown hard-walled cyst, which, although only as big as a pinhead, may contain 400 eggs, each of which can hatch to become a larva able to attack potato roots. Most larva in their turn can develop into cysts and the rate of build-up can be very great.

True immunity from eelworm would mean that the larvae could not damage the roots and there is no commercial variety which possesses this quality. Research is being actively pursued using South American potatoes as breeding stock, and promising eelworm resistant strains are being developed, but so far none is on the market.

Some of our commercial varieties are not so badly affected and are therefore immune to a certain degree, for example Kerr's Pink does not suffer so much as Majestic.

There is no satisfactory soil treatment to get rid of eelworm, but there are one or two ways of avoiding attack. One is to plant early varieties such as Epicure or Duke of York which can be lifted before the eelworm attacks; if you have enough land, practise crop rotation, keeping known infested land free of potatoes for at least four years, but if you haven't sufficient land then it will be advisable to grow only such other crops as lettuce, carrots, beans and peas.

If your garden is too small to allow rotation and you want to grow potatoes in spite of eelworm infection, a soil sterilant based on metham-sodium is effective but fairly expensive. It is irritating to eyes, nose and mouth too, so considerable care must be taken in its application.

Keel Slugs and Wireworm in Potatoes

Mr P. R.'s potato tubers are often pierced by one or more small diameter holes, and upon cutting them up he finds the centres are also eaten out. Is this the damage caused by keel slugs, and can the Team suggest a remedy?

The tubers examined appear to have been damaged by both keel slugs and wireworms, and for the former slug pellets should be used, and for wireworms a moderately effective control is to use BHC powder.

When planting potatoes, scatter the slug pellets in the bottom of the drill underneath the potatoes and sit the potatoes on top of them, because the keel slugs come up from fairly deep down. As successive earthings-up are carried out, sprinkle some slug pellets on the surface soil before earthing up.

The recent wet summers have meant that keel slugs have appeared in districts where they are not usually troublesome: they are the small black slugs which seldom appear on the surface, except about late April when they come to the surface for a fortnight or so. The rest of the time they spend under the soil and may go down as far as 2 ft. They are omnivorous and will eat anything, living plant material, decayed manure or compost, and the more manure is put into the soil the more slugs there will be. On very bad land for slugs, particularly in the north and north-west, where there is a high rainfall, it sometimes helps to omit manure and compost and rely entirely on artificial fertilizers for a year or even two.

Potato Blight

What can Mrs P. of Derby do to prevent or cure potato blight?

Potato blight is a disease caused by a fungus, *Phytophthora infestans*, which attacks the potato in two ways. In the first instance, it will attack the leaves and turn the tips brown and eventually black, gradually progressing down the plant until all the foliage dies off leaving bare green stalks sticking up. The disease usually starts in the south of England in June, working its way northward as the warm weather progresses.

The other way by which the potato blight causes damage is that it very often attacks the tubers by virtue of spores which fall off the leaves and land on any exposed potatoes. There the disease will enter the tuber and set up a rot which can eventually destroy the tuber itself. Thus not only will the yield be reduced by the attack on the leaves, but the actual crop which is produced can also be diseased and maybe destroyed.

One good way to avoid this disease is to plant early varieties such as Duke of York or Sharpe's Express or Epicure. These varieties mature in late June or early July and in consequence they can be dug safely out of the ground before the potato blight arrives. It is a useful coincidence that damage by keel slugs is also avoided by this method.

Most farmers, however, have to grow late potatoes, and where this is desirable or even unavoidable it is a good plan to spray with a liquid copper fungicide early in the summer. This spray should cover not only the upper side, but also the under side of the foliage and should be applied before the blight is due to arrive. An important point to note is that if spraying is carried out in districts where the air is industrially polluted, the application of the chemical should only be at half strength or the haulms may be damaged. The reason for this is that the atmospheric pollution already contains certain substances which will help to reduce the amount of blight, and are chemically active.

Good Eating Potatoes

Mr A. M. of Glasgow asks the Team to recommend a good eating potato for growing in the west of Scotland, and to give briefly the culture to ensure a good quality crop.

Two good late potatoes are Golden Wonder and Kerr's Pink; the former does not crop very heavily, but the latter gives a reasonably heavy crop. The earlies, Epicure and Midlothian Early, are both quite heavy croppers and of high flavour and would do well in Scotland.

Potatoes should not be grown on the same land for more than two years in succession as they tend to exhaust the soil fairly quickly and there could easily be a build-up of pests such as the potato root eelworm. Although they will grow in nearly any kind of soil they prefer to be planted in areas in which humus has been liberally added the previous year and, if possible, it always helps to add a little compost or grass cuttings along the drill before planting the tubers. In areas where slugs are troublesome many growers scatter slug pellets between the tubers and as the shoots come through they are earthed up in order to protect them against early frosts and in order to give them a longer underground stem. Halfway through the growing season it often pays to give a sprinkling of fertilizer along the drills and to earth up again to the stems. On sandy soils where the drills are liable to get flattened down by wind and rain it is advisable to repeat this fertilizing and earthing up process again. This will ensure that the crop gets two feeds during the growing season and this will be reflected in the number and size of the tubers.

Carrots in Stony Soil

Mrs G. of Kemsing in Kent would like to know what the Team considers the best method of obtaining long, straight carrots and parsnips in a stony soil?

Although this may sound a very simple question and one affecting not too many gardeners, it is important: there is nothing more infuriating than to have good crops of roots ruined by fanging and forking. The old gardeners' technique is, of course, to bore a large funnel shaped hole in the ground with a crowbar, fill up with John Innes compost and then sow the seeds in the hole. This is one way to achieve a good-shaped root without interference from stones but many gardeners dislike the technique saying it compacts the soil around the hole and makes for drainage problems.

An alternative way and one that is practised by many people who specialize in showing carrots and parsnips is to grow them above ground. This is usually in a 6 in drainpipe. The procedure is to dig in plenty of manure, stand the drainpipe on its end in this soil and fill with a prepared soil free from lumps and rich in organic matter. The seeds should then be sown and a little cloche or even a jam jar placed over the top of the pipe. Then when the seeds grow you should thin out to the strongest plant. This method gives an added bonus in that the height of the plant above the ground means that it will be safe from attacks of carrotfly – they seldom go much above ground level.

One last thing – another reason for carrots particularly forking is the use of fresh, raw manure – so don't!

Salsify

Mrs G. C. of Norwich would like to grow the vegetable salsify. She has tried once or twice but the roots have been small with wispy fingers and the germination has been poor.

Salsify, the vegetable oyster, is a root vegetable with a tapered root rather like a small parsnip. It has a very distinctive flavour and is usually scraped and cooked gently in salted water. There are no named varieties.

It isn't a difficult thing to grow. It needs a good open soil so

165

that the roots are able to ramify, fairly rich but with well rotted manure, not new. Growing on newly manured soil will cause the roots to fork.

Seedlings can't be transplanted so the seeds should be sown in April in drills, then thin out to the best plants roughly 4–6 in apart. The drills themselves should be approximately a foot apart and roots may be lifted from late October onwards and stored in moist soils. If they are left in the ground for late lifting, protection from frost will be necessary.

Vegetables under a Sycamore

Mrs T. B. of Bolton-le-Sands, Lancashire, asks, 'Which vegetables would the Team suggest I should grow under two large sycamore trees?'

The dense foliage of sycamores in summer causes considerable light restriction and so precludes the growing of summer maturing crops. Some of the lower branches could be removed to let in more bottom light, and then it might be possible to grow some of the brassicas reasonably well and maybe potatoes.

The safest solution would be to grow early maturing spring vegetables which would be more or less harvested before the densest foliage was on the trees, and would include spring onions, early radish, and early carrots. Another crop which might do well is white turnips as they only take about six or seven weeks to mature and three crops a year can normally be obtained. Leeks could be transplanted into this area from another part of the garden in the early autumn, where they will grow through the winter and can be used during the winter and early spring.

In such an area, however, there would always be the problem of drip and maybe the soil becoming acid and inhospitable. On the whole this would be part of the garden where vegetables would always be rather poor, and it would be more satisfactory to grow shade-loving bulbs or flowering plants.

Vegetables for Exhibition

How and when should Mr T. G. B. of Chepstow prepare the soil for growing vegetables, such as onions and kidney beans, for exhibition?

If one is really intending to go in for exhibition of crops such as onions and kidney beans, then quite certainly preparations should be going on all the time for it is impossible to get the soil into exactly the correct condition in one year. Nevertheless, if we start from the assumption that the questioner has not hitherto prepared the soil at all, then, as soon as the previous crop has been lifted, the area in which the onions are going to be grown should be enriched with plenty of farmyard manure, at least one heaped barrowload per 2 sq yds. This does not constitute a completely adequate fertilizer and so it is advisable to add, per 2 sq yds, 4 oz bone meal, 4 oz hoof and horn, about 2 oz sulphate of potash, and any wood ash that is available. This mixture should then be dug in and the ground left rough during the winter in order that the frost may get to work on it. This area will form a good onion bed, but before planting the following year, the ground should be trodden down firmly.

This may seem a lot of work and it may look as if a great deal of food material is going into the soil for a very limited return, but, in fact, one of the greatest advantages of onions is that they can be grown in the same bed year after year without any ill effects. This means that if you can start off with a really rich soil you do not need to apply similar quantities each year, but can simply keep the soil topped up with roughly half these quantities in subsequent years.

In the case of kidney beans, the soil need not be in such a rich condition as it is for the onions, and growers can therefore easily reduce the amount of hoof and horn and the amount of farmyard manure to half quantities, but they should be careful to include some superphosphates, about 2 oz per sq yd. The reason for this is that beans require plenty of phosphates and the mixture which is used for the onions does not contain as much of this as would be necessary. In addition to this, beans require a warm quick draining soil, so one should choose a site which will warm up quickly in the spring and which contains a certain amount of sand in the soil.

Exhibition Cauliflowers

Mr D. F. A. wants guidance on the timing of cauliflowers for show dates from August to November, having regard to the heavy clay soil he has to deal with. Also what is the Team's opinion of the Australian varieties of cauliflowers?

The best way to time cauliflowers is by successional sowings of one variety, say a good strain of All The Year Round or Everyday. For an August show, seed should be sown about the first week in April, followed by successional sowings every two weeks, so that you have a few plants to put out at fortnightly intervals. Sow in boxes very thinly, then prick off into 2 in peat pots in really rich soil, and eventually plant the lot so that there is no root disturbance, as a good root system is vital to the production of good heads.

Particularly for the first planting make a V–drill at least 4 in deep, preferably running north to south, and put the plants at the bottom of the drill so that they are protected from cold winds. As growth proceeds, draw the soil up to the stems to encourage stem rooting which will reduce the effect of any maggot or club root attack.

With this clay soil, heavy amounts of organic matter should be added, and also some lime; make sure it is well drained, for cauliflowers insist on really high fertility.

The Australian varieties of cauliflowers are autumn

heading hybrids that are generally more leafy than English varieties, the curds are solid and even, and quite well protected by foliage. These varieties mature very evenly, which is a good thing for the commercial grower, but not always so for the amateur.

Curd on Cauliflowers

Mr S. of Dunchurch has difficulty in obtaining cauliflowers with a good thick curd. Those he grows tend to break out into a mass of thin florets and he asks whether this is caused by feed or cultivation faults?

Several things can cause this to happen but the usual reason is an attack of rootfly and the answer would be to apply a dressing of BHC powder around the roots about once a fortnight to deter egg laying.

The point should also be made that cauliflowers need very careful handling, much more so than the others in the brassica family. They should even be pricked out into boxes or pots and planted with a trowel to eliminate any root disturbance. If they are pulled out of a drill like cabbages or savoys they will almost certainly bolt and they need a rich, well-manured soil with soil pulled up to the stem to encourage stem rooting.

Seeds may be sown under glass from January onwards and later on outdoors in a well prepared seed bed – young seedlings are best pricked out at 4 in apart to ensure a good root system.

For the beginner a good variety to grow is All Year Round as it may be sown, as its name implies, at varying times under glass for transplanting or in the open in a prepared seed bed. It produces large white heads which mature according to the season of sowing, making it a good variety for the exhibitor as it can be had in good condition for the show date. To help your calculations – reckon back 14 weeks from your sowing date.

Two more good varieties to note are Suttons Classic to produce good heads in early June and dwarf in habit; Suttons Arcturus for a good successor later in the season.

Brussels Sprouts not Buttoning up

Mr G. F. of Winslow in Buckinghamshire would like to know why his Brussels sprouts don't button up properly. This seemed to be a widespread problem in the area.

There could be several reasons for this. The most common cause is too lavish feeding, especially with nitrogen, or too loose a soil. This gives a large, soft plant which tends to catch a lot of wind, causing root rock which makes the sprout blow rather than make a tight button. In fact if there are very strong winds in autumn, even well grown and properly fed sprouts will suffer the same fate.

Variety also comes into this and if sprouts are to be grown on light soil in windy areas, it is advisable to grow smaller or dwarf varieties and, by the way, it is always as well to grow sprouts on land that hasn't been dug the previous year.

Brussels sprouts need a long season of growth and in most areas are best sown in late summer and treated in the way you would spring cabbages. Alternatively they can be raised in heat under glass from a January/February sowing, in cold frames and by sowing thinly in drills outdoors. Unfortunately, most people seem to treat all sprouts alike without any regard to variety and successional planting.

Where possible, sprouts should be planted in soil that has been well manured but consolidated. They can follow crops such as beans or peas without digging over the soil. If weeds are a problem they can be killed with a paraquat weedkiller just before planting. And in fact it doesn't matter if you have to make holes with a crowbar for your plants as Brussels sprouts are even better than potatoes at breaking up the soil. However you grow them, at the end of the summer, tread down the area around the plant thoroughly, give a sprinkling of National Growmore and earth up the stems to a height of 4 or 5 in. Roots will be emitted into this and help to steady the plant, reducing the risk of rosetting.

Anchoring Brussels Sprouts

Mr A. M. of the Riseholme and District Horticultural Club in Lincolnshire follows his potatoes with sprouts. The sprouts do well and crop heavily, but by August they almost invariably flop over. Can this be avoided by growing a special variety or by different cultural or fertilizer treatment? The sprouts get a little complete fertilizer and no nitrogen.

Where this problem is widespread it is very good practice to avoid growing tall varieties of sprouts and concentrate on the smaller, almost dwarf varieties. There is a very good one which is only about 2 ft high called Jade Cross, or there is one grown quite extensively on a commercial scale which is about 2 ft 6 in high which is called Ashwell's Strain. These will not produce such large sprouts as varieties such as Wroxton, but they should produce tight buttons of a very high quality.

Apart from choosing a dwarf variety, sprouts have to be grown on land which is not too wet, for if the soil becomes waterlogged at all there is a decrease in the growth of the roots which results in the plants being unstable. In order to overcome this instability and flopping over, many growers put the plants at the bottom of a deep V-shaped drill, maybe 5–6 in deep. As the sprout grows, the soil is brought into the drill to level it up and eventually the soil is built up to the stem until the sprout is coming through a ridge. B.H.C. powder is added to the soil as the plant is being earthed up, and by so doing not only buries the roots more deeply and, therefore, gives them a firmer hold on the earth, but it also encourages stem rooting, and by this means plants are very much more strongly anchored than they would otherwise be.

Club Root

Mr G. A. B. from Chepstow, in Monmouthshire, asks, 'What is the cause of and the remedy for club root?'

The cause of club root is a fungus named *Plasmodiophora brassicae.* This fungus lives in the soil and when any members of the brassica families are planted it is likely to attack the roots. It is a very primitive fungus and it possesses spores which can swim in water. This is important because these spores spread the disease and, therefore, if the soil is wet as a result of bad drainage, undoubtedly the disease will be fostered and be much more severe. Club root is also very much increased by having an acid soil and so the application of lime to the soil will reduce the acidity and, therefore, reduce the disease.

At the same time, of course, any method to increase soil fertility is of importance, as this will very often allow a crop to be produced even though the plants have been attacked by club root. Cultural methods are also helpful in the control of this disease. For example, if during the growing season soil is heaped up around the stems of the brassicas, roots will develop from the stems into this top soil and these roots will have less chance of being infected by the disease than roots deeper down in the rather moister soil, and so one can perhaps get a crop where one otherwise would not.

Another approach to the control of club root is to use chemicals. The chemical which is in widest use is mercury in the form of calomel dust or paste. Many growers before they plant out their cauliflowers will dip the roots in water and then in calomel paste. They may also dust some of the calomel around the base of the stem before planting. The application of this substance will certainly reduce the amount of club root, but will not eliminate it from the soil as only a

172

very long period of crop rotation is able to do this.

Gardeners and allotment holders who have club root are, therefore, well advised to adopt a different system of rotation and try to grow subjects such as peas and beans, lettuces, potatoes, carrots, etc., which are not attacked by this fungus.

Nine Star Perennial Broccoli

Mrs F. C. of Devizes says, 'Bearing in mind that Nine Star perennial broccoli will be remaining in the same piece of ground, how can I keep the plants healthy and in good heart?'

The average cropping life of this broccoli is about 3 years, so altogether it will be in the same piece of ground for 4 years. They produce anything up to a dozen heads about the size of a fist and to get good results they need a good rich soil as this heavy cropping takes a good deal out of the soil. An annual mulch of compost or rotted manure and then the usual applications of artificial fertilizer should be adequate.

Half a dozen plants are excellent in a small garden as according to weather conditions, they will produce unexpected heads almost at any time of the year with little or no effort on the part of the grower.

Space the plants at least 2 ft 6 in apart and as this is a longstanding crop, plant in a square, say of nine plants, rather than in a single row where they are exposed to the weather.

The Taste of Vegetables

Mr W. J. W., a retired miner with fifty years' gardening experience, feels that vegetables grown today are not up to the standard of years ago and asks whether the Team support this view.

This may not be just a 'good old days' story, for vegetables and fruit generally are not as good in quality or as highly flavoured as they used to be. One reason is that many highly flavoured varieties of fruit and vegetables through the years have succumbed to diseases, other varieties have proved too low yielding or would not keep, with the result that the hybridists have bred new varieties which are disease resistant, crop heavily, but frequently are not so highly flavoured.

This certainly applies to raspberries, strawberries, tomatoes and potatoes. But the amateur gardener does not need to grow commercial, heavy cropping varieties, and should concentrate on the better quality, highly flavoured kinds of fruit and vegetables. Some suggestions are, raspberries – Lloyd George; strawberries – Royal Sovereign; tomatoes – Ailsa Craig; and potatoes – early, Epicure, and late, Golden Wonder.

Feeding also contributes largely towards flavour, and unfortunately there is a feeling amongst gardeners that the main fertilizer they must use is sulphate of ammonia. All this particular fertilizer does is to provide nitrogen, which increases the size and at the same time reduces flavour; if more compost was used and less nitrogen, and slightly more potash, then fruit and vegetables would taste a lot better.

Transplanting Cabbages

Mr R. H. of Four Marks in Hampshire asks whether it is better to transplant cabbages or sow in position and thin out?

Although it's not always best to follow the practice of commercial growers, this might be one instance when it might be acceptable. In recent years they have been sowing direct and thinning out to the strongest plants; the reasons for this are economic as it saves a lot of labour. If you grow a lot of cabbages you may wish to do this, but on the other hand there is considerable virtue in transplanting. The mere act of transplanting induces a more vigorous root system giving a better end product.

One big mistake made by many amateur gardeners is sowing the seed too thickly in the drills and then waiting too long before transplanting. The closeness of the plants makes then drawn and leggy and less able to withstand the shock of transplanting.

Ideally the seed should be sown in a seed bed and depending on whether you want spring and summer or winter cabbages you have to sow at different times. For spring and early summer cabbages it is best to sow in July very thinly in shallow drills. The soil should be kept moist and when the plants are a reasonable size they can then be moved to their final situation in September. If they are then kept growing well and given a little feed of ½ oz per sq yd of nitrate of soda they will be usable not only through the spring, but into the early summer.

The cabbages you will eat in the late summer and the autumn should be sown the previous September or else early in March. They can then be transplanted to their final stations in April and their heart should be ready for cutting by August. Depending on the variety you choose you will then be able to have a succession of cabbages all the year round.

For winter cabbages, sowing should be done in April and the plants put out as soon as they are large enough to handle. The soil for winter cabbages should be rich, well supplied with old farmyard manure and special care should be taken to firm the plants in very well as winter cabbages are very often damaged by the high winds which blow in the late autumn. In every case it is advisable to treat the roots with either calomel dust or some other similar substance to protect them from cabbage root fly and club root.

Spinach Running to Seed

Summer spinach sown in April on light soil by Mr F. H. always runs to seed. What causes this?

As in so many other cases, bolting or running to seed is the result usually of some unfavourable condition, most often in the soil. In some cases it can be attributed to poor seed and some varieties are more prone to bolting than others, but on the whole it is soil or atmospheric conditions which can bring about this phenomenon. In the case in question, the spinach was certainly sown too early, for summer spinach should never be in the ground until about 10 May. On a light soil, too, there is always the tendency for the ground to be too dry and any check through dryness will undoubtedly make the spinach bolt. If, therefore, this condition is likely to hold, a good dressing of compost or farmyard manure should be incorporated into the soil as this will reduce the tendency to excessive dryness.

Very few commercial growers will touch summer spinach as it is recognized as one of the most sensitive and difficult crops to grow, and commercial people naturally avoid difficult crops as this can result in a loss of income. Most amateurs would probably find that New Zealand spinach is easier to grow, as it thrives in dry weather and can be picked over a very much longer period.

Control of Rabbits

In the garden of Mr A. A. M. of Uffculme, Devon, rabbits have eaten up cauliflowers, young cabbages and generally played old Harry. What can be done?

For a very long time rabbits constituted a real problem in the garden, but when myxomatosis appeared a very large number of the rabbit population died and gardeners and farmers began to breathe freely again. Now this problem has to be faced once more, for the rabbit population has started to increase and we are getting an increased number of reports of damage being done to gardens.

On the whole, deterrent sprays are not of much use. They have some value when applied to the bark of trees to prevent rabbits from eating bark but, as most people know, this problem only really arises in winter when there is a shortage of green food material. In the summer the general problem is where the young green things are being eaten. Under these conditions the best way undoubtedly is to use 1 or 2 in wire netting all round the garden, burying the netting some 6 in below the surface of the soil and leaving at least 2 ft 6 in above soil level.

Another much more laborious way, but certainly a much more effective way, is to dig a trench around the garden boundary. This trench should be made about 1 ft 6 in to 2 ft deep and the bottom foot should be filled with broken bricks, stones, broken bottles, any materials of this kind which are hard and which will resist a rabbit burrowing through. This ditch, filled in this way, will also act as a drain. Having filled the bottom foot with these materials then wire netting should be erected on top of it, having the bottom of the netting in contact with the broken bricks and the top of the netting 2 ft 6 in above soil level and the rest of the garden. The trench can then be filled in, and in that way you have what is virtually an impassable barrier to any rabbits. Gardeners ought also to remember that when this is done, sometimes as well as keeping rabbits out, the perfect fence will help to keep any rabbits in, and so, before any such construction is undertaken, everyone should be sure that they have no rabbits at all in the garden, and, thereafter, gates should be kept shut in order that a fresh invasion should not occur.

Greens to Withstand Frost

January King cabbage, curly kale, sprouting broccoli, and savoys have failed to withstand the winter. What greens do the Team recommend Mr T. A. J. to grow to get through the winter?

In cold districts it is advisable to plant winter greens early. With January King cabbage or savoys or sprouts, for instance, have them in, at the latest, by the second week in May, so that they will get up to a good sized, tough plant by October or November, and they will get through the winter safely. The secret is to grow them hard and not to feed at all.

There are two kales which will stand virtually any amount of frost; one is Labrador and the other Hungry Gap. Whilst these are not the choicest of winter greens, the young shoots are quite pleasant and tasty.

Halo Blight on Runner Beans

Mr L. F. of Aldershot had halo blight on his runner beans last year. He'd like to know what to do to prevent it in future.

This is generally a disease of French beans but will attack runner beans occasionally. It takes the form of a discoloration of the leaf, rather like the eye in a peacock's feather or a dark spot with a halo round it – hence the name.

This is a seed borne disease so it is important not to save seed from infected plants although the seed may look perfectly healthy. It is unwise to grow beans in the same area for some time – long enough to make sure that any material that has fallen from a diseased plant has completely disappeared.

Good cultivation can also help to discourage halo blight. Prepare a trench, break up the bottom well to help drainage and put in farmyard manure or compost. It is important that the beans get plenty of phosphates in the form of super-phosphate, 2 oz to the running yard of trench, and make sure that the soil is firm. This disease is always worse in a wet season so make sure that on heavy soils the trench or prepared site doesn't become waterlogged.

It should be said that halo blight is due to a bacterium and cannot be eradicated chemically. Fortunately, it is neither widespread nor very serious and providing ordinary hygiene is observed such as burning the old plants and not putting them on the compost heap, there should be little further trouble.

Maggots in Peas

Maggots which are found inside pea pods are most repulsive, and Mr E. K. of Swindon asks if there is any way to avoid them.

The cause, quite simply, is that the pea moth, *Cydia nigricana*, lays its egg on the flower after it has opened or on very young pods, and the egg eventually hatches into a little grub. At the same time the pod is developing so that eventually the grub is inside the pod. It is important to realize this because the pea moth can only be controlled if the plant is sprayed at flowering time with derris or nicotine. As peas flower over a few weeks it may be necessary to spray twice to cover the flowering period.

People are quite naturally worried about spraying open flowers with an insecticide because they think this may affect the pollination. In the case of peas this doesn't matter because peas are largely self-fertilized and don't need insects to pollinate them, so you still get a crop even if you spray with an insecticide when the flowers are open. Open apple blossom, however, should not be sprayed with an insecticide or there may be serious losses of bees and other pollinating insects.

Another way is to practise crop rotation, because the pea moth pupates in the soil where the peas have been grown, and if the peas are planted on the same land the following year the moths are there ready and waiting. Still another method is to dig very deeply so that the pupae are buried and can't get through to the surface. The previous year's pea-sticks should also be burned and not used again as sometimes the pest over-winters there. If the pest is very serious, early varieties often escape serious damage, whereas later varieties may suffer considerably.

Cultivating Mushrooms

Mr N. R. wants to cultivate mushrooms in orchard grassland and asks what preparation is required?

The main difficulty is growing edible mushrooms in grassland in an orchard is lack of humus. If mushroom spawn is just put under the turf, a crop might result for two years or so and then the land would run out of the essential 'ingredients' to grow good mushrooms.

Most mushrooms which are produced commercially are grown on beds which contain at least 50% of rotted straw or horse manure and, in order to do it successfully on a lawn, some well rotted manure has to be incorporated in the soil. If well rotted manure is not available, one can prepare reasonably good synthetic manure by composting straw with one of the 'starters' especially made for this purpose.

The job should then be begun by removing some turfs from the lawn or meadow and also some of the sub-soil beneath them, down to a depth of 6-9 in. This hole should then be filled with the well rotted compost and, in this compost, mushroom spawn should be placed. The spawn will then ramify and grow through the compost, and eventually some mushrooms should appear above the surface. The best time to do this is in early August and the turfs should, of course, be replaced and firmly stamped down over the spawned area.

This technique will certainly produce a few mushrooms for a few years but it does a certain amount of harm because, no matter how carefully one tries to fill in the hole so that the surface is level once more, after a few years the compost begins to break down and rots away and it is found that a depression will occur which could be quite deep. As the compost rots away still further, this depression will get deeper and deeper until it can be an absolute hollow, and a lawn therefore would become very difficult to mow and would require levelling by the addition of sand. On the whole, therefore, this is a rather chancy job to do in a lawn, although it could be done in an orchard where levels do not matter a great deal.

Vegetable Marrows

'What is the best time to put vegetable marrow plants in the garden, the best compost to use, and the best position in the garden?' asks Mrs B. of Barnsley. In her case, the marrows always rot off before reaching maturity.

It is best to think of marrows as being as tender as dahlias so that whenever it is safe to put dahlias out it is also safe to plant out marrows. This time, of course, varies with different parts of the country, but in the north of England, the first week in June is usually reasonably safe.

Marrows are very gross feeders and, if possible, they should be planted in a bucketful of soil which has been placed on top of a well rotted compost heap. The plants should have been grown in heat, preferably in a 3 in peat pot, so that plant, pot and all can be planted in full sun.

An alternative method is to dig out a hole which you fill with manure and compost and then you put the dugout soil on top of the compost. This creates an artificial raised bed on which the marrows can be planted. Further, they are not likely to dry out under these conditions. The best situation for either the compost heap or this raised bed is where they will be grown under the hottest possible conditions.

Rotting of the marrow fruit can very often be caused by imperfect fertilization. In order to avoid this difficulty when the plants are growing well, say, at the beginning of July, one can find both male and female flowers being produced. A male flower should be taken, the petals pulled off, and then it should be placed inside an open female flower. The female flower can easily be recognized because there is a tiny embryo marrow behind the petals. Whereas in the case of the male there is no such embryo. This is a much surer way of fertilizing female flowers than by relying on nature, and one can very easily get 100% fertilization under these conditions.

The production of a marrow puts a considerable strain on a plant, and so a wise gardener will never produce more than two or at the most three marrows on the one plant. Fruit rotting may also be caused by damage following slug or earwig attack. Into the areas which have been damaged soft rot bacteria can enter and thereafter the fruit will just rot steadily. This sort of damage can be minimized by raising the fruits a little from the ground and placing a piece of glass or slate below them.

VIII
Flowers

Rose-growing Calendar

Mr A. M. of Kemsing in Kent would like a brief run-down on the year's cultivation of roses (established hybrid teas and floribundas).

Obviously the first step is planting your rose and these days this can be done at any time of year by using container-grown roses which can even be planted in flower.

However, let us assume that these have been bought as dormant bushes which can be planted at any time after leaf fall and until they start to make growth in the spring. Both the hybrid tea and floribunda roses are in two parts, a particular variety grafted on to a rootstock, and the recognition of this fact is most important as it is at this point where the bush is most vulnerable. An examination at planting time will reveal that at the junction of the root and the top, there is a pronounced bulge and this union should be about 1 in below the soil after planting.

To plant, take out a hole a full spade depth and break up the bottom, mixing into the soil peat, into which has been added a double handful of bonemeal to a bucket of peat. Use about a third of this to each rose. Mix part of this to the soil at the bottom of the hole and the rest into the soil you've taken out. Settle the rose in, spreading out the roots carefully, filling in the loose soil and firming it gently as the job proceeds. Finally tread it down well and then scrape some of the surrounding top soil to level over and take out the footprints.

To make planting easier it is better to prune the bush before you start, cutting it back to about four sound buds and removing damaged or thin wood. No more pruning will be necessary the first season. The following season, shorten back the top growth in November even if the bush is still carrying a few bedraggled flowers. Shortening back to knee height reduces the risk of wind rock and certainly removes strain on the bush in trying to carry blooms into the winter months when it should be resting.

In the spring, which so far as rose pruning is concerned covers a period from mid-March to mid-April, the knee-height growths can be shortened to about 6 or 9 in, depending on variety. Very rigorous varieties such as Fred Loads, Queen Elizabeth or Peace can be left with 2 ft of growth or more – again, dead or weak growths should be removed. After pruning, remove the footmarks in the soil and give some good rose fertilizer, failing this a handful of National Growmore.

Roses have their share of pests and diseases but a well fed, strongly growing bush will be better able to resist these so you should try to achieve this by at least three applications of fertilizer during the growing season. Anticipate attacks of greenfly by spraying as soon as the foliage is formed with a systemic insecticide, this will give protection for several weeks. Systemic fungicides are now available also and if these are applied in good time they will keep mildew, black spot and other fungal diseases at bay for a considerable period. Fortunately the insecticide and fungicide can be combined and, if you add to this witches' brew a little foliar feed, almost complete control of pests can be achieved.

The cutting of blooms for the house is a form of pruning, so the first flush of roses should be cut with long stems, even if they are not required for the vase. And the second and third flushes which occur later in the season should be cut with shorter stalks. When the blooms fall, remove in the case of bush or hybrid teas with about 5 in of stalk and in the case of floribundas and polyanthas, to an evident new growth. This encourages formation of new wood which will give you another supply of bloom.

Keep the rose bed free from weeds, either by regular hoeing or by using a recommended weedkiller which can be sprayed or watered on the soil to keep it clear for the whole of the season. It is not recommended that other subjects be planted in amongst the roses but there is no harm in surrounding the bed with a border of pinks, violas or auriculas which give a good display of colour when the beds are bare and which enjoy the shade of the roses during the summer months.

Preparing Soil for Tea Roses

Mrs D. of West Bromwich asks about soil preparations before planting a bed of hybrid tea roses.

Most varieties of roses prefer a sunny position, so if the bed in which the roses are to be planted is at all overhung with trees, or shaded by a building, then it might be advisable to consider another subject. If, however, branches could be removed to allow full light on to the bed, then roses would do well.

Drainage should be made satisfactory and well rotted compost incorporated into the soil two or three months before the ideal planting time which is around mid-November. Additionally apply bone meal at one handful per sq yd before turning in the compost.

Adding the compost to the soil well ahead of planting time allows plenty of time for the soil to settle and reach a natural level, whereas if roses are planted on newly dug land as the soil settles around them the bushes can stick out like a sore thumb and so will suffer from wind rock. They should be planted with the budded position at least 1 in below soil level and, if the bushes have not been pruned, cut them back to about 12 in so that they are not blown about too much during the winter, as this damages the root system which is still young and trying to establish itself. In fact the death of many newly planted rose bushes can be due to this very cause.

Pruning Newly Planted Roses

Mr P. of Sunderland is bewildered by the amount and variation of the advice he has had on pruning his newly planted roses. Can the Team put the matter to him clearly?

Newly planted hybrid tea or floribunda roses should be pruned back by about a half to reduce wind rock during the winter. The final pruning preferably should be in March when they should be cut back to not more than two buds from the rootstock, with the topmost bud pointing outwards to that the bushes eventually will be of attractive shape, and the growths will obtain the maximum amount of air and light. Newly planted climbing hybrid teas should be pruned back to a sound bud, leaving approximately 2 ft of growth above the rootstock. First year rambler roses can be cut back to a sound bud 3 or 4 in above the grafted position. Weeping standard roses need pruning back to 3 in or so of the graft, and the same applies to standard hybrid teas.

After pruning, spray with nicotine or derris wash, and repeat during the growing season at frequent intervals to control pests.

Pruning Established Roses

Mr T. of Cardiff is concerned about the pruning of established bush roses.

It can be taken as a general guide that the more vigorous the habit of a bush rose, the less pruning it requires, and the

188

weaker the habit then the harder it should be pruned back. Established bush roses should be partially pruned in early December, so that they are not rocked about excessively by the winter weather, and then finally pruned in March. All thin and dead wood must be cut out and stronger canes should be pruned less hard than the weaker ones.

Rambler roses should have the old flowered wood removed completely to give the young growths a chance to ripen, and this is best done in August. Shorten back the tips of the current season's growth on climbing hybrid teas in August and, if any varieties have been shy to flower, then the growths should be bent so that the tips are below the horizontal. This will result in lateral branches being produced the following year more or less at right angles to the main growth, and these usually flower freely.

Established weeping standard roses should be pruned as ramblers, and hybrid tea standards be pruned as bush roses.

Reducing a Rambler Rose

Miss M. C. wants to know how to reduce the size of a rambler rose without harming its ability to flower.

Rambler roses flower usually on wood made in the previous year. This means, therefore, that any pruning has to be done after it has flowered in June or July so that August is the pruning time. Then it is perfectly good practice to cut old wood right down to the ground, leaving only the one- or two-year-old canes to bear next year's flowers. In this way the size of the rose can be very considerably reduced. If this is not sufficient, then even the one- and two-year-old canes can be tipped back a little, and if the bush is still too big rambler roses are so pliable that they can be bent into circles or made into arches, and this near distortion of the branches very often encourages flowering. In fact, it is an old gardening habit to tie the tips of branches below the horizontal in order to encourage additional flowers.

Treating Rose Mildew

Mrs D. of Sidcup had a poor display of roses last year, which she thinks was due to mildew. What would the Team recommend?

Rose mildew is caused by the attack of a fungus named *Sphaerotheca pannosa* which is most prevalent and does its most serious damage when the rose is not growing well. This is very often the case when the plants are in a sandy poor soil of low fertility or when they are near a wall or a fence where there is something to impede free air circulation. This is the reason why climbers and ramblers are more often attacked by mildew than bush roses in the open. Good growth should be encouraged by feeding the soil around the roses in spring with compost, and then later on through the growing season by feeding the roses with a compound rose fertilizer. Anticipate mildew trouble by spraying, certainly at three weekly intervals, with karathane fungicide, and in clean air districts, where black spot is troublesome, spray frequently with a fungicide containing captan. Frequent sprayings with these fungicides, as well as regular insecticidal sprayings, are necessary because it must be remembered that when growth is active new foliage is constantly being produced which has not been protected.

Black Spot on Roses

C. L. of Shincliffe, Co. Durham, wants to know what a gardener who is elderly but who has plenty of time should do about black spot on roses. Last year his roses had a little of it and his neighbours' a great deal.

Black spot is caused by a fungus (*Diplocarpon rosae*) and is a very common disease of roses, especially in areas with clean pure air. The typical symptom is best described by the name, the circular black blotches appearing on the leaves usually in July. This is a disease that can never be cured, but it can be controlled, and it is most important to start early in the season. Before the disease is apparent the foliage must be sprayed or dusted. One spray is not sufficient, you have to keep on spraying right through the season. One of the best sprays is captan, now reformulated with phaltan, and this, coupled with giving the plants good growing conditions, will ensure reasonable control.

A technique which has proved effective is that of spraying the roses with water during periods of high temperature, although it is possible this technique may induce mildew. It is also a good plan to pick off and burn infected leaves as soon as they are seen. Partial pruning in autumn, say down to knee height, will help a great deal, and it is important that any prunings should be removed and burned so that no dead wood or leaves are left lying on the soil to act as a source of infection the following year.

Feeding roses prone to black spot with purely nitrogenous fertilizers will increase the trouble, and it is wise to make sure that there is sufficient potash available to the bushes. Use a specially formulated rose fertilizer at least twice during the season.

Budding Roses

Mr G. D. would like to bud some roses. He needs some advice on how to go about this, when to do it, the best rootstock to use, and how long he must wait before he sees the results of his labours. His land is heavy.

This is a fascinating hobby and a good amateur gardener can get a great deal of pleasure and save a considerable amount of money if he can bud his own roses. The first essential is to obtain the correct rootstock and the most suitable one for fairly heavy land is Rosa canina. The rootstock should be planted and then grown on for at least a year until a good root system has been established, because only on a good root system will budding be satisfactory. The actual operation of budding should be carried out in July when there are plenty of ripe shoots of the varieties which you wish to bud on the rootstock, and also when the bark lifts readily. With a sharp knife, a bud should be scooped from the stem; when this is done, a small portion of the stem will be taken too and this is rather hardish white wood. This wood should be carefully trimmed off the back until there is no white wood there at all, and you can see the base of the bud with a green sheath beneath it.

In the bark of the rootstock a T-shaped slit should be made by making first of all a horizontal cut and then a downward cut from it. In this way the flaps of bark can be eased back with the spatula end of a budding knife and this will allow the insertion of the bud. The bud should be fitted in and carefully bound tightly with a grafting bandage specially sold for this purpose. The bud will sit all winter but the following year will begin to grow, and once it is well established the unwanted top part of the original rootstock, that is the Rosa canina, can be cut away and the bud will then grow as the main plant. With care it should be possible to have the variety flowering the year after the budding has been done.

Roses in Pots

From Mr B. B. comes the question, 'Is there a special type of rose for growing in pots to flower indoors in early spring?'

Any hybrid tea or floribunda rose can be grown indoors successfully, but perhaps the best varieties for this are Lady Sylvia, Baccarat, Super Star, Garnet and Dr Verhage. To be successful, the roses should be grown in 7 in pots, well crocked in the bottom and filled with a good, stiff loam with which some bone meal has been mixed. Once planted firmly, the roses should be cut hard back until only two buds above the rootstock are showing. They can then be grown in a cold or only slightly heated greenhouse, or in the window of a house, but at all times it must be remembered that their main requirement is plenty of natural light.

Once they have flowered indoors it is a good plan to put them out in the garden around June and to take them back indoors in early December before the really severe frosts come. At this period they should again be cut hard back and this will induce early flowering the following year.

Although it is quite often suggested that miniature roses are more suitable for indoor cultivation, it is quite often the experience of ordinary growers that the outside roses are equally successful. Care must be taken not to coddle these plants as they are tough and can stand quite a lot of mishandling. The main problem usually associated with growing roses indoors is that of greenfly, for under household conditions the greenfly can multiply abundantly. Care should therefore be taken to watch for this pest and as soon as it appears to apply a good remedy. If the plants look a little bit off colour they can very easily be stood outside for a while and this generally allows them to return to full health.

Hardy Annuals

'What does the Team suggest for hardy annuals in pinks and blues, and what do you do with them when they've finished flowering – throw them away or dig them in?' asks Miss V. L. of Cheltenham.

Seed catalogues can be very helpful here as colours are given, and the plants are classified into hardy, half-hardy, biennials, perennials, etc. A few suggestions for pink flowers would include asters, stocks, antirrhinums, cornflowers, clarkia, saponaria, godetia, and petunias, and for blues, cynoglossum, cornflowers, flax, myosotis, convolvulus, nemophila, and ageratum.

They should not be taken out at the end of the season, but chopped up and dug in. Alternatively, the plants could be dug up and added to the compost heap with the reminder that dry woody stems might take a long time (two years) to break down. This is probably the better plan as it gives a chance for inspecting the plants to see if they carry any pests or diseases, and should be burned rather than composted. If they are simply dug in they might build up a reservoir of infection in the soil.

Growing Pansies

Master R. H., 11 years old, grows pansies; in the first crop the flowers are large, but the flowers get smaller as the season goes on. Why is this?

There may be various reasons. The first pansy flowers thrown have the benefit of all the food and nutrients that the plants have been able to store up, but subsequent crops of flowers have to use food that has been made very recently. Secondly, very often when pansies first flower, or round about that time, they are attacked by greenfly which weakens the plant so that future flowers are smaller. The third explanation is that the flowers are setting seed and there is competition for plant nutrients, so to avoid this the dead flower heads should be removed below the seed-box.

Growing Violets

From Mrs D. of Sawtry a request for a good strain of violets, preferably with large purple, scented flowers and easy to grow. She would also be grateful for some hints on their cultivation.

Although violets may seem simple, uncomplicated plants their continued production in a garden can be difficult. They are at their very best in a moderately rich, heavy soil and if

194

your soil is light or sandy then incorporate into it as much humus as possible.

The area in which you are going to plant the violets should be dug deeply and planting up can begin from March until the end of April. The best position to grow them is a southern aspect with a certain amount of shade and if you really want to grow them well, then you must be prepared to grow them for part of the year under cloches or in a cold frame as many of the best varieties are not hardy under frost conditions.

It is always best to propagate violets each year either by division, cuttings or from new seed. If cuttings or runners are used for propagation they should be removed from the parent plants in April and planted firmly, just deep enough to bury the base of the crown. They should be in their summer quarters by the end of April and will produce flowers all through that same year. If on the other hand you propose to use seed then this should be sown in shallow boxes in early autumn; the boxes can then be placed in a cold frame and, in the spring, the seedlings can then be planted into other boxes if they are getting on too quickly, or else directly out into the garden at the end of April.

The main problems facing growers are red spider and greenfly. These can be controlled by spraying with malathion – if necessary, repeating this spray as often as you see signs of the tiny white dots produced by the red spider on the leaves.

One of the few present day varieties which has retained a strong scent is Princess of Wales and another nearly as good, Princess Marie Louise. There are one of two very good blue varieties, for example Blue Heaven and Azure Blue. Very often the largest flowered varieties are not very highly scented but a good one which is a pale mauve is John Bradbury. This has a good scent as has Arkwright Ruby which is a ruby crimson with very fragrant flowers.

Antirrhinum Seedlings Damping Off

Mrs M. S. of Northampton would like to know the best remedy for preventing antirrhinums damping off at the seedling stage.

Antirrhinums are very prone to this disease. It's a fungus and often carried in the water used to water the seedlings. It's always best to use John Innes or a loamless compost when sowing the seeds, as these are sterilized and free from this damping off disease. Even so, they are very susceptible to over-watering, and it is better to keep them a little on the dry side. Water the compost before sowing so that they won't need any attention until the seedlings are well grown and when they do need water, water from the bottom, i.e. immerse pots or boxes in a shallow tank of water and let the water make its way up the compost. If seeds are sown in unsterilized compost, damping off can be prevented by watering with Cheshunt compound.

It is very important that the seed be sown thinly, and if this proves difficult, mix the seed with a little dry sand so that they can more easily be distributed.

Make sure, too, that the container – that is the box, tray or pot in which they are sown – is scrupulously clean, as this group of fungus diseases called loosely 'damping off' can persist in soil crumbs, which adhere to the inside of the container.

Furthermore, prick out singly into a suitable compost, such as John Innes No. 1, or a soilless compost at a very early age, roughly when the seed leaves are ⅛ in in diameter.

Very often the source of infection is the greenhouse water tank. Moisture drips off benches, etc., where there could be infected plants, and is collected in the tank. It is best to clean it out every year.

Autumn Sown Annuals

Mr W. C., an apprentice seedsman, asks whether the Team advise autumn sowing of annuals in Scotland, without a greenhouse although a cold frame could be used? If so, what varieties do they recommend, particularly for cutting?

In favourable districts it is certainly worth experimenting with the autumn sowing of annuals. The main factors which the annuals will have to cope with are the incidence of frost which can cause a great deal of damage if it comes following heavy rain, and the intensity of the light during the winter. Thus the idea should not be experimented with in industrial areas where there is a lot of fog and cloud, but might be worth doing in high intensity light areas, especially by the sea where there is not so very much frost. If autumn sowing of annuals is attempted, then cloche protection would certainly be valuable, and it would be very good policy to ensure that the ventilation through the cloches was good in better weather. To ensure reasonable drainage, it is very often good practice to raise the soil beneath the cloches about 6 in or so above the surrounding ground. If cold frames are available then, of course, this is a very good procedure as one can certainly protect the annuals against the worst of the weather.

Suitable annuals or biennials for sowing in September or October are calendula, godetia, larkspur, statice, lavatera, sweet peas, clarkia, cornflower, forget-me-not, candytuft, Brompton stocks and East Lothian stocks. These would provide flowers for cutting in the spring, maybe anything up to a month earlier than one might normally expect.

197

Potting Chrysanthemums

Is it essential to pot chrysanthemums in stages through 3 in to 5 in and then to 9 in pots, or could Mr F. R. produce good blooms by potting rooted cuttings straight into 9 in pots?

If rooted chrysanthemum cuttings are put directly into 9 in pots, then each cutting will have a great volume of soil from which to find food. This will be very easy for the chrysanthemum and the sheer excess of good things would tend to make it grow soft and sappy. In the same way there may be large volumes of soil in the pot which are not inhabited by the roots of the cutting and this soil could easily go sour and acid. When the roots eventually reached these areas they might find conditions rather inhospitable and so growth could suffer.

Under the system of progressive repotting the plants will receive a series of slight checks which do very little harm if care is taken. In addition, however, the plants are grown a bit 'hungry' and this encourages the production of strong tissues and later improves the quality of the flower.

Another point to be borne in mind is that if cuttings are put immediately into 9 in pots there may not be sufficient room in the greenhouse or cold frame for many other plants you may be growing at the same time.

One way to cut down the repotting operations when the chrysanthemum cuttings have rooted is to plant them out in a cold frame. Put in a layer of ashes, tread this down hard, then add 5 in of soil and plant the cuttings 4 in apart. The chrysanthemums can then be potted up later on, or if they are early varieties planted straight out. The success of this method is the result of the cuttings again being grown tight because of competition from each other, and they will lift easily with a good ball of soil because of the hard layer of ashes underneath.

Planting Out Chrysanthemums

Miss A. of Pinner, Middlesex, asks, 'When planting out my new chrysanthemums in the garden, should they be put into any special soil; also should they be watered if the weather is dry?'

Chrysanthemums are usually planted outdoors about mid-May and like a fairly rich soil with plenty of compost added. If there are any doubts about this, some John Innes Base Fertilizer should be added to the soil before planting. If the weather is dry at the time of planting, water should be put into the planting hole and the plants might well benefit from regular watering if the weather remains dry. All watering should, of course, only be done in the late evening.

Spray regularly to keep down greenfly, capsid bug and cuckoo spit or frog hopper. Stake securely and, if you know nothing about variety or stopping times, pinch out the growing point when the plants have made six pairs of leaves, but allow them to become established for at least a fortnight before any stopping is done.

Keep free from weeds by hoeing and give occasional feeds of fertilizer during showery weather.

If specimen blooms are required then they must be disbudded by removing all except the central bud.

Six to fourteen single blooms may be expected from one plant depending on variety and whether the plant is stopped once or twice.

Over-wintering Korean Chrysanthemums

'Is it safe in a normal winter to leave Korean chrysanthemums in the border, and is it best to take cuttings in the autumn or in the spring?' asks Mr J. E. M.

Most varieties of Korean chrysanthemum would certainly over-winter in the garden border in milder districts of the country. In more severe districts of the country, such as the North of England or maybe over in Lincolnshire where the winters are cold, a considerable amount of damage can be done if a severe and prolonged spell of keen frost occurred. It might be that even in milder districts of the country an exceptionally severe winter would kill off the chrysanthemums, but, generally speaking, they will survive most conditions.

In the milder districts one of the greatest problems is not the actual over-wintering of the plants, but protecting them from slug damage. Under winter conditions slugs will do considerable harm to the fleshy shoots and the roots of Korean chrysanthemums and it pays usually to surround the clumps with slug pellets in order to keep trouble away.

In the less favoured districts it is best to lift the chrysanthemums and to store them in boxes of soil in a cold greenhouse or in the garden frame. They should be left there until growth starts again in the spring and then one can take cuttings.

In the milder districts where one would not bother to lift the chrysanthemums, one can take out an insurance policy simply by giving the plants some form of protection during the winter months. This could be by means of cloches or, if they are not available, by covering the plants with straw or bracken. In these areas where Koreans may stand year after year in the ground without being dug up, it is very often good policy to replace the old plants with fresh young ones each fourth year. The reason for this is that older plants very often become infected with virus disease and may, in fact, harbour soil pests and diseases, and by replacing them with fresh clean stock the garden will be kept in very much better condition.

The Dahlia Bed in Winter

Mrs J. H. of Brentwood, Essex, sends us this problem. 'In our household we are dahlia enthusiasts. For two months of the year our garden looks like a bamboo plantation; for four months it is a mass of bloom; for the rest of the year it looks naked and unloved. Can the Team suggest ways of introducing colour into the beds between December and May?'

Less love of the dahlia seems indicated in order to leave some room for interplanting, say with lupins, delphiniums or sidalceas, which would flower earlier than the dahlias and give colour in May, June and July, with the dahlias to follow on in August and September. Another possibility is to interplant with heathers of which there are summer and winter flowering varieties but, of course, any interplanting with permanent subjects would lead to some difficulties in cultivation and in providing the high fertility which dahlias demand. If you want to dig the whole area over each year, then there is really nothing that can be done except to put in bulbs for spring flowering, and to move the bulbs each spring after they have flowered.

Pom Dahlias

How to prevent small pom dahlias from growing too large for exhibition is Mr M. C.'s problem. Can the Team help him?

The first essential in growing small pom dahlias is to choose the right varieties and it is suggested that Diana Gregory, Glow or Gay Look should be chosen for preference. Thereafter it is usually found advantageous to use the method used by commercial growers, namely, to grow them 'tight'. In order to do this, you have to try to restrict not only the root growth of the dahlia but also the amount of food to which the plant has access, and a good method is to plant the dahlias in a 6 in pot and sink the pot in the ground. Plenty of crocks should be put in the bottom of the pots in order to prevent rooting through into the sub-soil and thus obtaining additional food materials. By this method the only food available to the dahlia is that in the pot itself and, in consequence, you will find that the heads remain small and compact, well-shaped and suitable for exhibition.

A variant of this method is to use a rather larger pot, say, an 8½ in, and to grow two plants in the one pot. This sets up a certain amount of competition within the pot and this competition helps to keep the flowers smaller and the plants tougher. During this whole period it is important to realize that because the roots are restricted there may be a certain shortage of water and it is always advisable to make sure that under these conditions adequate moisture is supplied.

Cut Flowers

A question that is itself something of a perennial, and this time Mr H. W. O. of Bristol asks it: 'Will the Team please give a formula for making cut flowers last longer?'

Cut flowers die basically from two causes. The first one is the normal process of decay which takes place in flowers as they ripen; the second one is that the cut surface is a pathway through which funi and bacteria can enter the bloom and kill it off that much more quickly. A great deal of research work has been done to try to devise a solution to make cut flowers last longer, but so far nothing of any outstanding value has been obtained; in fact, it is almost certain that a solution of about one teaspoonful of ordinary sugar in a quart of water will do as well as anything. This water should be changed frequently, at least every second day, and this solution will help to slow down the process of decay. The Consumer Research Council have investigated this subject and their

202

finding showed that very few of the proprietary flower life prolongers were of any value whatsoever and were certainly no better than the sugar solution. There is a certain amount of evidence, too, that if the flowers are stood in a copper container they may last a bit longer. The reason for this is that the copper will act as a fungicide and a bactericide, and so prevent infection of the cut blooms.

It is important also to realize that the situation in which the flowers are kept has considerable importance, so they should not be stored in a hot room or near a radiator, but should be kept as cool as possible. Many people will have noticed this for they will remember how their cut flowers will last very much longer in the winter than they do in the summer, and this is simply because of the lowness of the temperature.

Preparing Cuttings

'When taking cuttings we are told to prepare a clean stem, removing lower leaves.' Mrs D. W. wants to know if this is necessary or does it rob the cuttings of nourishment?

There is evidence that the amount of roots produced by a cutting is directly related to the number of leaves which it carries, in that the more leaves there are, the better the cutting will root. There is, nevertheless, the other posibility that in softer subjects the lower leaves of cuttings will undoubtedly rot and so provide a means of entry for fungi which could completely kill the plant, or even of fungi which by growing in the soil will hinder the development of roots. So the answer really is that with soft subjects the lower, older leaves should be removed so that an inch or so of clean stem goes into the compost and the leaves at the growing point are just above the compost.

A further point is exceedingly important because most leaves are losing water all the time by the process known as transpiration. This water has to be replaced and normally the roots take water from the soil. In the case of a cutting, however, no roots have been developed and if the process of water loss goes on indefinitely without any water replacement, the cutting will simply collapse and die. For this reason also, therefore, it is a good idea not to leave too many leaves on a cutting.

The production of roots from many cuttings is also influenced by light, and the gardener has to run a rather nice gauntlet between allowing plenty of light and so encouraging rooting and water loss, or shading the cuttings, reducing the amount of light and rooting but also reducing water loss. Each gardener will get to know his own circumstances best and take appropriate action.

Growing Anemones

For years Mrs A. F. S. has been trying to grow anemones. They bloom well for a time but very few continue, and even fewer flower the second year. What does one do to grow good anemones?

These would probably be the De Caen or St Brigid anemones which have been very highly bred and are today really a florist's flower. They will only bloom sporadically year after year, and should be replanted each year. This is how they are grown commercially, although in favourable districts it is possible they may produce a good crop of flowers the second year.

Anemones insist on very good drainage. They like to be in full sun, in a fairly limey soil, but even given these ideal conditions, in difficult areas they will not do very well unless spring planted, as frost and excess moisture will cause heavy losses. Under these conditions they should be planted in March, in rich soil, and you should be prepared to replace them each year.

For those who live in difficult areas the answer is to grow the herbaceous type of anemones, of which there are many grand varieties like the pasque flower or Anemone pulsatilla, Anemone nemerosa, Anemone magellanica and Anemone blanda. Given reasonable conditions these will give a good show and come up year after year.

Transplanting Sweet Peas

Mr W. A. G. finds that transplanting sweet peas retards their growth by six weeks. Can the Team help?

If the sweet peas are sown in heat in February and planted out in early April then the seedlings haven't sufficient time to become hardened off before being put outside. It is much better to sow in October, to keep the sweet peas in a cold frame all winter, and to give them plenty of air. It may be, in this case, that the soil temperature was too low, so cover the planting position with cloches about three weeks beforehand so that the soil warms up.

Another method to avoid a check at transplanting time is to sow and grow the sweet peas in small peat pots. These break down in the soil for the whole pot is planted, and the best type of peat pot contains fertilizer elements which also helps the plants to recover from the move.

Autumn Grown Sweet Peas

Mr J. C. who lives in Lydiate, Lancashire, has difficulty in over-wintering autumn sown sweet pea plants. The main trouble appears to be caused by the sun thawing the plants out too quickly in the frames, which makes the sap rise too quickly, resulting in brown collar rot. Having lost the autumn sown plants, should he sow in the spring to get first class plants for planting out time?

The problem really with the sweet peas in this case is not the sun but is, in fact, the brown collar rot. This is caused by a soil-borne fungus which is always at its most damaging when the soil is too wet or when the root system is in very moist soil. This very often does occur in winter and where this disease has been experienced before, it is a good idea to water the soil with Cheshunt compound which will kill most of these harmful fungi.

Of course, the problem should really be tackled at its source and the best method of doing this is to try to improve the drainage and to be sure that the soil which is used is healthy. This can be done by having about 4 in of rich sterilized soil on top of a layer of ashes in the frame. This provides for good quick drainage and there is a certain measure of safety in plants being relatively dry through the winter. An alternative method would be to put a little electric soil-warming cable in the frame for this could help during cold weather and would lead to earlier plants. Before embarking, however, on electric-soil warming cable it should be pointed out that in the north of England there is very little point in having plants all ready to go out of doors before conditions are favourable for them.

For spring sowing it is best to sow in heat in late February, and plants will be produced that will only be fourteen days or so behind autumn sown stuff at flowering time. Sowings made without heat will be another week or two later still.

Wallflowers as Perennials

'If wallflowers are perennials, why are they always grown as biennials?' asks Mrs W. of Snitterfield.

The short answer to this question is simply that if wallflowers are grown as biennials they flower more brightly, they produce more flowers and they are much more attractive. They also do not occupy the ground when they are unattractive and this is very important to someone with a small garden who wants the maximum amount of pleasure and colour from it.

Thus, if wallflowers are grown as perennials, leaving them in the same bed year after year, they tend to become rather unsightly; some will grow tall, some may die, and they will not bear flowers most of the year but will only look attractive in spring. It is much better, therefore, to treat the wallflower as a biennial by sowing in early summer and then planting out in September to flower the following spring. One can treat wallflowers as perennials if one grows them really as 'wallflowers' and plants them in a dry wall where they will thrive for ages, and they will produce flowers which, although not nearly so large as those produced by the garden specimens, will be much more fragrant and look very attractive.

Moving Paeonies

When is the best time to move paeonies without retarding growth? When Miss R. G. moved hers, it did not flower for years afterwards.

The best answer to this question is in fact to say, 'Don't move paeonies at all unless it is absolutely necessary.' The reason for this is that the paeony plant makes rather fleshy brittle roots which are very easily broken during the process of transplanting. When they are put into their new home, they therefore take a rather long time to settle down and it may be three or four years before they are really established and have arrived at a constant flowering rhythm.

If, however, it is absolutely necessary to move paeonies, the best time to do this is September, as this allows the plant to rest through the winter and then in the early spring to start forming new roots with the least possible delay. September is also the best time to divide paeonies but the golden rule should be to leave them alone and they will do far better than if they are treated in any way.

Malmaison Carnations

Mr N. W. wonders if the Team can tell him why the Malmaison has dropped out of collections of carnations, when it used to be so popular and so beautiful.

The original *Souvenir de Malmaison* was raised in France in 1857 and was given its name from its resemblance to the rose. It is a rather larger, stiffer type of carnation with broad leaves and usually with pink flowers. The reasons why the Malmaison has been dropped out of collections are that it is not easy to grow, there is not the same variety of colour as in other types of carnations, being limited usually to shades of pink, and the tendency towards calyx splitting rules it out as a show carnation. Another disadvantage is that you seldom get a crop through the winter, even with the modern perpetual Malmaison.

Perpetual Malmaison is still available, but the best types of carnations to grow nowadays are the modern border carnations, and particularly the Elizabethan pinks. This is a very good race of border pink, non-calyx splitting, with a good colour range, and of good habit.

Phlox

Can the Team please tell Mrs W. of Pinner why the leaves of her phlox lose their colour and have patches of white and brown, eventually turning black?

This could be the eelworm disease of phlox caused by a nematode, *Anguillulina dipsaci.* The usual symptoms of this pest are that the leaves become crinkled and wavy and very often brittle, in fact the whole plant can become brittle and split. The leaves may become discoloured, starting at the bottom of the plant and working their way upward, and under favourable conditions the parasite can completely ruin beds of phlox.

The pest lives in the soil and it is very easily carried from one part of the garden to the other on tools or on boots or on wheelbarrows. It is thus very important to take immediate steps to restrict the spread of materials from infected beds. Any diseased plant should be cut off very low down at the end of the season and burned. This helps a great deal because the phlox eelworm very rarely gets into the roots and if one can get root cuttings from which all the soil has been washed away, it is quite possible to grow healthy plants again.

Unfortunately, there is no known chemical control. Certainly if the phlox are treated with sulphate of potash they will do rather better as this chemical seems to harden the phlox up and make them less affected by the attack. The land should be heavily manured, using farmyard manure or well made compost and it is very often wise to adopt a rotation and grow crops which are unrelated to phlox. The eelworm will attack a number of other subjects such as Sweet William, evening primrose, schizanthus, etc.

Protecting Michaelmas Daisies

Last year Mrs G.'s Michaelmas daisies were ruined by mildew. What can she apply to protect them this year?

Michaelmas daisies are very prone to attacks of mildew. This is a fungal disease which is most troublesome when the air around the plants is moist and not moving very freely. In Michaelmas daisies this condition often arises because the growths have not been thinned out sufficiently, and so in the centre of the clump there is perfectly still air which is moist and which, therefore, provides an ideal breeding ground for the mildew fungus. The plants should also be top-dressed each July with a good compost, as this helps to keep them healthy and also increases the resistance to various troubles.

Surprisingly enough Michaelmas daisies thrive best in rather damp soils, but this means that although the roots are in damp soil the tops of the plants should be in a fairly brisk moving air.

Chemically, one can protect the plants against mildew by using a proprietary fungicide based on karathane. This is a very effective protection against many fungal diseases, and the secret is to apply it early and to apply it regularly, and if this is done then you will find the attacks of mildew will vanish altogether or will be very much reduced in intensity.

Hollyhock Rust

Mrs E. J. of Newcastle, County Wicklow, has hollyhocks but the flowers get covered in little rusty nodes. Would the Team tell her what it is and if there is a cure?

This is hollyhock rust which, like black spot on roses, is a disease which flourishes in a clean atmosphere. It is a difficult disease to control as it stays with the hollyhock from year to year, over-wintering on the stools at the root of the plant. Dusting with sulphur will reduce its severity but not eliminate it and at the moment there aren't any varieties resistant to this hollyhock rust.

Single varieties of hollyhock will stand up to rust better than doubles and it's said that a flourishing plant has more resistance than one in poor soil. So the only remedies would appear to be a liberal application of farmyard manure and either spray with a fungicide or dust with sulphur.

Hollyhocks, because of their height and need for support, are usually grown close up to a wall which in the summer can become extremely hot and dry. Furthermore, the base of a wall is usually dry and the soil hungry. The wall should be sprayed as thoroughly and as regularly as the plants and if the wall is whitewashed then add a handful of sulphur to the limewash.

210

Under such conditions regular watering and mulching is essential to help the plant to combat this disease.

Dividing Delphiniums

The advice given to Mrs S. of Tisbury, Wiltshire, is that she should divide her delphiniums every three years, and she asks if the Team think this is good policy.

With the old varieties of delphiniums this advice certainly is very good. By dividing them one could increase the number of delphiniums and in a sense could also rejuvenate them by putting the divided clumps into fresh soil.

Modern varieties, however, are largely based on strains which come from California. There the weather is very much better than ours, and in Britain these new varieties may die off in the winter, either through slug damage or through the stem rotting. Because they are much more tender than our own varieties it is best not to divide new varieties introduced within the last ten years or so. If new plants are desired, then it is better to take cuttings from the young growths which appear early in the spring. Since these newer varieties are often also short lived, many of them dying before they reach three years of age, in many cases it pays to take cuttings each year and so be sure that the strain is perpetuated.

Hardy Pinks

Mrs H. W. of Pulborough tells us that she is trying to establish a permanent border of hardy pinks. She wants to know if a good show can be achieved without them becoming untidy and straggly so that they have to be replanted every few years?

First of all let us look at the growth requirement of pinks –

they need ideally a well drained soil and, if this isn't available, the bed should be raised to give good drainage. Work in plenty of gritty material; rotted manure or compost is preferable to adding peat which will produce a certain amount of acidity and pinks like lime. They revel in the sun, will tolerate dryness but must have lime which can be added as crushed limestone or old mortar in preference to the powdered forms.

Mrs W.'s ambition to have a trouble-free border is almost impossible to achieve as it is the very nature of pinks to go straggly after a few years. The length of time depends to some extent on the variety: the Old Elizabethan which grows up to 15 ins high soon looks untidy but some of the dwarf varieties, particularly Alpinus, will go much longer.

The essential of a good pink border is frequent propagation — every third year is the ideal and it really isn't too difficult. If some good compost is put into the heart of each flower you will get stem rooting and in fact it is easy enough to get cuttings to take – if these are taken before August they will flower the following year.

Iceland Poppies

Mr J. N. of Bury would like advice on the care and propagation of the Iceland poppy. Although its name seems to indicate that a cold climate is a desirable habitat it seems to flourish in the Bury area.

This is properly known as Papaver nudicaule and although originally from the Arctic and sub-Arctic regions it has been so hybridized as to have lost a good deal of its hardiness.

They should be sown from May to July, pricked off into nursery beds or boxes and planted out either in the autumn or early spring. They can be regarded as a hardy biennial but in wet districts it is probably more satisfactory to treat them as a half-hardy annual, sowing each year.

Some of the new hybrids are extremely attractive and a new F.I. hybrid called Champagne Bubbles contains many beautiful colours with large flowers – some bi-coloured.

Dividing Christmas Roses

Mr C. S. of Harlow, Essex, has a Christmas rose that has been established for two years; it has just finished flowering and he would like to give some to a friend. How and when should he divide it?

In one respect Christmas roses are rather like paeonies in that they do not like to be disturbed and grow at their very best when they are left alone in a settled soil. This particular plant has been in the ground for only two years and it is asking rather a lot of it to attempt to divide it at this early stage. If however, a promise has been made and division becomes necessary it is better not to divide the whole plant, but in March after flowering, or in September, gradually to take away soil from one side of the plant and to try to tease off one of the crowns. With a certain amount of care it is often possible to tease off a crown to which some roots are attached and if this is then used as a separate plant it will settle down very much more quickly.

It must be clear, however, that if the divided part is going to settle down and flower freely, it should be given more or less ideal conditions for growth. In the case of Christmas roses these are: shaded from direct sunlight, and a soil in which there is a large quantity of organic matter at the roots and which can therefore hold considerable quantities of moisture. Christmas roses also like lime and it is often a good plan, especially in sandy areas, to give a light dusting of ground limestone every second year. The plant may take two or three years to settle down, but is such a lovely thing it is well worth persisting with.

Lily of the Valley

The most beautiful lilies of the valley ever seen by Miss M. E. G. were growing amongst rhubarb – was it the shade of the leaves or something in the soil that caused this?

Lily of the valley, of course, is a shade loving plant. As well as being shade loving it does also like plenty of air movement which is the reason why it can often be grown so successfully in narrow passages between houses, where there is shade, a fairly high degree of moisture, and where there can be a strong through draught. Rhubarb leaves are large and are held fairly high up from the ground, and so they do provide shade; they are also so high off the surface that there is plenty of air movement and, once again, lily of the valley would be helped by these conditions. It should further be noted that if the rhubarb is growing well then it is being fed with lots of organic material, and these constitute absolutely ideal conditions for lily of the valley.

Gladioli for Show

Mrs E. W. of Erdington asks how she can get gladioli spikes equally developed for showing? Hers do well but the end flowers don't come as early as those lower down.

Nature has arranged it so that the florets open progressively to be fertilized and to extend the life of a flower over a longer period. They are natives of a hotter part of the world extending from the Mediterranean through Africa and under hotter, dryer conditions they open fairly rapidly. Under our climatic conditions, development is slower and when grown outdoors the lower blooms are so weather beaten that they may have to be removed by the time the top florets are open.
However it is possible to influence their behaviour slightly,

214

firstly by restraining the lower florets which open first and secondly by stimulating the top ones. Cut the spikes when the first four or five florets are open but restrain the bottom ones earlier by tying them lightly with soft wool and shading them by cutting a cross-shaped slit in a piece of cooking foil and slipping this over the spike.

Cut the spike early in the morning of the day before the show and plunge the stem into about 4 in of hot water, not boiling but about as hot as you would normally wash in. Repeat this a few times then cut off 2 to 3 in of the stem and stand in water almost as deep as the lower florets. By doing this you can usually encourage two or three more florets to open which could well tip the scales in your favour at the show.

Increasing Gladioli Corms

From Mr R. W. of Coleford, Gloucestershire, a question about gladioli. He would like to know how he should set about increasing his stock of corms.

When a gladiolus is grown through the summer it produces flowers and leaves. The production of these takes food from the old corm, but as the flower dies down the food made in the leaves passes back down the stem and a new corm is produced on top of the old one. This new corm is usually termed the primary corm and around it a large number of tiny cormlets about ⅛ in in diameter may be produced. These tiny corms can be grown on, and if this is done carefully, they will eventually produce flowering plants. When the plants are lifted in the autumn all the plants should be dried in a cool, dry place. They should be stored through the winter in a frost-proof, airy shed and all the little corms separated from the big ones.

The cormlets can then be either planted outside in a special position or they can be brought on in pots or pans in the spring. No matter which way you choose be sure that the soil is rich, open and well drained. Many people like, in fact, to bed the corms or cormlets down on sand and to cover them with sand and then complete the planting by levelling off with good soil. If there are dry periods the corms do like some watering.

In the first year the cormlets will not produce flowers, but will produce slender green leaves which are often referred to as grass. This grass should be treated with a fertilizer, either a foliar feed or a solid fertilizer and allowed to grow and die down naturally when it will be found that the cormlets have increased considerably in size. This process can be repeated a second year as it usually takes three years for a corm to arrive at a flowering size.

Gladiolus corms, on the whole, are fairly cheap and it is economically hardly worth while taking up the time and the labour in order to grow on your own cormlets, unless you want to do it purely out of interest.

Planting Corms

Mrs W. of Presteigne asks for advice in planting corms. Which way up should they be planted as many show no signs of old roots or growing point? Last year she bought a corm or bulb called apios which looked like a small fat mouse with a long tail. Was the tail the top or the root?

For a start the 'mouse' apios is a hardy, tuberous rooted, twining perennial climber with long racemes of brownish purple scented flowers. It is a kind of ground nut and the tubers are edible. As far as this is concerned it doesn't really matter which way up it is planted, just lay it down and it will soon work out its own salvation.

In fact in quite a few cases it isn't critical to know which way up to plant corms, with begonias for instance if they are put in the wrong way you will soon see which way they are

216

going and if necessary, turn them over. Generally you plant begonias with convex side down.

With most tubers you can clearly see a leaf or root scar and, with crocuses, the growing point is fairly obvious.

Without wishing to seem flippant it very often doesn't matter which way you plant a corm or a bulb for that matter and if you are in any serious doubt then you can plant it on its side. This will make little or no difference to the final growth and you may be saved some nerve racking sleepless nights wondering if you have done it the wrong way. In most cases the decision as to which side to plant uppermost is fairly easy, for there is usually what is termed a basal plate on which you can see the scars or the remains of the old roots and the other end should then point upwards. But if in doubt then plant it on its side.

Crown Imperial

Mrs T. B. of Oxford grows crown imperial in her garden. It comes up each spring looking very healthy, grows well and then just fades away without flowering. Any suggestions to bring it into flower please?

The crown imperial or the giant fritillaria is not an easy subject to flower year after year in ordinary garden soil. It requires rather special conditions and certainly needs planting 6 or 7 in deep, and if one could create conditions similar to a gritty, sandy river bed these would be ideal.

The nearest one can get to these conditions in an ordinary garden is to dig quite a big hole, about a foot square and a foot deep, and half fill this with sand and gravel, working in a bit of leaf mould, plant on this and top up with similar material.

Possibly an easier place to create these conditions would be the pocket of a rockery and grow a group of these lovely subjects. Failing this one mostly has the mortification of seeing a marvellous show of bloom the first season and then each year getting progressively worse and finally with just a few leaves, as a token of growth. Late frosts can also nip this subject, and again this means no flowers. This doesn't happen too often but it helps to make sure you aren't planting them in a known frost pocket.

Naturalizing Daffodils and Narcissi

'How do we keep drifts of daffodils and narcissi healthy?' asks Mrs D. R. of Osgodby in Lincolnshire. 'Ours are planted in grass, we allow the leaves to die down before scything the grass and we take off the dead flower heads.'

Well, Mrs R. seems to have done all the right things: it is important to let the foliage die well down before cutting; and taking off the dead flower heads stops the plant wasting its energy making seeds. It could well be that the fly in the ointment, so to speak, is the narcissus fly. These crawl down into the bulb through the hole that is left when the foliage dies down and lay their eggs in the neck of the bulb. These attacks are particularly bad in dry years and a very effective remedy is the application of a BHC powder. The best way to do this is to make a mixture of equal parts of sand, peat and soil plus the BHC and apply this to each plant in June. This gives a good feed boost and gets rid of the narcissus fly in one operation.

Bulbs of any sort don't thrive in waterlogged conditions so the choice of site is important as is the choice of bulbs as not all varieties are suitable for naturalizing. Above all avoid the use of hormone weedkillers when the bulbs are actively growing.

Some varieties which lend themselves to naturalization are the doubles including Vonion and the short cupped Sir Watkin and Fortune; Polyanthas such as White Cheerfulness and Rembrandt.

218

Leaf Spot of Arum Lilies

For several years Mr G. H. has had two quite handsome pots of arum lilies which come into bloom at Easter time. The last few years the leaves have been attacked by a brown spot (at the tip) which eventually spread all over each leaf which had to be cut off, spoiling the appearance of the plant. Would the Team comment?

There are about four different leaf spots of arum lilies caused by fungi, but these can appear on any part of the leaf and usually have a light brown centre with a dark brown edge. However, as the spots which worry this questioner appeared in each instance at the very tip of the leaf when the flowers were in full bloom, it would appear that the lilies were not being well enough fed. All the nutriment in the plant is going into the flower itself and, therefore, the oldest part of the leaf, which in arum lilies is the tip, is dying because it is exhausted. To overcome this they should be fed or repotted in December in a richer soil.

When they have finished flowering and the weather is a bit milder, it is wise to knock them out of the pots and plant them outside in rich soil (for example, where peas or celery have been grown). They should be left there until autumn when they can be repotted and divided as necessary. For the final potting use John Innes No. 3 or a mixture of loam, manure, peat with a little bone meal, leafmould, and sand to keep it well drained, using a fairly large well crocked pot.

Lifting Tulips

What is the point, asks Dr S. D., in lifting tulips annually?

There are basically two reasons for lifting tulips annually. The first of these is that as tulips die down the leaves become very untidy and quite often they rot off and suffer from slug damage. They will, therefore, look very unsightly during the summer and most gardeners prefer to remove them and use the space to accommodate summer bedding plants.

The second is that garden tulips, such as the early singles or Darwins and Mendels, do not naturalize well as they are not natives of Britain. The best recommendation for them is that after flowering, flower heads should be removed to prevent seed production. Foliage should then be allowed to die down naturally, when the bulbs should be lifted and dried and stored until the following autumn. Because of the inclemency of our climate it is usually found that tulips, especially in the colder parts of Britain, do not maintain their full vigour in the second and subsequent years. One usually finds a gradual deterioration in the size and quality of the bloom. It is good policy, therefore, to buy some new bulbs each year in order to keep a first class display going.

A number of people are now moving away from what is sometimes called the 'garden' tulips and planting species tulips. These are not quite as showy as the garden varieties, but they flower earlier, they have beautiful shapes, and they are very hardy. Species of tulips such as Tulipa Eichleri, Clusiana and Kaufmanniana will naturalize successfully and easily, and, in fact, it is generally found that they multiply and tend to spread. If these types, therefore, are planted in a rockery or in a herbaceous border, they will persist and the whole trouble of lifting will be avoided. These tulips also have foliage which does die down rather more quickly than that of the later garden varieties and so they do not remain unsightly for very long.

Alpines for a Small Sink

Miss M. S. asks the Team to suggest some alpines which she could grow in a small stone sink, 3 ft × 2 ft × 1 ft, to flower over as long a period as possible.

Trough gardens can be made really attractive and the best way of doing this is to ensure that the surface is not flat. In order to do this, it is unwise to create a hill in the middle with slopes running down to each end, but rather to create a hill on one side and to 'landscape' the surface with small undulations and even small pockets. In these pockets special types of soil can be put, in which special subjects can be grown. The drainage hole in a sink of this type should be left open and the sink tilted very slightly towards the drainage hole in order to prevent waterlogging.

In such a trough garden, dwarf plants are of course the things to go for and it is useful here to plant one or two miniature trees, such as miniature dwarf roses or dwarf fuchsias, or maybe even some of the dwarf cupressus. One or two of these trees planted discreetly in the trough will lend variety to the surface. Then a number of other dwarf subjects, such as miniature phlox, sedums, thymes, veronicas, lithospermums, etc., will add cover, and it is sometimes useful to have trailing plants tumbling from the edge of the trough in order to hide a rather unattractive sink. These could simply be aubrietia or any other tumbling plant. Other suggestions that might be made are dwarf iris, candytuft, hypericum, hepatica, gentians, campanulas, and so on.

Any good catalogue will give lists of dwarf plants, but it is most important when dealing with a garden in miniature to avoid very vigorous or invasive subjects as they can easily smother out the rest of the plants in the garden and necessitate a complete replanting.

Gentians

Mrs H. of Arnside in Westmorland has a bed of Gentiana acaulis which eight years ago had sixteen flowers. Numbers have gradually dwindled and now she has only one left. Could the Team give some hints on the correct cultivation of this beautiful plant?

Very few of the four hundred or so species of gentians are easy to grow outside in Britain. They are a genus of alpines, chiefly European or Asian and valued for their glorious blue flowers. Acaulis is one of the European varieties; it grows to about 4 in high and has bell-mouthed, funnel-shaped flowers during May and June.

The conditions gentians need to flourish are difficult to achieve here. If one thinks of the conditions prevailing in their alpine home you can easily understand this – they need to be moist in the summer and dry in the winter with a growth bed that is well drained but having plenty of moisture a few inches down.

The best one can do is to give the gentian a gritty compost with plenty of leaf mould, a bit of peat and a sunny or only partially shaded position. They should be grown where no root disturbance is likely.

Plants for a Garden Pedestal

Miss L. S. has in her garden an earthenware pot on a pedestal, the pot being 5 ft 9 in in circumference and 3 ft 4 in deep. What do the Team suggest she grow in it?

A pot such as this can be made very attractive, but it must always be borne in mind that it will contain a considerable amount of soil, and in dry weather it may need watering as often as twice a day. For this reason its permanent position should not be too far from a source of water. It is also worth remembering that you should put into this pot a soil which will be moderately retentive of moisture, that is, which will contain a reasonable amount of humus or of peat. Once you have done this, then nearly anything can be grown in it provided the proper precautions are taken.

It is very easy, for example, to start off with all the spring bulbs, then follow these with the summer flowering subjects such as pendulous begonias or fuchsias. Ivy-leaved geraniums could also be used and maybe the more exotic African lily, named agapanthus. A very attractive display can sometimes be made by having a standard fuchsia in the centre which will be there all the year round, surrounded by bedding plants such as petunias and nemesias, or even by some of the new geraniums such as the Red Nittany Lion which comes true from seed.

If something more permanent, but not quite so colourful, is desired, then maybe some of the horizontal varieties of broom or juniper or cotoneaster could be grown, for they would spread down the sides of the pot and might help to hide it if the pot itself was not a thing of beauty.

A further suggestion might be that in areas of the country where the natural soil is chalky, within a pot of this type one could artificially create an acid soil. Here subjects such as azaleas, rhododendrons and ericas could be grown successfully, especially the dwarf types.

Fertilizer for Herbaceous Borders

Mrs A. N., who lives near Birmingham, has a long and wide herbaceous border very full of plants, and she wants to know which is the best fertilizer to use on this?

Herbaceous borders can constitute a problem, for if they are full of plants it is often very difficult to apply any fertilizers or to do any cultivation without actually doing damage. This point becomes especially apparent when it is realized that many herbaceous plants have their roots well towards the surface and such 'surface rooters' can very easily be damaged. The best advice, therefore, that can be given is simply to top-dress with a good sterilized compost or a good leafmould. This, of course, is best only if the plants are already growing well which is an indication of a reasonably fertile soil. In most cases the top-dressing can be left lying on the surface and it will be carried down by worms, but if there are not many worms in the soil, then about the end of March it could be forked in very lightly, care being taken all the time not to damage the roots.

If the plants are not in very good heart and seem to be growing poorly, top-dressing with a compost such as John Innes No. 1, or even No. 2, would be useful, because these manufactured composts contain fertilizers and food materials and, being sterilized, would avoid the problem of adding weed seeds.

A herbaceous border which has been established for a long time tends very often to become the home of perennial weeds and it may in fact be overrun by these pests. If this is the case, it usually pays in the end to remove all the plants and start afresh. This can be done in September; the plants can be dug up and collected; the weeds can then be carefully killed and dug in; the soil then could be enriched with compost, and the whole border replanted.

IX
House Plants

How to Choose House Plants

Mrs E. B. wonders if there is any way of telling by the appearance of a plant – the shape or type of its foliage – whether it will make a good house plant or not?

There are two kinds of plants which will stand the conditions of a house, and the best are those called shade plants, such as ivies, cissus, rhoicissus, philodendrons, and tradescantias. Next to these for suitability are the ones with thick textured leaves, like Ficus elastica, monstera, and peperomia. If two of the best house plants are compared, e.g. tradescantia and aspidistra, it will be seen that they have little in common which is outwardly visible. The fact is they are both tolerant of shade but give little or no outward and visible sign of this. Plants with hairy foliage are usually poor house plants.

It should be stressed that the plants mentioned are only tolerant of house conditions but don't prefer them and it is perhaps true to say that most house plants suffer from too little light and too much water. House plants should never be watered overhead, or excess water allowed to remain at the bottom of the pot. For those that require a moist atmosphere,

227

such as the saintpaulia, fill a saucer or container with shingle or gravel, add water, and then stand the plant pot on top of the gravel.

The Effects of Hard Water

Swindon water is very hard. Does it have a bad effect on house plants if used continuously? If so, what can be done to counteract it? These are questions which worry Mrs P. J. B. of Swindon.

This is not really a serious problem with the normal run of house plants, such as cactus, primulas, rhoicissus, ivies, and the like, but hard water can have a harmful effect on azaleas and some of the ericas which are grown indoors.

Where the water is chlorinated as well as being hard there can be harmful effects on pot plants, and the best way to avoid this is to collect rainwater for use on indoor plants. Another thing which may at first seem queer is plants should be repotted rather more frequently than normal, because in this way you are getting rid of the old sad soil and replacing it with fresh potting material which will help to keep the concentration of lime in the soil always at low levels.

Insecticides for House Plants

Malathion applied to a scented leaved geranium by Miss J. J. made the geranium's leaves shrivel, so she asks for an insecticide for greenfly and white-fly on house plants.

Some insecticides are unsuitable for house plants, for example, malathion should not be used on ferns, petunias, crassulas, and some others, so do read the instructions on the tins or bottles before using. The best method indoors is to use one of the natural insecticides based on pyrethrum, derris, or

228

nicotine which, whilst perhaps not as effective as some modern chemical insecticides, are much safer. Another point in favour of pyrethrum and derris is that they are non-poisonous and can be stored in the home.

Indoor Hyacinth Bulbs

Miss E. H. of Rushden, Northamptonshire, asks, 'When should hyacinths be brought from the dark into the light in order to have them flower for Christmas?'

Prepared hyacinth bulbs should be planted in August in order to have them in flower indoors by Christmas. They should not be brought into the light from their cold, dark rooting position until there is a good show of leaves above the soil, say about 2 in. To have them in full flower for Christmas, bring them into light and warmth about two weeks before Christmas, but it is really no use doing this unless the flower bud is clear of the neck of the bulb.

Sometimes if the flower bud is not elongating as it should, they should be put for a week or so in a warm, dark position.

The secrets of hyacinth growing are good bulbs, early planting, twelve weeks or so of cold and dark, and then warmth and light.

Amaryllis

Mrs M. L. of Ranskill in Nottinghamshire would like advice regarding her amaryllis. It has produced eight flowers but no leaves and she wants to ensure it flowering next year.

It is quite normal for an amaryllis to flower like this: it produces one or more flower spikes on the side of the bulb and these spikes carry perhaps four blooms.

When the plant has finished flowering it shouldn't be

allowed to set seeds, i.e. the flowers and stem should be removed. Then concentrate on feeding and watering to produce the large, strap-like leaves and in July it should be put outside to get thoroughly ripened off in the sunshine. Water should be gradually withheld at this time and the leaves will eventually turn yellow and some will die off. If stood outdoors to ripen as suggested, cover with a frame-light or lie the pot on its side or the rain will keep it moist and it will continue to grow. We seldom get a sufficiently hot summer for them to die off completely and at the onset of cold weather they should be brought under cover.

Even single bulbs will eventually produce offsets and these can either be removed and potted up or allowed to remain on until repotting takes place. Amaryllis bulbs resent disturbance and should only be potted up every third year and, to increase the food supply, 2 in of the soil should be scraped off the top of the pot and replaced with a good mixture such as John Innes No. 3. Do this each year and at the end of three years repot into a slightly larger pot.

To end with, two good points to remember: when dry bulbs are first bought they need an initial heat of 70° F to start them into active growth; and amaryllis come readily from seed and you can produce your own hybrid crosses.

Freesias

From Mrs L. of Four Marks in Hampshire, a question about freesias. She says that freesias in pots always seem to produce plenty of leaves but not many flowers. What treatment would the Team suggest to improve flowering?

Most people tend to give their freesias too much water early on and keep them at too high a temperature; in consequence this combination of high temperature and high humidity does produce too many leaves and few flowers.

They should be kept on the dry side until they come into

bud, then they can be watered more freely.

Freesias can be grown very successfully from seed: sown in, say, mid-March they will flower in September/October. Sow them in a deepish box, say, of up to 7 in deep, plant the seeds 2 in apart and give them a highish temperature to start them off: 65–68° F. Once they have started to grow they should be kept in a cold frame all summer. Keep moist and then bring into a gradual warmth.

Plant bulbs 2 in apart in pots in August/September for winter and spring flowering. Place in cold frame for about a month. Pink Giant, Gold Coast, Orange Favourite and Sapphire White Swan are all beautiful varieties.

Streptocarpus

Miss E. B. of Banwell, Somerset, would like to grow streptocarpus. She has tried but the leaves turned brown and died back from the tips, spoiling the plant's appearance. Could the Team give her some advice on growing them well?

Streptocarpus, sometimes known as the Cape primrose possibly because of its primrose-like leaves, can be grown quite easily from seed and once you have established a stock, special varieties may be propagated from leaves inserted in sandy soil. From seeds sown in January, for example, flowers will be produced in September and the plants can be over-wintered nicely in a temperature of around 50° F. The plants will grow well into October or even November when the water supply should gradually be reduced so that the soil is kept on the dry side during the winter. They can be repotted in early March, using John Innes No. 2 or one of the soilless composts.

The most likely cause of the leaves turning brown is the dryness of the atmosphere – the leaves of the streptocarpus extend anything up to 12 or 15 in and pumping moisture to the ends of the leaves can put severe strain on the plant. Once the damage starts it can soon spread more than halfway down the leaf. In fact they seem to like the sort of atmosphere you find in a bathroom. They will grow quite happily in a north window without ever seeing the sun and, if placed in a room with radiators near the window, they will do better moved away from this area of local dryness.

In a greenhouse they benefit from light shading or the shade given by taller subjects such as palms and grevilleas. They like an occasional feed and spray over with clear water. Like many house plants, streptocarpus derive great benefit from an application of foliar feed now and again.

They are becoming a very popular house plant these days and this popularity dates back to the introduction of a much wider range of colours a few years back. They are now available in various shades of pink, blue, violet and, of course, the white of the older varieties.

Watering Cyclamen

Mr R. W. G. asks, 'What is the correct method of watering a cyclamen plant in the house?'

The correct way to water a cyclamen plant in a house is quite certainly to stand it in water halfway up the pot for about twenty minutes and then to allow the pot to drain completely. This may seem a bit tedious but, in fact, if water stands among the young buds or growths, it very often causes rot and the plant would ultimately die.

In a greenhouse, commercial growers, of course, do not do this. They water from the top simply because any moisture which falls on the corms or on the young leaves and flower buds very quickly dries off in the warm conditions of a heated greenhouse. So if you have a heated greenhouse, you can water in the normal way from the top, but in the home these ideal conditions very rarely apply.

One of the other reasons for cyclamen dying is because they are generally grown in a greenhouse to begin with, and then, having been given as a present at Christmas are transferred to an ordinary house. This change is a very drastic one and, in order to overcome it, cyclamen should always be kept fairly dry and in a cool light place where they will not be frosted.

Growing Aphelandra

Mrs E. W.'s aphelandra plant is three years old and about 23 in high, but most of the growth is now at the top. It is grown in the house and not in greenhouse conditions. Can she take cuttings, and when, and what potting mixture should she use?

Aphelandra is not an easy plant to grow in a house and Mrs W. has done very well to keep this one going for three years. This is a plant which likes fairly high temperatures and it is generally classified as a stove plant. However, many people do grow it in the house and the best way to do this is to keep it in as light a window as possible, in a warm room. It should come into flower in the autumn and once the flowers have died down, the plant should be allowed to dry out, given a reduced supply of water, maybe only once a fortnight and just enough to keep it ticking over. During all this time it should not be allowed to get frosted and, if possible, a night temperature of about 50° F is best.

When the spring comes and the aphelandra begins to throw up new shoots from the base in March or April, these new shoots can be taken as cuttings. They should be about 2 in long and inserted into a nice open mixture of half peat and half sand. The ends of the cuttings should be dipped into water and then into a hormone rooting powder and a small number of cuttings, say half a dozen, should be inserted round the edge of a 4 in pot. It is sometimes a good plan to enclose the pot in a polythene bag and give it the maximum light until rooting has taken place.

The best soil for the parent plant is a mixture of fibrous

loam, leafy soil and peat with a good proportion of sand added. It should not be fine soil but is best if it is rather lumpy as this helps to improve the drainage and soil aeration. Once the cuttings have struck they can be inserted into a pot of this type and grown on. The parent plant can then be cut down to within 3 in of the soil level, and if it is given a light regular feed it should throw out new growths from the base and these will produce once again a nice dwarf plant.

Poinsettias

> Mr B. P. of Alwoodley, Leeds, received a poinsettia plant as a gift. His greenhouse is heated to 45° F. Can the Team give him some advice on how to keep this plant going – watering, feeding, etc.?

Poinsettia is really a hot-house rather than a house subject and to be at its best it requires a temperature of about 55° F. When it is taken into a house, it very often produces an inferior plant, usually as a result of the poor quality of the light. It is possible, however, to grow the hardier varieties of poinsettia as house plants by keeping them in the lightest window in a warm room through the winter.

The best technique is as follows: they should be allowed to flower and then dried off for a few weeks and the leaves and the brightly-coloured bracts will begin to fall. Once they have dried, they should be kept dormant for about a month and then started into life again with gradual watering, when it will be found that the old stem will produce new growths, which can be used as cuttings when they reach 3–4 in long. These cuttings can easily be rooted on a window-sill and they should then be potted singly and placed in a cold frame during the summer. Once the cuttings have taken, the parent plant can be cut hard back and will then throw new growth to produce the coloured bracts later in the year.

This is a plant which benefits from a rich soil and so the

potting compost should contain a considerable amount of both humus and sand and it requires to be fed regularly every three weeks. When the brightly coloured bracts have been produced, that is, when one usually says it is 'flowering', the plant should be fed every two weeks with a good liquid fertilizer.

The Prayer Plant

From Hartley Wintney in Hampshire, Mrs O. writes to tell us that she has what she knows as a 'prayer plant'. It isn't doing so well, and she wonders whether the Team can help. That is if they can identify it from this brief description.

The proper name of this subject is maranta, and it is a native of tropical America with dark green leaves blotched with lighter green and purple underneath. It's an attractive foliage plant, but not particularly suited to the house as it needs fairly high temperatures and a humid atmosphere. It is really a greenhouse plant and should have at least 55° F.

With its liking for warm, humid conditions it does well in a bottle garden as long as it is given plenty of nitrogen to keep the foliage colour and is not allowed to flower. It hasn't a very attractive flower in any case. It will stand a fair amount of shade too, and it's interesting to know how it got this name 'prayer plant'. At night, either under the influence of darkness or lowered temperature, it folds its leaves together and these look like hands in an attitude of prayer.

Marantas grow best in a compost which consists of 5 parts of good 'humusy' loam or leaf mould and 1 part of sand. It is obvious from this mixture that they must like rather damp conditions at the roots, and so one should water them liberally while they are growing, and keep them so far as possible in an atmosphere which is very moist. When growth is finished you should start to withhold water, and let them dry out, not completely, but fairly dry, until the following spring when they can be taken out of their original pots and repotted in a slightly larger container.

Cinerarias

From Mrs E.K. of Port St. Mary in the Isle of Man a request for advice on growing cinerarias from seed. She has had some success, but some of the plants collapse and all are affected by blackfly.

The cineraria which is commonly grown in greenhouses today has its origin in the Canary Islands. The cinerarias we now grow have coloured daisy-like flowers and are sown usually in the summer of one year in order that they may flower in the next. They are very attractive and useful house plants since they do not need much heat, but since every plant has its little peculiarities they do require a great deal of light throughout the winter.

House plants are best grown by sowing the seed in John Innes No. 1 compost at the beginning of June. Seed of cineraria is fairly small and you just dust it lightly over the pans, and stand them in a shaded position in a cool greenhouse. Once the seeds have germinated the seedlings can be pricked off into 3 in pots, and then as they outgrow each pot they can be potted on later into 3, 5, 7 or even 10 in pots. Some of the largest varieties will grow to 3 ft high and 2½ ft across, but most of them are rather smaller than this, being about 18 in high and perhaps 10 in across.

Cinerarias, although attractive, are on the whole rather troublesome plants. They are often referred to as 'lousy' since they seem to attract all manner of insects which live and thrive usually on the under surface of the leaves. The simplest way to deal with this is to water the plants very early in growth with a systemic insecticide, and renew this watering every three to four weeks.

The cause of Mrs K.'s cinerarias collapsing is not easy to diagnose from what she tells us. Very often such plants will collapse if the seed is sown too early, for under these conditions the seed will lie for a long time in the soil before it germinates, subsequent growth will be very slow and the plant will not thicken and toughen up so that it very easily falls prey to fungal diseases. This is especially so in a house for plants are often watered too frequently and kept too hot. They perhaps sit on a sunny window or in a porch where the temperature gets very high during the day, and under these conditions a collar rot caused by one of the many soil fungi may bring about speedy collapse of the plant. This collapse can often be accelerated if the pot is badly drained.

There are one or two insects which attack the roots of cinerarias and these should always be looked for and, at the first sign of the presence of any insects, the soil should be watered with a weak solution of insecticide. This attack is most prevalent in the autumn and especially careful watch should be kept at that time.

Although these diseases and pests are not uncommon, the most frequent cause of cinerarias collapsing is over-watering or bad drainage. Most people will say, 'Well, how can I tell if I am over-watering or whether the drainage is bad?' In the case of cinerarias it is a good maxim to give them a fairly heavy watering and then allow them to dry, even to the point of the leaves wilting before you water again. Only by this technique will you avoid a build up of water in the soil.

The Shrimp Plant

Mrs S. of Greenod, Lancashire, would like to take cuttings from a Shrimp Plant. She tried some last year, but they didn't grow so she'd like the Team's advice to see what she did wrong.

The shrimp plant is Beloperone guttata and takes its name from the pinkish-brown flowers which look very much like shrimps. It is a shrubby plant some 2 or 3 ft high with fairly dense foliage, and these spikes of small flowers which are

237

covered with overlapping brown scales or bracts look like the shrimps. The plant is best grown in a warm greenhouse using a compost made up of three parts loam, one part leaf mould or peat and one part of coarse sand, plus about one oz of bone meal per 5 in pot. Once it starts growing it flowers practically all summer provided the air is kept moist. The ideal temperature for it is about 65° F.

The best growers water it freely during the summer, but during the winter they tend to let it dry out a bit. Under these conditions it tends to become a bit leggy and therefore must be cut back fairly regularly. It is the cuttings that you get following the cutback that can be used in order to propagate the plant. The cuttings are frequently dipped in a hormone rooting compound and then rooted in a double pot: you take a 5 in and a 2½ in pot and you put the smaller inside the larger. The space between the two pots is filled with the compost and the cuttings are then inserted in that compost. Full light and plenty of water will help the cutting to root quickly, but they will not do very well unless they are given considerable heat.

Cuttings are best taken in late spring, even May or June, and at that time of year it is found that they root easily. It has been noted by the most successful growers that when the plant is in flower, it is a good idea to keep it in a much cooler greenhouse for the lower temperature seems to increase the coloration of the shrimps.

Solanum Capsicastrum

Mr A. of Onchan on the Isle of Man can't get his solanum plants to bear berries. They are grown indoors in pots and flower profusely but the stems of the flowers turn yellow and then the flowers drop off.

The Solanum capsicastrum is probably better known as the winter cherry and bears small red berries. There is also a variety that bears yellow berries and one giant berried species. It is a half-hardy shrub and in favourable districts can be grown outside, making a bush of up to 4 ft high and wide.

In less favourable districts they should be grown in pots and brought inside in the winter and if Mr A. keeps his inside all the time, this is probably what has gone wrong. The yellowing of the flowers is a clear sign of imperfect fertilization or non-fertilization and this can often be overcome by spraying the flowers with a tomato setting hormone.

Lack of feeding might also be a contributory cause and the following régime could well be followed to advantage. Sow the seed thinly in a pot or pan of light soil in gentle heat in February or early March and then when about 2 in high pot up into 3 in pots and grow these on briskly near the glass. When the roots touch the side of the pots, pot up into 5 in plant pots using John Innes No. 2 or the same compost as you would use for tomatoes or chrysanthemums.

Harden off the plants and stand them on an ash base or in a cold frame, pot close. This means that as the growths extend, they will intermingle and this will assist in fertilization as the pollen can then easily be transferred. Put outside at the beginning of June and leave them outdoors until the end of August or beginning of September, keeping free from greenfly and watering regularly, including liquid feed with every second watering.

Bilbergia

Mrs R. of Camelford in Cornwall would like advice on the treatment of the pot plant bilbergia. When shoots have once had flowers they don't seem to flower again and, if they are divided, spend a year or two making new shoots before flowering.

Bilbergia, a stemless herbaceous plant originally from South

America, has a narrow grasslike leaf and spikes of colourful bracted flowers in late winter or spring. It is usually grown in a cool greenhouse or as a pot plant and needs a minimum temperature of 60°F. The main problem of growing it in a house is the lack of humidity and probably the best answer to this is to have some moist florist's moss in a container. Stand the pot in this to keep moisture rising through the foliage.

Potting compost should be loam, leaf mould and peat, no manure and, of course, the plant should be in the lightest possible position. One of the easiest varieties to grow is Nutans which has yellow–green flowers and rose pink bracts.

Probably one of the reasons for Mrs R.'s disappointment is that in the early stages they need temperatures of up to 80°F as is the case with many other tropical plants – these are normally grown in this country in a 'stove', i.e. a very hot, damp greenhouse.

Offsets and cuttings and sometimes seeds need this high initial temperature to initiate growth but when the plants become adult they can tolerate much lower temperatures for several months. To get them growing again they need these high temperatures. In fact some of these stove plants need a temperature as high as 85° and 95°F to break their dormancy and get the young growths rooted.

Growing Saintpaulias from Seed

Mrs K. Y. of Bedford would like the Team's comments on growing Saintpaulias from seed as opposed to leaf cuttings. Which would make the best plants in a given time?

It is easier to propagate Saintpaulias from seed but the main drawback is that they are variable in colour and habit and tend to give a preponderance of singles. With leaf cuttings it is nearly certain that the offspring will take after the parent in all ways, so always propagate from your best plants. However, many people enjoy the element of chance in growing from seed and don't mind finishing up with Saintpaulias in many different colours. As far as the time factor is concerned they should flower just as quickly from seed as they do from cuttings.

Two nice varieties are Blue Fairy Tale, and Pink Fairy Tale. To get the seeds away successfully they need a brisk heat, at least 55°F and the plants should be kept in a warm, light position, though direct sunlight is neither necessary nor desirable. A moist atmosphere assists flowering, so always put the pots either on a tray or saucer covered with pebbles or some other material which can be kept moist.

The Saintpaulia comes from East Africa and from a distance looks rather like a violet and in fact it is generally known as the African violet. They have become very popular house plants these days and the hybridists have produced a large number of new varieties including many doubles. These produce few or no seeds so the chances are that when grown from seed the seedlings will be all singles. This means that double varieties have to be propagated vegetatively.

A good compost for the Saintpaulia consists of leaf mould with the addition of some rotted manure and some pieces of charcoal. Organic material should make up three-quarters of the compost but avoid the excessive use of peat and whatever you do keep them in small pots. They shouldn't be repotted unless absolutely necessary and feeding should continue about every ten days while they are growing.

Saintpaulias are liable to rot, especially when the temperature is low, and drops of water on the foliage should be avoided. Don't water with cold water either – leave it standing in the room until it has reached room heat.

Zimmerlinden

Mrs R. W. of Cheam has a plant which she knows only as a zimmerlinden. It is planted in ordinary soil and is constantly losing its leaves. It is also turning rather yellow. Any hints would be welcome before it is too late.

241

This plant is a quick growing, handsome leaved shrub which can grow as large as 15 in high. It also produces white flowers in April/May and is correctly Sparmannia africana or African hemp.

It could be that Mrs W.'s problem is too much water and lack of light. Sparmannia must have plenty of light and it would probably do much better if put out into the garden during the summer months. As a matter of interest this plant is quite easily propagated from cuttings of firm shoots in spring. They will root quite readily with some bottom heat of say 65°F. A good compost is 2 parts loam, 1 part peat and a little sand and when established it should be fed occasionally between April and September.

Although this subject is evergreen, reduce moisture slightly from October until March and during this period the temperature should be lower – 40°–50°F with a higher temperature while it is growing.

A light position and no shading or syringing is required; any pruning that needs to be done should be in November/December.

Cypripedium – Lady's Slipper

Mrs D. of Croydon has a cypripedium kept as a house plant in a cool window. It is potted in John Innes compost with charcoal and small stones; it has good foliage but the flowers are scarce and rather small. Any hints please?

While orchids will keep for quite a long time on a windowsill, they won't grow well in such a position. Cypripedium or lady's slipper is about the easiest of the orchids to grow. We are now assuming that the questioner is talking about the greenhouse variety as the hardy variety will grow well outdoors in many parts of the country. The latter are most attractive, particularly the hybrids which have tessellated and

242

whorled foliage making them very decorative even when they aren't in flower.

Coming back to the indoor varieties: John Innes compost isn't a good medium – a better one would be two parts of rough fibrous peat and one part sphagnum moss and sand. The pots or pans should be well drained for about one third of their depth. Keep in a temperature of 65° to 85°F from March to September and from September to March about 60°F.

It is a good plan to stand pots of orchids on trays filled with aggregate and pebbles. Keep them damp and tuck in some sphagnum moss over the top of the pot to maintain atmospheric moisture around the leaves. They must never be allowed to dry out and, if the atmosphere is at all dry due to central heating, then they should be syringed with clear water at least once a day.

Brunfelsia

Mrs G. of Wisbech says she has heard the Team, particularly Fred Loads, extolling the virtues of a house plant called, she thinks, brunfelsia. It sounds most attractive and could Fred repeat what he said about it?

The brunfelsias are a group of small shrubs which are native to the West Indies and to parts of South America. They have large glossy laurel-like leaves and very large, mostly fragrant, flowers. Brunfelsia calycina are violet or purple and probably the best for the house. Naturally, coming from such warm countries they need reasonably warm conditions and the temperature should not drop during the winter months below 52°F but during the summer they can stand a much higher temperature.

I find that the soilless composts are excellent for these and if John Innes is used then more humus in the form of leaf mould should be given.

It will last for several months in flower and the general

treatment is at the end of our season, say in early October. Gradually reduce the water but do not, of course, allow it to dry out. Do not have it in a room with a high temperature, 50°F is fine, and allow it just to tick over during the winter months. In the spring, water, give a little plant food in solution, spray with a foliar feed, expose it to the brightest light possible and it will soon be smothered with flower buds.

The only complaint I have about mine is that they make so much flower that they make very few new growths from which to propagate, as they can be increased by taking cuttings of young half-ripened growths.

Syringe them, particularly on the undersides of the leaves, at least once a week as, if grown in a dry atmosphere they tend to be attacked by red spider. Generally spraying with a systemic insecticide will take care of these.

They may be obtained as plants or they can be raised from seed.

Treatment of Christmas Cactus

Miss D. P. of Oxford waters her Christmas cactus (Zygocactus truncatus) three times a week in winter and gives it dried blood every fortnight. It is in a centrally heated room on a south facing window-sill. In spite of all this, eight promising blooms fell off. Mrs G. of Bexhill says hers does very well up to flowering time, then all the ends turn yellow and the developing buds drop off. What should they do?

This is not a true cactus and will not stand the extreme drought conditions tolerated by desert cacti. Nevertheless, watering a Christmas cactus three times a week in winter is too much, although the temperature of the room really determines the amount of water needed. In winter this plant needs full light and should be in a south window in a warm room. It mustn't get chilled and needs watering, say about once a week. Feeding should be once every three weeks or so with a complete liquid fertilizer which would contain potash, phosphates, and some nitrogen; dried blood supplies only nitrogen.

The bud drop would probably be due to excessive watering and perhaps too little light and the leaflets turning yellow could indicate the same faults.

After a Christmas cactus has finished flowering it must be kept fairly dry, and when the weather gets warm and sunny, say June for the north and perhaps a bit earlier in the south, it should be stood outside on the window-sill and have a really good baking. Later on, in August, start watering; it does not need repotting every year as it will go on for several years in the same pot providing it was put in decent compost to start with. John Innes No. 1 will do very well. Keep it moist and bring it indoors in early October. It should then be put on a light window-sill with not too much sun and just an occasional feed.

Growing Fuchsia

A listener in an Invalids' Home has to have wide open windows night and day, and wonders whether this is the reason a lovely fuchsia given to her dropped all its buds within a week. She also asks whether used tea leaves are any good for it, and has bone manure any value for pot plants?

The fuchsia which was given to this lady has probably been brought from a greenhouse, and under these conditions it would be growing in an atmosphere which was moist, where the light would certainly be at a maximum, and where conditions would be ideal for the growth of this plant. Bringing it into a hospital, one would naturally find that the air would be dry, the light would possibly be indifferent and, as a consequence, most plants under these circumstances will shed their buds. She can be reassured, however, that if the

245

fuchsia manages to hold its leaves it will slowly become accustomed to these changed conditions, and will produce more buds rather later in the season which will eventually become flowers. This problem of humidity for indoor plants, especially in hospitals and nursing homes, is a very important one, and a simple way to provide the necessary humidity is to place the pot which contains the plant in an attractive container or else in a larger pot. The space between the two pots should then be filled with moist florists' moss or with moist peat or with sphagnum moss. By this means the water vapour from the florists' moss, etc., will evaporate up through the leaves of the plant and help to keep it alive.

Used tea leaves have some virtue in the garden and in pots, but not very much. They tend, if put on the surface of the soil, to become wet and soggy, and so choke up the surface and prevent free air movement. It is very much better indeed to use peat itself or leafmould rather than a material such as tea leaves. Very much the same sort of comment should be made about bone meal. This is one of the best fertilizers for mixing in potting soil but, once again, if it is placed on the top of the soil it will cake, go mildewed and become crusty in a few days and the air movement will be impeded. One further tip on household plants, especially on established pot plants, is to remember that the roots are the parts that have to be fed, that the roots are buried in the soil and not on the surface of the soil, so that any feed which you give the plant should be given in a soluble form, and preferably as a very dilute solution in water, fairly frequently. If solid foods are given to the surface of a plant pot they tend to lie there for a very long time because one never waters sufficiently strongly to wash the food material down. Under these conditions the sheer concentration of food materials on the surface can cause damage as well as encouraging the growth of moss and algae on the soil surface.

Camellia in a Sun-lounge

*Could a camellia be grown in a sun-lounge with
windows facing south and west as a pot plant? If
so, Mrs T. would like some hints on culture, and
the names of some good double varieties.*

Surprisingly enough, camellias are rather tough plants and
they will stand a great deal of mishandling. Certainly a
camellia could be grown in a sun-lounge whose windows face
south and west, but here the greatest danger might be that it
will become too sunny and too hot for the plant, for the
camellia really prefers growing in slight shade. If possible, the
best way to grow this camellia in the house would be to try to
provide some shade and during very sunny weather the plant
should be sprayed each day with water. In the height of
summer, the camellia would certainly be under too stringent
conditions in a sun-lounge and, to overcome this problem,
take the pot outside in the month of May or early June and
plunge it up to the rim in soil in a partially shaded position. It
could stay in this place until the end of September when it
could be brought back into the house and the régime
described above could be continued.

A pot not less than 12 in in diameter would be suitable or,
better still, a wooden tub which would not be so easily
affected by variation in temperature. The compost should
contain quite a lot of humus so that it holds enough moisture,
yet be light and open enough to drain fairly quickly. A good
mixture would be three parts peat, two parts loam, plus a
little coarse sand, bone meal, and an annual top dressing of
good flaky peat.

It is conceivable that after a number of years the camellia
might be too big to move out into the garden and, if possible,
it would be wise to remove part of the flooring in the sun-
lounge, enrich the sub-soil, and to stand the tub on top of this
so that the camellia could root down into the sub-soil.

Good double varieties are Nagasaki, one of the biggest
double flowers, crimson and about 4 in across, Noblissima

(white), Donation (peach pink) and Mathotiana rosea (double rose pink).

Growing Coleus

Can the Team give Mrs J. B. of Walsall any information on coleus? Are they annual or can they last longer, and what is the best way to propagate them?

There are different types of coleus, some grown for their flowers and some for their foliage. The most attractive of the foliage type, a half-hardy perennial, is Coleus blumei which is easily raised by sowing seed in heat in early spring. Plants raised in this manner tend to run into flower which reduces their attraction, and they should be kept deflowered to encourage the production of foliage. The old plants do not over-winter easily, and it is best to treat them as annuals unless a minimum temperature of 60°F can be given.

There are many named varieties of coleus which are propagated only by cuttings, as they do not come true from seed, and some do not produce viable seed at all. This type is the easiest to over-winter and to produce standard plants, and is known as the perennial or tree coleus.

But many gardeners prefer the fun of sowing seed and seeing what colours turn up, and then discarding the less desirable ones at the seedling stage.

Treating Aspidistras

Mrs L. H. tells us, 'I have a variegated aspidistra that belonged to my grandmother and it is at least forty years old. I was offered quite a lot of money for it by an antique dealer (£5 per leaf). Should I take the offer whilst the plant is healthy? Is the plant likely to live for many more years? I wouldn't really like to part with it.'

I think the dealer must have been joking as aspidistras are still fairly common. Keep it in its present 7 in pot, leave it there, pot-bound until it cracks the pot, and then and only then, put it in a slightly larger one. If you over-pot or over-feed the variegated type they will tend to revert to green. One way to maintain the variegations in a highly coloured state is to keep the plant in a strong natural light, because as happens with most variegated plants, the variegation will fade in a dim light. Keep the foliage clean by sponging with a soft damp cloth or sponge, but do not use castor oil. The aspidistra flowers at soil level, bearing purplish, squat, tulip-shaped flowers, which in nature are fertilized by snails.

When the plant is knocked out of the pot the individual leaves will come away with a root system of their own, but if they don't they can be rooted fairly easily in a light, open compost. Take the leaves off at the base, plunge them 2–3 in into the compost and roots will begin to grow and a new shoot appear.

Monstera Deliciosa

Mrs S. of Kirkby Fleetham in North Yorkshire has a flourishing specimen of monstera and would like to know how she can propagate it?

The name aptly describes the plant as it has the appearance of a monster or serpent – it's also known as the Swiss cheese plant. It is a South American aroid with a thick round stem and a creeper rather than a climber. Although very hardy in the house, tolerating indifferent light and quite low temperatures, they make very big plants and could cause problems in the smaller house.

The leaves are characterized by deep serrations and are also perforated with large holes; they are not likely to fruit under house conditions but in their natural habitat produce a delicious fruit with a pineapple flavour – hence deliciosa. The monstera requires a wet soil but it should never dry out completely and a peaty soil such as a soilless proprietary compost which suits begonias will do nicely.

Propagation is by seed or cuttings and curiously enough the top cuttings will root quite easily but the leaf joint cuttings need a very high temperature – somewhere around 75–80°F. Because of this, layered shoots are a better bet and to do this, select a suitable half-ripened stem, scrape the underside with a knife or even a grater and put this into a pot containing a mixture of sand and peat. Stand the pot adjacent to the plant or even on top of the large pot and when you put in the layer, bend it into a U-shape. This will hold it securely in the pot. When the layer is well established, cut it off and you've got another monstera. The bending of the layer into a U-shape stimulates growth cells and encourages quick rooting.

With such a large leaf area, they are sometimes 2 ft across, the foliage can get very dusty in the house and it helps to sponge it periodically. If the plant grows leggy the top can be cut off, in fact with this vigorously growing plant it can be cut back hard whenever occasion demands it.

The monstera has one thing in common with the aspidistra – it will live quite happily in a room with a gas fire.

Thrips in Pot Plants

Mr P. M. of Christchurch in Hampshire has got thrips on his house plants and would like to know where they come from and, more important, how to get rid of them.

These are very small white insects which cause small white dots on the foliage of plants looking rather like some form of fungus disease. They come from small pupae in the soil and are often in the pot in which a plant is bought. Thrips are very, very small and cling to the nooks and crannies of the pot and plant, and are, therefore, difficult to get rid of. The ideal way to completely eliminate them is by fumigation with an insecticidal smoke but this is difficult for many people who haven't the proper equipment. An alternative way if the plant isn't too large is to place the whole thing, pot and plant, in a malathion solution. A word of warning, though, malathion is very poisonous and can be absorbed through the skin, so rubber gloves must be worn and great care taken with the operation.

Although pot plants can be fumigated thoroughly in a greenhouse, it is much more difficult and perhaps impossible in a house and the way to tackle this is to make a cabinet.

A simple way of doing this is to obtain a large box such as a tea-chest and make this smoke or gas proof by papering the inside with ordinary wallpaper.

If it is likely that there are a number of plants to do, a cabinet can be made larger and fitted with shelves which can be taken out so that larger plants can be put in and the shelves put back for smaller plants.

A thick wet sack or even an odd piece of carpet soaked in water will make a gas-tight curtain or door and part of a fumigating pellet may be used, basing the quantity roughly on the cubic capacity of the cabinet which can be obtained by multiplying length by breadth by height.

Plants for a North-east Room

Miss A. B. G. takes delight in watching things grow. Her room in an Invalids' Home faces north-east and she'd like suggestions as to what to grow in the window. So far she has been lucky with winter bulbs but unlucky with seeds and summer bulbs, and mixed dwarf annuals planted in early April soon died off.

It is a matter of choosing subjects which will tolerate the indifferent light of a north-east facing window; bulbs will stand these conditions, and that is why they have been successful, but dwarf annuals will not, as they need good natural light.

Some good foliage plants, very attractive in growth, and tolerant of poor light, include tradescantia, Cissus antarctica, philodendron, and the various ivies in yellows and greens. Busy Lizzie (Impatiens) would flower well in summer and autumn, and winter flowering or Lorraine begonias would do well in winter and early spring.

For something a little out of the ordinary in the way of flowering pot plants, epiphyllum (crab's claw or Christmas cactus) would do quite well in this situation. The larger summer flowering epiphyllums would also thrive under these conditions. And don't forget to get a few dwarf Iris reticulata and plant them in a pot in October. They will flower in January and their perfume is delightful.

Bottle Gardens

Mr K. F. of Luton asks, 'Should a bottle garden be tightly corked after it has been planted and watered?'

Bottle gardens are very useful objects in centrally heated rooms or in hospitals, or even for anyone who is house-bound, for in these little gardens one can watch a whole cycle of plant life being displayed in miniature.

The idea really is that within the bottle you provide a closed environment in which the plant will maintain itself more or less indefinitely. Thus, the moisture which is lost from the leaves into the air simply condenses on the glass of the bottle, runs back into the soil and is re-used. In the same way, the oxygen which the plants need keeps on being re-used and re-used, as also does the carbon dioxide. Provided, therefore, that the soil is clean and the plants are healthy when they are put in, and provided that plenty of natural light is available, these bottle gardens should go on for many years without watering at all.

The reason for Mr F.'s question is probably that he has seen bottle gardens on exhibition stands or in shops in an uncorked condition. This is in order that the plants may be seen easily, because when the bottles are corked the condensation on the glass quite often forms a film which makes observation difficult for a time. However, it will be found that this condensation is not a permanent feature, for a balance is reached in which condensation will occur on the glass in the morning but this will usually have cleared up by midday when the whole of the mini-garden will be visible.

Condensation in smaller sweet jars is not so troublesome as in the large carboys, mainly because the smaller sweet jars provide a large area in which to grow plants and therefore there is less condensation per unit area. It is advisable in these smaller jars to concentrate on dwarf, slow growing subjects and, if possible, to avoid those with conspicuous flowers because the flower parts will tend to decay and look rather unsightly. It is best, therefore, to confine the vegetation in a bottle garden to foliage plants.

Replanting a Cactus Garden

Miss L. K. P. of Charmouth, Dorset, has a small cactus garden which has been in the same 8 in diameter clay saucer for several years and now needs replanting. At what time of the year should this be done, and what kind of compost should be used?

The first point that must be made to Miss P. is that so long as the cactus garden is doing well there is no necessity to replant it. Replanting should be done if there are obvious signs of deterioration in the plants, otherwise it is simply a waste of time.

Assuming, however, that replanting has to be done, the best time in which to do it is in April when the temperature is beginning to warm up. The compost to be used should be gritty, containing about one-third part of fibrous loam, crushed brick rubble, and coarse sand. To many people, ingredients such as crushed brick rubble might be impossible to obtain and, if so, it is possible to buy a cactus compost from most horticultural sundriesmen. These composts are quite complete in themselves and no feeding at all should be done for at least two years, for if the cacti are fed too well they will grow out of character and become softer and more liable to damping off and to diseases. Many good cactus gardens have small granite chippings or pebbles scattered on the surface of the compost in order to imitate the appearance of a miniature desert or mountain scree. This is a very useful addition because it helps to prevent the growth of any algae or mosses on the surface of the compost, but care must be taken that granite chippings are used and not limestone chippings because most cacti do not like limestone.

Growing Dwarf Trees

Mr G.S. would like to grow dwarf trees, and he asks what are the best kinds for this? He has tried oaks and conifers without success.

Growing dwarf trees is definitely a very interesting but long term project. The treatment has been developed from the Japanese Bonsai method which will work with any type of tree but which demands considerable time and patience for success. The best trees to use are undoubtedly evergreens, for the deciduous trees naturally lose their leaves in winter and do not look nearly so attractive as dwarf junipers or cupressi done in this way.

The dwarfing process is brought about really by producing starved trees. To do this, the seed is sown in a pot, the small tree is allowed to develop and every year the tree is taken out from the pot and the roots pruned. This restricts the growth of the tree and in time the top begins to be starved. This top growth of the tree can then be trained, pruned, and tied into various interesting shapes and this process of arranging the top growth is the really skilful part of the business and should be begun usually in the third year. After the third year the little tree can be transplanted into 3–4 in stone or plastic pots, in a compost which is well drained, that is with a fair amount of gravel in the bottom and some sand throughout it, and in which there is no food material whatsoever. The drainage is exceedingly important because these dwarf trees in their starved condition very easily succumb to root rots and damping off unless the drainage is good.

Any kind of tree can be treated in this way and a good book by a Japanese expert would be very helpful in describing the types of tree and the types of shape which have been proved attractive over the years. An easier way, of course, of doing it, is to use some of the dwarf naturally occurring varieties. Species such as Juniperus communis compressa can make a very attractive dwarf tree grown in a pot and they do not require any pruning or root trimming at all. For ordinary household purposes, therefore, I think it is best to stick to dwarf varieties and only if one is interested in the process should one use the naturally occurring large oaks and conifers and try to dwarf them by the Bonsai method.

House Plants Adapting to New Conditions

Mr W. S. of Four Marks in Hampshire used to be a journeyman gardener in his younger days. He says that then plants such as Brunfelsia calycina were grown under stove conditions, i.e. min. 55°F, and woe betide the gardener if it fell below this. Now he grows the same plant in the north-facing window where the temperature often goes down to 40°F and it does well. Was it ever necessary to maintain these high temperatures and have plants adapted themselves to our climatic conditions?

This particular plant is a free flowering evergreen shrub which originally came from South America and is still listed as a warm greenhouse plant, requiring a minimum temperature of 50°F. In fact it will adapt itself to lower temperatures than this.

In the days when fuel was cheap (and labour) a great many plants were grown under stove conditions that didn't really need them: dracaena is another in this category. Nowadays it is impossible for most people to provide these conditions and many plants formerly regarded as stove plants are adapting themselves to a much harder life.

Although the adult plants can and often do adapt themselves, even if they produce satisfactory cuttings and offsets these often require conditions of high humidity and temperature to root satisfactorily and for the young rooted cuttings to grow into decent plants.

The difficulty is very often the time factor; for example, although aphelandras will eventually produce side shoots, they do this so late in the year that there is seldom time enough to root them and get the plants established before the onset of winter.

In heated propagating houses these high temperatures can be produced in the early part of the year. And as people such as Mr S. will appreciate, it would take several heated greenhouses to keep a conservatory, which is cooler, furnished with suitable plants.

Keeping Plants during Holidays

How to keep potted geraniums and ivies alive during a six week holiday period is Mr E. S.'s problem, and he would welcome the Team's advice.

If this is a summer holiday then the easiest and most satisfactory method of keeping the plants happy would be to plunge them in a garden border with enough peat over the top to hide the rim of the pot. An ideal situation would be one where the plants would be in shade for half the day.

This idea of plunging pots is a very good one as there is always a considerable reserve of moisture in the soil and the sides of the pots are protected against the direct rays of the sun which could very easily dry them out.

Where a garden border is not available, then the plants should be placed on the kitchen floor, or in some other cool, light room, preferably with a concrete floor. They should be stood in a washing-up bowl filled with peat that is quite moist, but not soaking wet. In this manner plants may safely be left to their own devices for up to three weeks, but they would demand urgent attention to feeding, watering, and improvement of light immediately on return.

Hanging Baskets

Miss J. C. in the Isle of Man would like some advice on hanging baskets. She has a basket hanging over the front doorway and although it gets little sun, the winds dry it out quickly, and the eaves of the house prevent much rain reaching it. Is there any way of retaining moisture a bit longer after it has had a good soaking?

Never embark on making a hanging basket with the idea that once it is made and in position it will need no further care. However carefully the basket is made up it will always require watering, so when positioning it, do not hang it too high up so that a stepladder is needed to reach it. On the other hand, if it is too low it could easily be a danger to someone walking into it. The ideal way is to have a rope pulley arrangement so that the basket can be lowered when watering is needed.

Use a largish basket and remember that, with the soil in, it will be quite heavy, so make sure that the hook it hangs from is firmly secured. Line the basket with moss and then put a saucer at the bottom or some plastic sheeting to come halfway up the sides of the basket. On top of this, put in the soil and start planting.

Many annuals are not suitable subjects for hanging baskets as they suffer considerably under these conditions, but petunias, dwarf phlox, annual sweet Williams, schizanthus and nasturtiums will be happy.

Better still are subjects like ivy-leaved geraniums, such as Madame Crousse, Galilee or, best of all, Eastbourne Beauty, also pendulous begonias and fuchsias which make a wonderful and even permanent basket if a greenhouse is available in which to over-winter it. Another subject, too infrequently used, is the perennial campanula, Campanula isophylla or Star of Bethlehem, in white or blue, and this again can be a permanent basket going on year after year.

Subjects for Window Boxes

Like many other flat dwellers, Mrs F. M. R. of Oxford is a keen gardener, and would like suggestions for plants in window boxes facing north. Should they be planted in John Innes compost or ordinary soil? Would geraniums be suitable, for example?

One of the problems faced by flat dwellers is that window boxes are often subject to very stong winds, especially if the flats are of the multi-storey variety. In the case of Mrs R. this difficulty is exaggerated because the flat faces north, and in consequence, great care has to be taken over the choice of subjects. This would not be a position for such subjects as petunia or mesembryanthemum or any of the sun-lovers, but plants which might prove fairly hardy would include the ivy-leaved geranium, perhaps the ordinary type of geranium (e.g. Chatsworth or Paul Crampel), phlox, trailing lobelia, and dwarf sweet peas.

Window boxes are easy to obtain and there are some made out of plastic which are practically indestructible. One of the first essentials is to make sure that the box is firmly anchored to the sill on which it will sit. This is often done by putting weights in the bottom of the window box, but this method has the disadvantage that if the box does get dislodged it can do very serious damage in falling from a height. It is probably more satisfactory and safer to ensure that, when the box is watered, the water does not go right through and pour down the front of the building, as this will, in time, cause an unsightly stain. One way of overcoming this is to put a tray underneath the window box or provide it with a shallow false bottom which will catch drips and excess water.

Ordinary garden soil is not a good growing medium to use in window boxes, as it tends to compact and go sour, and John Innes No. 2, which is not too rich, would be better. Another idea would be to use one of the soilless composts now available, which are made up from only peat and sand, and which will 'do' the plants well, providing they are given a liquid feed from time to time. This also has the advantage of being lighter than normal compost, and cleaner to handle.

X
Greenhouses, Cold Frames and Cloches

A Beginner's Greenhouse

From Eastbourne, Mr A. A. asks for the Team's advice on the most suitable size of greenhouse for the weekend gardener, and also what use to make of it.

Really the answer to this question depends on the amount of space and money available. The length should not be less than 8 ft, but perhaps the ideal for the amateur gardener would be 10 ft × 8 ft wide. If the choice had to be made between a smaller heated greenhouse, or a larger one unheated, then the former would be the wisest choice especially if it was of the type that could be extended later by adding a section. With a very small house, difficulties arise as it gets hot quickly, but also cools down quickly, and it is difficult to grow good plants well in such an atmosphere. The bigger the greenhouse, the easier it is to maintain an even growing temperature and atmosphere.

It is usually better not to buy the glass-to-ground type of greenhouse. Firstly it takes more heat, and secondly plants are put in at ground level and run into trouble with dampness and mildews. It is much better to have a brick or stone wall, say, 2

263

ft 6 in high, a central 3 ft path, and a 2 ft 6 in bench on each side. The staging or benches should be arranged so that the pots of boxes stand on gravel, and the space under the staging can be used for forcing chicory, or rhubarb, or for storing dormant plants in winter, such as begonias, gloxinias, and fuchsias. In summer, shade-loving subjects could be housed under the staging.

What to grow depends a lot on to what extent the greenhouse can be heated. If the temperature can be kept to around 45°F during the worst of the weather, then almost anything can be grown. Such plants as geraniums, fuchsias, cinerarias, and calceolarias can be over-wintered, and hydrangeas, cyclamen, azaleas, begonias and gloxinias be grown for the home. Another use is to sow vegetable seeds to produce plants that will crop much earlier than outdoor sown stuff.

A good idea also is to set aside a portion of the greenhouse for growing something of special interest, such as perpetual carnations, cymbidium orchids, or attractive twiners like stephanotis, lapageria or Hoya carnosa.

When starting a greenhouse, it is perhaps best to grow all that you fancy for the first year or two until you can decide what gives you most pleasure, and then specialize.

Fitting Out a Greenhouse

Mr A. T. of Pinner in Middlesex is buying a greenhouse for cultivating flowers. Have the Team any suggestions for extra fittings and equipment which might be advantageous? Electricity is available.

First there's the obvious need – heating. As electricity is available then tubular heating is the obvious choice for the amateur gardener. It is fairly cheap to install as against hot water heating, but the latter, used in conjunction with an immersion heater, is cheaper to run. A thermostat to keep the greenhouse at an even temperature is a very good investment too. For most subjects the heating should be adequate to maintain 45-50°F during the winter months. It should be quite clear that the number of tubular heaters which are required depends on the size of the greenhouse which is going to be heated, and there are lots of fairly complex calculations which take into account the volume of air in the greenhouse, the frequency with which the air is changed, the amount of heat that is lost through the glass, etc., in order, eventually, to reach as many tubular heaters of a given capacity as are required. It would be unwise to attempt to make these calculations yourself. It is far better to get the local Electricity Board to make them for you, for if you supply them with the dimensions of the greenhouse and the temperature you wish to maintain, they will then be able to advise you correctly on what to buy.

If Mr T. wants to grow flowers out of season then he will need additional lighting – mercury vapour lamps are ideal: they are expensive to buy, but cheap to run. One or two of these lamps suspended over the benches will increase the rate of growth and sharpen up the colour of the blooms. To grow things out of season it is necessary to adjust the day length systematically and to do this properly, a time switch is a must.

Another useful, practically essential, piece of greenhouse equipment is an extractor fan. This, used with a thermostat working on a rising temperature, enables a buoyant atmosphere to be maintained throughout the year and, of course, ensures that there's plenty of CO_2 in the air – a most important point.

Coming to what might be called the 'optional extras', these are legion and are a matter of personal preference or depth of pocket. Electrically controlled blinds are available which reduce the sun's glare during the summer months, electric fungicide and insecticide aerosols might even be considered a necessity as these give a pest-free greenhouse. Water equipment, humidifiers – you name it, someone is bound to make it, but the basic essentials for Mr T.'s purposes are proper heating and lighting.

Disinfecting a Greenhouse

Mr D. G., a member of the Civil Service Gardening Club, at Oxford, would like advice on disinfecting his greenhouse after the tomato crop has finished.

Most amateurs grow tomatoes and usually they like to follow the tomatoes with a crop of chrysanthemums. Usually there is an interval of two to three days between the tomatoes being taken out and the chrysanthemums going in, and quite often this is the only opportunity the amateur can get to clean his greenhouse. In such a short period of time it is difficult to do this thoroughly, but as careful a job as possible should be done.

The first step naturally is to get rid of the old tomato plants, including the roots, and burn them, for by doing this one can eliminate pests or diseases which they might harbour. If possible, the soil should than be taken out and stacked outside to be weathered by the frost and the rain. Many growers now use the ring culture method and, if this is the case, the amateur must not only take out the soil in the ring to be weathered, but must also remove a considerable amount of the aggregate because this too can harbour root fragments in which diseases may be preserved. One thing at all costs which should be avoided is leaving soil in the greenhouse during the winter, for there it is dry and protected and there are none of the naturaly chilling effects of frost on the insects and fungi.

Once the dead plants and the soil have been removed from the greenhouse and it is completely empty, it is a good plan to burn inside it a sulphur candle. This is cheap, easy to obtain, and it will help to kill insect eggs which may have been laid in nooks and crannies which you do not easily find. Very often it pays to wash down the woodwork and the glass and to lime wash any brickwork, especially if you remember to add a little sulphur to the lime wash, and this too will have a disinfectant quality.

This disinfecting of the greenhouse is a job which is very often skimped by the ordinary amateur, and it is very well worth while doing a good job of this and actually delaying getting the crops in, for an advantage will certainly be reaped in the long run.

Mildew on Greenhouse Subjects

> *Mr J. H. of Evesham is growing garnet roses in one half of his greenhouse and cymbidium orchids in the other half, with one or two various pot plants. What fumigants can he use to prevent mildew on the roses without adversely affecting the other plants?*

Mr H. raises here one of the problems which worries a large number of amateur growers: in a greenhouse in which you have a number of different subjects, how does one treat individual subjects in such a way that the others will not be harmed? In this case, Mr H. wants to have a fumigant which will prevent mildew on his roses, but at the same time will not adversely affect his cymbidium orchids or the other pot plants which he has. It is very easy to prescribe a spray or a smoke which will be effective against mildew on roses. Most commercial growers use karathane smokes or karathane sprays. This substance is very effective but it has been known to cause damage to a number of different chrysanthemum varieties and it will also affect open flowers of nearly anything and discolour them.

It will be seen, therefore, that the problem is fairly difficult and one can only recommend that a karathane spray be used directed specifically on to the rose trees, but before this is done a little of the spray could be put on to one of the poorest or weakest of the cymbidiums in order to see if there is any detrimental effect. If there is no detrimental effect, Mr H. can go straight ahead and spray the lot.

It must, therefore, be realized that in a mixed house it is impossible to provide conditions which are ideal for all the subjects which might be grown there and, in consequence, not only are pest and disease control rendered more difficult, but so also is the provision of the correct temperature and water régime.

Painting a Greenhouse

If Mr H. W. paints the inside of his greenhouse in June, will it have any adverse effect on his tomatoes?

Most paints carry a turpentine base or some substance related to turpentine, and the fumes from such paints can harm tomatoes in hot weather, especially if the door and ventilator are closed. 'Plastic' or 'rubberized' paints also contain solvents which may be equally harmful to plants. Painting the interior of the greenhouse, therefore, is much more safely carried out in winter. Outside painting should be done in summer for obvious reasons.

In wooden greenhouses white lead paint is best, as not only does it preserve the timber, it also provides considerable reflection of light. In addition, the paint seals up cracks and crevices in the timber, thus providing a clean smooth surface which is easily washed, thereby reducing the amount of pests and diseases. You should make sure that the paint contains no zinc, otherwise, if sulphur is used as a spray or fumigant in the greenhouse, the paint may turn dark grey due to chemical reactions.

Keeping Humidity in Greenhouses

The small greenhouse, 10 ft × 8 ft, owned by Mrs K. S. has good ventilation, with green roller blinds for shading, and also a tank of rainwater inside. It gets very hot though, up to 90°F, there is never any humidity, and the plants get dried up and scorched. The centre path, between the benches, is of concrete. Could this be the cause of the trouble?

Although concrete paths in greenhouses are clean and neat they do tend to absorb water very strongly, and in dry, hot weather can be a contributory factor to drying up the house. It is, therefore, a very good policy to soak the path frequently in the summer and, if the greenhouse must be left untended during the day, to put old sacks or coconut matting on the path and give them a good soaking each morning. This will help to keep the air moist.

The sides of the path and below the benches could be covered with a layer of ashes, and, when soaked, this also will help to ease the problem. Finally, if the plants are on the staging, the pots could be set in a few inches of peat or vermiculite, and if this is kept saturated the plants will, at least, have some damp air moving about them.

It should also be remembered that adequate ventilation will help to keep the house cool, and although it might increase the rate of drying out, more damage can be done by high temperature than by a small degree of drought. Besides, if the soil is well prepared with lots of compost, the surface may get dry but there will be plenty of water deep down to satisfy the needs of the plants.

Loamless Culture

Mr E. R. C., a winner of National Cups for carnations, asks, 'Some gardeners are having success with loamless culture (peat and sand compost) for greenhouse plants. In view of the advantages claimed, would the Team advise the use of this compost?'

Originally composts were mixtures of peat, sand and loam in differing proportions, but two things have acted to make gardeners take a fresh look at compost. Firstly, it has proved very difficult and expensive to obtain a supply of good loam and, secondly, loam is a very variable quantity which could not be standardized.

269

Accordingly a loam-free compost was devised which simply consisted of a mixture of peat and sand.

This is a good medium in which to grow most things; it is not a perfect medium, but it certainly is a lot better than a compost made up with bad soil. Soilless composts have many advantages for they are clean, warm up quickly, and it is easy to add the necessary food materials. On the other hand, with this type of compost, the feeding, i.e. the addition of potash, nitrogen, phosphates and trace elements, is much more critical than with a compost that contains loam, for in the latter there is a reserve of nutrients, trace elements, and bacteria, which acts as a buffer. There is also the question of texture; for instance, carnations should be potted quite firmly, which is difficult with a compost made up of peat and sand.

Care must also be taken to see that the compost does not dry out, as when dry it is extremely difficult to wet without immersion.

On the whole, therefore, the advantage lies with the traditional method if the appropriate materials are available, but if there is a doubt about the quality in the supply of loam, then the loam-free compost should be tried and with attention to the above points excellent results can be obtained.

Orchids in Unheated Greenhouses

Miss P. G. has heard orchids can be grown in an unheated greenhouse. If this is true how should one set about it?

It is not possible to grow orchids satisfactorily in a completely cold greenhouse as even the hardier kinds require a minimum night temperature of 40°F. Possibly some of the cymbidiums, cypripediums, oncidiums, and odontoglossums would survive, but they would certainly need some protection during exceptionally cold weather.

Orchids are fascinating and satisfying subjects to grow, as

they will give beautiful flowers for twenty years or more, and each flower will last anything up to three weeks. Plants are fairly expensive, and it is better to start in a simple way by buying a few plants, say a cypripedium and a cymbidium, which are fairly easy to grow. The soil should contain plenty of fibrous humus and as they are slow growing they should not be fed heavily, and concentrated artificial fertilizers should be avoided. Water should be given quite frequently during the summer months but only moderately during winter. At the base of practically all orchids there is a pseudo-bulb which stores up food, and it is important that this doesn't become shrivelled, and that each year it develops to the size of the previous year's bulb. Most orchids like shade, and it is best to keep them at one end of the greenhouse where a little shading can be put on the outside of the glass or, better still, a blind fitted on the inside which can be lowered and raised as required.

Growing Begonias

Mr S. J. S. would like to know the best method of growing begonias for exhibition.

It is important to obtain a good strain and the best way of doing this is to approach a specialist grower and ask for tubers of exhibition varieties. A cheaper, but maybe slower and less reliable way, is to sow first class seed, as begonias usually come true from seed.

Where tubers are used they should be started off in April at a temperature of around 50°F by pressing them into a box containing a mixture of sand and peat. Under these conditions they will start to grow and when the growths are 1½ to 2 in long they can be repotted into 4 in pots.

In the 4 in pots they prefer a compost which while retentive of moisture will drain easily, and this can be achieved by using John Innes No. 3 with, if possible, a little dry cow manure in the bottom. Later the begonias can be transferred to a 6 in pot, in which they will flower. They can be grown very successfully in the soilless composts, providing they are fed with suitable nutrient solutions.

It is, of course, desirable to have a greenhouse or a glass structure and equally important in bright weather, particularly in July and August, to provide some shading, or the plants may get burned up and lose the colour of their foliage. Any single flowers should be removed. These are distinguishable quite easily by the three cornered seed-box behind the petals. Light but regular doses of a soluble feed should be given from the time the stems are about 6 in high.

Leaf Curl in Cineraria

Mr H. J. E. has cineraria leaves which curl up at the ends, and asks if this is caused by the use of a paraffin heater? The cinerarias were repotted from 5 in to 7 in pots just before flowering at Christmas time.

The use of a paraffin heater is not ideal in a greenhouse in which cinerarias are being grown. These plants like a medium to low temperature and should be brought on slowly. The moist atmosphere and shortage of oxygen resulting from the use of this type of heater could result in the curling of the leaves. Other causes of the leaves curling would include being pot-bound, dry at the roots, or they may have a pest at the roots, or indeed be suffering from earlier aphis attack.

However, the main cause would perhaps appear to be the lateness of the repotting, for cinerarias should be in their final flowering pots certainly by the second or third week in October. Transplanting at Christmas time would result in a check and the breaking of some of the roots at what would be the worst possible time for recovery, and the symptoms described could be caused by this factor alone.

Growing Freesias

A longing to grow freesias has proved to be Mrs C. G.'s problem; so far indoors she has only succeeded in growing long, strap-like leaves and no flowers, and the outdoor ones have been a complete failure.

It is almost an impossibility to grow good freesias in a house, as the temperature, light, and humidity are usually against this. Freesias demand maximum light, they need to be kept cool (the temperature of a living-room may be too high for them), and humidity must be high. One or two flowers might be produced if seeds (not corms) were sown in mid-April, and kept in a cool, light room, such as a bedroom. But much better results would be obtained by keeping the seedlings outdoors till September then moving them into a slightly heated greenhouse. Plant corms in late August for spring blooming.

For outdoor cultivation, buy the special varieties of freesia corms, and plant around 1 June. If a greenhouse or frame is available put them in peat pots on 1 May to start them off, and then plant out on 1 June. Put the freesias in rich soil where they will be in full sun, yet sheltered, and they should flower about the end of August.

Using Frames and Cloches

Miss M. W. of Ipswich – a beginner with garden frames and cloches – asks four questions. Should the soil and manure in the frame be cleared out every year? How soon should the cloches be placed on the ground before sowing? Should an end pane be put at either end to prevent a draught through the length of the cloche? How much earlier can one sow if a cloche is used to warm the soil?

273

To prepare a garden frame, dig out the bottom to a depth of 3 or 4 in and put in a layer of coarse clinker, broken bricks or similar material, with 3 or 4 in of fine ashes on top. This should be rammed hard down and 4 or 5 in of good soil placed on the top of this. An important point is that to prevent waterlogging the level of the soil in the frame should be higher than that of the surrounding soil. The soil should be changed or topped up each year and the drainage base soaked with disinfectant: at the same time whitewash the frame and generally clean it up as for a greenhouse.

It is important that the plants should be quite close to the glass or they may get drawn; and, if possible, slope the frame soil slightly to the south and, for the same reason of collecting the maximum light, the frame itself should look and slope south.

Cloches should be placed on the ground a fortnight or three weeks before sowing in order to warm up the soil, and as a result of this protection, sowings can be made under cloches about three weeks to a month before similar sowings can be made outside.

End panes are useful, as not only do they reduce draughts which cause cloches to lift in high winds, but they prevent birds and even cats from getting underneath the cloches and damaging young growths. Plastic end-panes are now available which do not buckle or break.

Growing Frame Cucumbers

Mrs W. of Northwood, Middlesex, would like advice on growing frame cucumbers in a cold greenhouse with top and side self-opening windows. She has had some success with a plant grown in a 12 in pot but the cucumbers were bitter.

The name 'frame cucumber' is a misnomer to start with! Under this heading one will find listed in catalogues such varieties as Telegraph, a variety which enjoys temperatures up to 90°F. Such varieties need high temperatures and high humidity night and day, which is impossible in an unheated greenhouse. These fluctuations are the cause of bitterness in cucumbers.

The first thing is the choice of suitable varieties – go for one of the new F.1. hybrids such as Nadir or perhaps Baton Vert or the Apple Cucumber. These would all be grown better in a cold frame (however crude) than in an unheated greenhouse and this is because in a cold frame the soil heats up and holds the heat and, as the area is small, the body of air keeps much more even in temperature than it does in the larger volume of the greenhouse. In addition an atmosphere of high humidity can be maintained in a cold frame because the water evaporates from the soil.

The *modus operandi* goes something like this: dig out a hole big enough to take a good bucketful of rotted manure or compost, replace the soil on the top and treat it down so that there is a slight mound. Plant the cucumber on this and when it has made three pairs of leaves, pinch out the growing point. Side shoots will then develop and can be trained outwards; when they reach the side of the frame the growing points should again be pinched out. Embryo cucumbers will form on these side shoots and the side shoots will in turn produce other shoots carrying more cucumbers so that as many as sixty can be taken from one plant.

Feed generously with dried blood or liquid manure and always use aired water, never directly from the tap. During midsummer the glass should be shaded slightly by splashing with whitewash but don't ventilate or humidity will be lost.

XI
Odds and Ends

The Team's Mistakes

Mr M. B. W. of Helsby in Cheshire asks a question that is somewhat off beat but brings out some useful points. He asks, 'Would each of the Team members please state, apart from the fact that they ever took it up at all, what was the biggest mistake he made when he first took up gardening?'

Fred Loads: I never regarded it as a mistake, I've enjoyed every minute of it although I've made mistakes every day of my life. The main thing is to learn by your mistakes and not do it a second time. My worst moment was more than 25 years ago when I moved up from Norfolk to Durham. I was going to show these cautious northerners a thing or two about gardening and during a fine spell in February, I got cracking and sowed the beans, peas, cabbages and radishes. The weather remained fine for a while and everything came up beautifully. Then the winter arrived! It rained, hailed, blew, snowed and froze and by the time the snow had gone several weeks later, so had my peas, beans, cabbages and radishes. I didn't dare tell my boss what had happened and had to replace the seed out of my meagre pay.

Alan Gemmell: I think my biggest mistake was really the same as Fred's, trying to do things too quickly. When I moved to Keele University I made a garden immediately, as I wanted roses, gooseberries, shrubs, etc., straightaway. It wasn't until the rabbits arrived and ate the lot that I realized my very first job should have been to erect a rabbit-proof fence. Ever since then my advice in any situation is to hasten slowly.

Bill Sowerbutts: The question implies that we took up gardening! As far as I am concerned the reverse is the case, gardening took me up. I was born on a nursery. I wasn't very good at school and spent maths lessons cleaning the windows and swept the corridors during English. As a result of this my father decided I was only fit to be a gardener. My biggest mistake has been the growing of crops that I liked but could not sell. An amateur gardener often makes a similar mistake – the growing of plants that he likes, but that his soil and situation don't like.

Easier Gardening for the Retired

Mr L. B. of Heathfield in Sussex is retired and would like some advice on how to cut down the work in his 3½ acre garden?

It is very important for even the most enthusiastic gardener to realize that as he gets older he will be able to do less in the garden, and he must plan ahead for retirement and lay out a garden that can still look attractive with the minimum of work.

Grass is one of the easiest things to look after and the herbaceous border one of the hardest, so – lawns, grassy walks and shrubs should be the things the older gardener goes for. Groups of flowering shrubs are easy to look after. Paraquat or simazine type weedkillers can be used to keep down the weeds until they grow out of the way, and instead of having gravel or crazy paving paths, sow grass paths, which can be kept tidy with a small rotary mower.

In fact, a great deal of the hard work can be done by machines these days, and it's a good idea to mechanize well before retirement, as it becomes harder to learn about machinery the older one gets. If it is financially possible, get a lawn mower with a seat on it.

It also helps if the work can be kept at a height which is easy to manage without a lot of bending and stretching, for instance grow shrubs which stay at about 4 feet high. Give up any thoughts of growing vegetables, use chemical weedkillers and chemical fertilizers as much as possible.

If one can afford it, a greenhouse or garden room with access from the house can provide facilities invaluable to the older gardener. This can extend his or her range of horticultural interests, perhaps allowing some form of specialization.

Gardening Developments

Mr T. S. of Aldershot asks this question. 'We have seen two minor revolutions in gardening since the war, one of them mechanization which took a lot of the backache out of gardening and the other instant gardening, flowers and shrubs in bloom in containers for planting out in any season. Can the Team suggest where the next step forward might be?'

Bill Sowerbutts: I think the next revolution is already taking place and it is in the field of weedkillers. The hormone selective weedkillers were the first and now we have paraquat, a total weedkiller which acts through the foliage, giving a total kill without harming the soil, and simazine which acts through root absorption. These are great steps forward in chemical weed control and I expect to see even more selective, safe weedkillers developed as time goes by.

Alan Gemmell: I have two ideas about what might happen in gardening or horticulture generally. During the last few years great developments have taken place in the plant-breeding sector – so important that they have been christened the Brown Revolution. For instance a new variety of rice has been bred which yields so well that some countries that previously saw famine very often have now become rice exporters. There is no doubt that these improved breeding techniques are going to be applied to many other food crops.

Another development which hinges on the availability of cheap electric power is the technique of heating gardens by the use of underground electric elements, rather like those installed on some football grounds. This could revolutionize gardening in Britain, making it possible to grow things we can't attempt now, minimizing the effects of weather and bad drainage.

Fred Loads: I am looking forward to the time when I can have a completely covered garden with an artificial sun that can be switched on and off as necessary, artificial rain and fertilizer laid on. I would then sit and pull the necessary switches, and this may not be so far away as you might think.

I am also looking forward to the advent of more systemic fungicides, etc., to take some of the work out of gardening, and I have heard of work on a chemical that could give plants immunity to frost. Having lived in the north for a good deal of my life and having no desire to move south this would give me a great deal of pleasure – to be able to grow some of the more tender subjects that I only see when I travel to the south-west.

Developments in Seed Packeting

Mr S. T. H. would like the Team's views on the new development in processing and packeting seeds so that they will remain in perfect condition for a number of years.

Normally seeds die for two reasons: the first one is that they simply get old and the embryo which is contained within the seed begins to decay and this will result in death. The second reason is that the seeds may be slightly damp and in this condition there will be enough moisture to enable moulds to grow which will produce toxic chemicals which will kill the seed, or if the dampness is even slightly greater, the seed can begin to germinate very slightly until it has used up all the moisture in the packet, and then it simply dries out and dies.

The modern technique which has been developed consists really of drying the seeds in a very controlled fashion in warm air so that just enough moisture is left to keep the seeds alive and then to pack these seeds in hermetically sealed packages.

The virtue of this system is that seeds from a vintage crop could be kept for years in a perfectly viable condition, but it must be realized by the amateur that as soon as the package is opened all the advantage of the processing is lost and the seeds must be sown in the usual way. Thus, although the amateur may buy excellent seeds, packed in the most modern manner, he will still have to use them the year he buys them if he opens the package.

Peat Varieties

Mr H. B. of Great Barrow in Cheshire would like to know the difference between moss peat and sedge peat and how to use each to the best advantage.

There are more than 270 different classified forms of peat, but for practical purposes they come under two headings, sedge and moss peat. Sedge is, of course, a collective name for grasses, sedges and broad leaved plants and often sedge peat also contains pieces of trees and shrubs. Moss peat is formed from sphagnum moss only and is yellow in colour.

As far as the garden is concerned a blend of the two is the most useful. Sedge peat alone takes too long to break down, but the long particles of roots, stems, etc., it contains helps drainage if anything, but does break down fairly quickly.

The use of peat by the amateur gardener has increased rapidly in the last few years, and has become looked upon as a cure-all for many soil deficiencies. It has its uses but used too liberally can cause trouble. It may possibly be blamed for the rapid increase of moss in our gardens as it always contains a great amount of moss spores.

Direction of Rows when Planting

Mr W. F. of Whimple in Devon would welcome some advice on the direction of rows of plants to get the best results.

Usually the shape of a garden dictates what direction the rows must run, but if there is enough room to vary this it can make quite a difference to cropping. The ideal is to have your rows of plants so placed that the sun shines along all of them and usually this means running them north to south. Unfortunately, there are usually other considerations. If a garden is on a slope it is desirable to run the rows along it, not up and down. If a garden is very exposed to wind it is better to have the rows so aligned that the prevailing winds will blow up and down the rows rather than sideways to prevent damage to foliage.

Quite frankly, in this country it does not matter a great deal for whichever way the rows are planted one side will be in shade at some time or other and at midday in the summertime the sun is virtually overhead.

Perhaps what is of more importance is to see that tall subjects do not unduly shade those of a shorter stature.

Subjects for an Indifferent Position

Mrs K. M. of Bolton has what must be the gardening problem of the year. Have the Team any suggestions as to what she can grow up the side of a garage – an area that gets no sunshine at any time of the year?

Obviously there aren't many subjects that would thrive or even survive under conditions like this. Polygonum baldschuanicum (Russian vine) is about the only thing that comes readily to mind; firethorn might do and possibly Hydrangea peteolaris. Forsythia suspensa is another possibility and golden ivy would certainly clothe the garage wall making it look more presentable.

If this situation was in an area of high light, the fact that actual sunshine doesn't fall on the wall or plants isn't terribly serious but in Bolton where the light isn't particularly good there aren't many suitable subjects to select from.

To screen a wall it isn't necessary that the subjects should climb up it or be fixed to it, in fact there are many tall-growing shrubs which prefer to have their backs to the wall. In many parts of the country you could add to the list of suitable subjects for a sunless area Garrya eliptica, Jasmine nudiflorum, kerria, symphoricarpus, many of the viburnums, Cornus alba and green hollies but not the golden varieties. A good cheap, rough screen would be Sambucus canadensis which is a golden leaved variety of elder.

Plants for a Hollow Wall

Miss H. L. of Newbury is planning to build a hollow wall about two bricks high on the edge of a lawn. This is for a few rock plants: gentians, pulsatilla, aubrietia, companulas. Can the Team suggest any other suitable plants, and say whether there should be any rubble at the bottom for drainage, and any special mixture to fill it up?

A hollow wall three to four bricks high would be preferable, as two bricks would not be high enough to give a really attractive show of trailing plants. Rubble at the base is not necessary for drainage, providing the soil at the bottom is broken up and not packed solid. It would be important to leave 'weepers' or small gaps in the brickwork to allow excess water to drain away, otherwise the cavity could become waterlogged, and in really hard weather the water could freeze and the walls collapse.

Fill the cavity with not too rich neutral compost, and then plant up with any of the following subjects: miniature bulbs such as species crocus, ranunculus, alliums, freesias, sparaxis, alpine phlox, hepatica, rock gypsophila, gazania, miniature roses, rock pinks, campanulas, soapwort, sedums, or pink arabis. There is really such a wide choice available that it would be wise to study a catalogue of rock garden plants, to decide on colour and form.

In a cavity wall of this type, it is a very wise precaution to add a top-dressing of a neutral compost each year. The reason for this is that the height of the wall increases the drainage and in consequence the soil tends to become exhausted as the water drains through it. The addition of fair quantities of compost helps to hold water and so prevent this exceedingly rapid drainage. Many people might feel that with this quick movement of water there would be a considerable depletion of the food for plants, and this is so. But the sorts of plants one is growing in a cavity wall are all rockery or alpine plants which thrive best and look best when they are growing on poor soils, for then the colours are at their most vivid.

Plants for a Bog Garden

Mrs A. E. wants to convert some low-lying land by a stream into a bog garden. The soil is sandy and the water varies from 4 in to 2 ft deep, flowing fairly swiftly where deepest. Frosts are severe. Can the Team suggest suitable plants?

Where the water is flowing slowly it is easy to establish plants, but in swiftly flowing water the choice is limited. Some suggestions would include water violet, water forget-me-not, water iris, water buttercup, buckbean, and ferns, which could be established at the edge of the water so that growth would tend to spread inwards.

Perhaps the best way to tackle this problem would be to create a by-water where the flow would be much slower, and then in addition to the foregoing subjects various water-lilies could be established.

On the banks martagon lilies, trollius, astilbes, bog arums, mimulus, and primulas would be very attractive.

Plants for a Small Pond

Mr G. H. T. is altering his house, and during the alterations he has taken out a bath. He wants to sink this bath in his garden to grow water plants and would like some guidance on the kinds of plants he might grow.

After the bath has been sunk in the ground the first thing to do is to disguise the edges and this is best done by using turf or stones from which trailing plants can be grown. Then a variety of depths of water should be arranged by putting cement or stones on the bottom of the bath. The thing is to have a shallow and a deep end as this allows a greater range of subjects to be grown.

In a restricted area, such as a bath, it would be better to limit oneself to miniature types, such as pigmy water-lilies. Plants can be used to provide a more natural appearance at the shallow end and here one might use water crowfoot, water forget-me-not, sweet flag, water iris, and reed mace. A useful tip is never to use too much of the same subject, otherwise, in a tiny pool, it looks monotonous.

Protecting a Fish Pond

Mr A. H. B. of Slinfold in Sussex asks whether the Team have any suggestions to prevent herons taking fish from an ornamental pond other than unsightly netting.

Although this is very much a minority problem, the answer has a bearing on a whole range of other problems involving birds, and how to keep them off crops of various kinds. Local authorities would love to know how to keep pigeons and starlings off town buildings and so on. It is really necessary to know something about the habits of particular species to take really effective action.

Generally the questions we get are how to keep birds off newly sown lawns and other crops and the best answer seems to be watch how the birds approach their food. Pigeons glide in to a few feet away and walk the rest, sparrows also alight some distance away and hop in, herons approach their prey in much the same way as pigeons, walking quite a way, and they will all be put off if thin wire or some other fairly strong, difficult to see, obstacle is strung across their glide path. They will hit it once or twice and then go off to more congenial surroundings.

Incidentally, herons will fly or glide in to within a few feet of the pond and then walk towards it, so if a few protective strands of strong black thread are supported on small stakes about 4-6 in from the ground this will frighten the bird.

Of recent years, since seagulls have become more accustomed to people and are aggressively tame, swooping down on to back lawns for food, a net is the only way to protect the fish. These need not be unsightly nowadays as there are fine monofilament and fine plastic mesh nets available.

Plants in Stone Walls

Mr A. F. W. of Wells, Somerset, would like some advice on establishing plants in a stone wall; also some suggestions for suitable subjects.

Whether plants succeed in or on a stone wall depends very much on the construction of the wall. Obviously, if the stones are cemented together then nothing will grow in it but you could grow plants on the top. On the other hand if the wall is made merely of loose stones, laid and fitted into one another, there will be no soil into which the roots can penetrate so the first job is to inject some soil into the spaces or possibly rebuild the wall, using layers of soil as you would cement or mortar.

If this method is followed then there is no limit, apart from size and suitability, to the types of plant you can grow in your wall – it is much more difficult to insert plants into an established wall as many of the young plants will die off before they can become established. Even if seeds are used, try to give them a good start by making a sort of mud ball around them, pushing these into the crevices of the wall, and don't forget that the south side of a stone wall can become very hot and dry and the young plants will need regular watering until they are well rooted.

On a very old wall there are deposits of rotting mortar and moss and you'll find that subjects such as stonecrop, barren ferns, Linaria repens (the creeping toadflax) and even antirrhinums will do well.

Cleaning Moss Covered Flagstones

Mrs M. S. of Norwich asks for advice on the best method of cleaning moss covered paths (paved) which she says can be downright lethal when you're not so young as you used to be.

This isn't quite as simple a problem to overcome as you might think. It is very easy to kill the moss on the path but all the substances used for this would run off on to any flowerbeds or grass alongside, killing off the vegetation. If this is the case probably the best method is to apply a dilute solution of ordinary household bleach (the ammonia based type) with a paint-brush. This dries very quickly, kills the moss and there is no run-off.

In cases where there is no vegetation beside the path you can use an algaecide or tar oil wash as used for spraying fruit trees. If the latter or any other caustic substance is used, care must be taken that it isn't walked into the house as it could damage carpets and furniture.

Mercurized lawn sand such as is used for killing moss on lawns is very effective and won't damage plants either. This is impregnated sand and can be scattered on the path or flag-stones when they are wet or dry and left until the algae die – this also gives a bonus in that it makes the path less slippery with the dying algae.

Going back to the use of tar oil wash – this is a very effective substance for cleaning gravestones and should be used at twice the strength recommended for spraying trees. It is useful too for killing weeds on paths, drives and hard tennis courts.

Propagators

> *Miss M. B. of Huntingdon says that she often hears the Team talking about using a propagating case. She is an enthusiastic but ignorant house plant fanatic and would like to make use of such a contraption. Could the Team tell her something about these and could she make one?*

In gardening parlance, a propagator is a small structure in which growing conditions of humidity, aeration and temperature may be controlled to enable plants to be raised from seeds and cuttings, particularly half-hardy or difficult subjects. There are many ways of achieving this sort of result and a very cheap, effective way is to place a small pot containing compost, seeds or cuttings in a polythene bag, folding over the top and clipping it on a line in a window with an ordinary spring clothes-peg. This gives a very useful sort of micro-climate essential to successful propagation.

Being slightly more ambitious, a simple home-made propagator can be made from a deep box, bisected by a shelf or slotted metal. Heat can be provided in the base by say a flat car oil-heater or by one or two 25 or 40 watt electric light bulbs connected to the mains. If one's knowledge of electrical engineering is slight, seek skilled help with the installation of these. Line the walls of the plant chamber with polystyrene: cheap ceiling tiles of this material are easily available.

Plants to be raised should be placed in containers, such as peat fibre pots, on the metal shelf and covered by a glass or PVC light. Add to this a thermometer and you have a propagator which will suffice for most amateur gardeners. You can, of course, buy them ready-made and they aren't too expensive these days.

Cactus from Seed

Mr E. H. of Ranskill in Nottinghamshire would like to know whether it is worthwhile for the amateur gardener to take seeds of cactus with a view to obtaining a new variety? If so, how should he go about it?

This is a difficult question to answer as it's impossible to tell whether the seeds will be fertile or not. Also there is no guarantee that they will produce a new variety. However, many people like to experiment and if Mr H. wants to have a go then the ideal time to collect seeds is when they are ripe, i.e., as they are ready to fall. Let them stay on the plant as long as possible and if they are to be stored for any length of time they should be kept cold and dry.

Sow the seed in gentle heat in April in a light, sandy open

compost. Some varieties will germinate within a few weeks, others may take months and it would be difficult to differentiate without writing a whole book about it as the cactus family is so large and a great deal depends on variety and growing conditions.

When the seeds have germinated they should be pricked out singly into a box of compost about an inch apart. Although the plants may be very tiny, not more than ⅛ in high, they will have a very good root system so handle them carefully. Eventually pot into 2 in pots and flowers may be expected from some varieties within three years.

Lastly you should remember that if plants are allowed to set seeds and carry them to maturity, it will reduce the chances of the parent plant flowering the next year. This is because it takes a lot out of the plant producing the seeds.

Growing Tobacco

Miss N. M. wants to know if tobacco plants will grow in North Cornwall, and, if so, when is the correct time for planting?

Tobacco plant (Nicotiana tabacum) will grow in almost any part of Britain. It is fairly tender and should be planted late in the year, probably the best time being in the month of May. This usually means that the plants have to be raised in a cold frame or in a greenhouse to be ready for planting out then. Many varieties of tobacco are grown for their lovely flowers and, more especially, for the beautiful perfume which they can emit in the evenings. There are some really lovely new varieties, such as Nicotiana sensation and the Nicotiana daylight hybrids. These open their flowers during the daytime, as distinct from the older varieties, such as Nicotiana affinis which opens its flowers only at night. This night scented variety, naturally not so beautiful as the daylight ones, is worth growing in some part of the garden because of the beautiful perfume which it produces.

If, however, Miss M. wants to grow the tobacco plants for

smoking, then the problem is a very difficult one. It is easy enough to grow the appropriate varieties, such as Nicotiana havana for making cigars, or Nicotiana virginica for making cigarettes or pipe tobacco. These demand a very rich soil in an open situation and given this will grow profusely. The difficulties really begin when one starts trying to produce tobacco leaf which is smokable, because the ripening of the leaf requires long sunny autumns to get into its best condition. Following the autumn the leaves can then be picked and cured. Curing is also a very tricky business, much experience being required if a smokable tobacco is to be produced.

Feeding Rhubarb

Mr G. J. from Swindon wonders what treatment and fertilizer should be used to get a good bed of rhubarb?

At the Government Horticultural Experimental Station at Cawood, Yorkshire, they have over 100 different varieties of rhubarb and through the years experiments have been made to determine the best methods of feeding rhubarb. The findings are that rhubarb does best with very heavy dressings of farmyard manure, forked in lightly, so that the crowns are not damaged, and then later a balanced fertilizer, with the accent on nitrogen, some potash, but less on phosphates. A tomato base fertilizer is suitable as there is not a specific rhubarb fertilizer on the market. Rhubarb cannot go on year after year, as it is mostly expected to, without being fed and, if farmyard manure is not readily available, good compost must be applied to the soil.

What must be remembered also is that rhubarb cannot be forced and then be expected to produce a hardy outdoor crop as well.

When planting new crowns the land should be prepared as well as it would be for potatoes, with manure or compost dug in. The small crowns, or individual buds, should be placed in the form of a triangle about 1 in apart, and will grow together until there is a good crown.

Preserving Bulrushes for Decoration

Mrs M. K. of Stratford-on-Avon would like some hints on drying and preserving bulrushes. She understands they can be varnished but this destroys their natural look. Is there any alternative?

The main factor in preserving any flowers or plants including helichrysum and the other so-called everlasting flowers is timing the picking. In all cases they should be picked just before they ripen and then dried quickly in a sunny greenhouse.

This applies to bulrushes also and a good tip is to spray them with a good quality hair lacquer after they have been properly dried. This prevents the seeds from dropping out of the head, but doesn't give them the artificial look achieved with varnishing.

Dried Flowers for Floral Decoration

Miss D. C. of Grimsby asks for suggestions of flowers, foliage, and berries for drying for floral decoration.

The most widely grown everlasting flowers are rhodanthe, acroclinium and helichrysum, and it is not always appreciated that for them to be at their best when dried they must be cut and dried just before they are in full flower.

There are many varieties of ornamental grasses, and some seedsmen offer packets of seeds of mixed grasses especially for floral decoration. Ornamental gourds are very colourful when dried and varnished, and some of the berried shrubs such as cotoneaster, pernettya, berberis, viburnum, honeysuckle and pyracantha, with their arching sprays of winter berries, are useful. Euonymus is attractive and the autumn colour of azaleas, rhus, cornus, liquid amber, ampelopsis, sorbus, spiraea, maple, and beech will light up any floral display. The most colourful and attractive shrubs to grow for floral decoration are the shrub roses with their brilliantly coloured hips of varying shapes and hues.

It is possible to force many shrubs and trees into flower indoors in the spring. The branches can be pruned off and the bases put in water as soon as buds appear, and when they are brought into a warm and well lit house many shrubs and trees will, in fact, produce their flowers. These flowers may not always be true colours but they are much more attractive in winter than dead or desiccated things. Plants which can be treated in this way are hawthorn, daphne, ribes, forsythia, prunus, magnolia, crab, deutzia, willow, lilac, mock orange and birch. Nowadays, when plastic flowers are so common, it is very refreshing to find floral decorations made from living flowers out of season, and it is for this reason that we recommend that the everlasting type of flower should only be used as a last resort.

What is a Graft Hybrid?

Mr S. M., a trainee nurseryman, asks what is a graft hybrid and how is it brought about? Can the Team please name some which could be grown in a small garden?

There is really no such thing as a graft hybrid; these words are often joined together and misused. There is only one way of producing a true hybrid and that is to pollinate one plant with another. What is wrongly described as a graft hybrid is known technically as a chimaera. This is a plant which is produced by grafting one individual on to another of a different species. Once the two have knitted together and started to grow, then a cut is made at the level of the graft. From this cut a number of new buds will very often arise and we usually find that some of these buds will arise from the stock, which is the bottom half of the graft, some of them arise from the scion, which is the top half of the graft, and others may arise at an intermediate point where the stock and the scion meet. In this case the bud may consist of half of one plant and half of another and quite often may produce leaves, half of which are of one species and half of another.

The original work in this field was done by a German named Winkler in 1907. He normally worked with the ordinary nightshade and a tomato. As a result of his work he produced plants of which half the plant would be nightshade and the other would be tomato. He also produced a type which is called a periclinal chimaera in which the outer layers of the plant were derived from one of the graft partners, let's say the tomato, and the inner layers of the plant were derived from the other graft partner, let's say the nightshade.

This form of chimaera is not very common but there is a well known one which is grown in a number of gardens and which originated from a graft between ordinary hawthorn and the medlar. There is another one which we see quite often which results from the graft between cytisus (the broom) and the ordinary laburnum. This latter one is often called Laburnum adami and is an easy plant to grow.

This is a fascinating type of plant and there are many interesting and important scientific discoveries based on this ability to grow, so to speak, two plants in one.

The Team's Gardens

Mr W. A. of Kingskerswell, Devon, feels the Team has helped millions of listeners to improve their gardens by answering questions on a wide variety of subjects, and wonders how they manage their own gardens?

Fred Loads has about an acre of garden, so designed and planted that it can be left, and his only problem is the greenhouse, and there his grandson does the watering in his absence.

Alan Gemmell has a man who comes in once a week every other week! It is quite a large garden, but he doesn't do a great deal in it, although his wife does. Like Fred Loads's garden, it is designed and planted in such a way that it requires the minimum of labour, with a lot of perennials, shrubs, roses and flowering trees that require infrequent attention. He finds he can keep on top of it with the odd potter around on a summer evening. Part of his garden is a paddock in which spring bulbs and daffodils can grow, and the grass in this is kept relatively short by grazing a few sheep. He has quite a large lawn, but motor mowing, of course, keeps this down and makes it quite easy. His long drive is kept free of weeds by using paraquat and other types of weedkiller.

Bill Sowerbutts has two gardeners – one seventy and one eighty! They don't and can't bend their backs very much and are happy rotary-mowing, and applying chemical weedkillers. Modern techniques are used such as paraquat for controlling weeds around roses, shrubs, hedges and fruit, and for moss or weeds on paths. Grassy walks are created by rotary-mowing between roses, shrubs, and the like.

Gardening is not only for the young and strong. Older and handicapped people can enjoy it too if some thought is given to the design and layout of the garden and the use of modern techniques. Fit the garden to the time and energy available, and be very careful who is the master – you or your garden.

XII
The Scientific Gardener

by Alan Gemmell

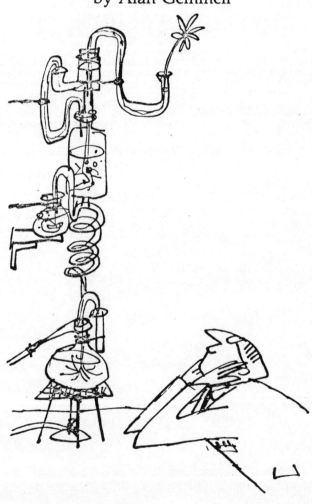

Plants and Iron

Everyone knows that one of the common causes of anaemia in human beings is a shortage of iron. This shortage is reflected in a reduction in the number of red blood corpuscles and the consequent paleness of the affected individual. It is an interesting fact that a shortage of iron also produces paleness in plants. In the plants, of course, this does not mean that there is a shortage of blood corpuscles but that there is a shortage of the green colouring matter, chlorophyll, responsible for the dark green appearance of leaves.

Plants which are short of chlorophyll are usually said to be 'chlorotic', and this shows itself as a pale yellowing of the foliage, a reduction in growth, and very often the premature death of the plant. But the outstanding symptom is the pale colour of the foliage.

The plant gets many food materials from the soil, and among the chemicals which it must have in order to live healthily is an adequate supply of iron. Usually there is no shortage of iron in the soil. But one factor complicates this matter – for not only does the plant require iron in the soil, it also requires that the plant should be able to extract that iron from the soil. In other words, there may be plenty of iron in the soil but if it is unavailable to the plant then the plant will develop the usual symptoms of chlorosis.

The next stage of the problem is to determine why iron may

be unavailable, and the first clue is found in fields which have been very heavily limed, for quite often it is there one finds iron chlorosis developing. In a similar fashion the chlorotic symptoms are evident in plants in soils which are formed from the breakdown of limestone or chalk. There is, therefore, a correlation between lime and iron, and it seems that when there is a lot of lime in the soil then the plant cannot obtain the necessary quantities of iron to maintain healthy and fruitful growth.

The actual chemical details of the interactions which take place between lime and iron in the soil are very complicated but they point to one clear conclusion, namely, that the addition of ordinary iron salts to such soil in fertilizers would be pointless, because it would simply be locked up by the lime in the soil and be unavailable to the plant.

There are two ways out of this difficulty. The first one consists of spraying the leaves of the growing plants with a solution of iron salts. If the leaves are chlorotic the effect of this spray may be visible within forty-eight hours. It is, however, very often impossible to spray iron solution over plants, and then one reverts to the other answer to the problem, namely, to use compounds, technically called chelated compounds, which contain iron tied up in such a way that the lime in the soil cannot fix it but that the plant itself can obtain iron from the chelated compounds. These substances are also called sequestrenes and they are now widely sold for application to plants suffering from an iron deficiency. At present they are rather expensive and, in consequence, people whose plants are showing signs which might indicate chlorosis should not apply chelated compounds to the soil wholesale without running a trial experiment first. The reason is that sometimes the yellowing of plant foliage is not due to a shortage of iron but may be due to bad drainage or to an insufficient supply of nitrogen or to one of many causes, but in limestone soils and in the chalk areas of the country many hitherto unexplained plant deaths might have been avoided had sequestrenes been used early and intelligently.

Plants and Power Stations

A large part of the charm of a garden lies in its gay splashes of colour. The well laid-out garden will take advantage of these contrasting colours and use them to create an overall impression which is both aesthetically pleasing and which helps to set off the house to best advantage. Very few people, however, have considered how these bright, gay flowers originate. It is clear that they do not simply arise through bringing wild plants indoors and domesticating them as one might domesticate a cat or a chicken. It is also equally obvious that they cannot all arise by crossing or hybridizing different strains because in so doing one might create differing shades but it would be rather unlikely that one could get the departures from the normal which some of our modern varieties show.

As every gardener knows, one of the commonest sources of variation is the 'sport'. A sport is simply a plant, or even a branch of a plant, which diverges from the ordinary parental stock. It may have bigger leaves, brighter flowers, double flowers, a different scent, it may vary in one of many different ways, but its essential characteristic is that it does differ from the parent and this difference is inherited. This variation is technically known as a mutation.

At one time mutations, of course, arose as 'acts of God'. They simply appeared in a garden, were propagated, and tended, and in due course were put on the market as a new or an improved variety, but what was not known was the reason for these sports.

In another field of scientific investigation it was found that sports of fruit flies would arise if they were exposed to X-rays. Thus a fruit fly which normally had red eyes might, after exposure to radiation, have offspring with white eyes, or the body instead of being relatively long could become short and dumpy, and these characteristics would be inheritable.

X-radiation is a tricky thing to handle. It is expensive, and to use X-rays for producing mutations in plants would be a very costly business. With the development of atomic energy a large amount of radio-active material has been produced, much of it as a by-product of atomic power stations, and this material is as active as X-rays in producing mutants and sports. So nowadays growers and scientists expose seeds or even cuttings to the action of radiation in the hope that new and better plants will be produced. In many cases the results are worse, and one obtains stunted and deformed plants which die when they are planted out. On the other hand, occasionally a winner appears, and so a new mutant is born which may improve either the yield of our crops or the beauty of our gardens.

A number of people are worried about these mutants as they feel that since they are the product of atomic radiation, the mutant itself might be radio-active and constitute a hazard. You can be very sure that this is not the case. There is no radiation attached to these mutant plants; this has all been dissipated long ago.

Already one or two new varieties have been obtained, and now that radiation is available on a large scale one can hope for more brightly coloured and better plants for the gardens and fields simply as a by-product of atomic energy. It is a pleasing thought that some of these power stations, which many people feel disfigure the landscape, may in a very indirect way end up by beautifying our gardens.

A Revolution in Weedkillers

Just as the discovery of the 2-4 D-type weedkillers revolutionized weed control in the Forties and Fifties, so the discovery of the bipyridylium substances such as paraquat and diquat bids fair to bring about a further revolution.

These compounds act on the green chlorophyll-containing parts of a plant and, it is suggested, produce hydrogen peroxide which results in the rapid death of most plants. They are total killers making no distinction between narrow and broad leaved plants, and are so rapid in their action that a dramatic kill can be seen in a day. It is important to realize that the action on the plant is via the photosynthetic system in the green tissues and is, therefore, limited to those times of day when good light is incident on the leaves. Paraquat and diquat accordingly are best applied in the morning when application will be followed by an extended light period.

This, in itself, is not so very important, for many other substances will kill plants dramatically. The significant thing about the paraquat-type substances is their complete and immediate inactivation on touching the soil, especially in soils which contain some clay. The problem of build-up in the soil is therefore non-existent, as also is the notion that some time must elapse between killing weeds and sowing a subsequent crop.

Paraquat and diquat can be used in a number of ways in the garden: for example, since they affect only the green parts of plants, orchards or even rows of gooseberry bushes can be kept weed-free provided some care is taken when watering or spraying the paraquat. Hand weeding of rose beds and hedge bottoms can also be avoided.

In a somewhat similar way, their use as pre-emergence sprays is already becoming widespread. The technique is simple, for the gardener prepares the ground and plants his crop, say potatoes, in ridges. He then waits, leaving the soil undisturbed, until the potato crop is just emerging (this can be judged by the first potatoes through the soil), and then sprays. All the weeds which germinated and grew between planting and spraying time will be killed, and an almost weed-free potato crop can be obtained.

It is important not to disturb the soil after spraying, for any disturbance will bring fresh weed seeds to the surface which will germinate and so reduce the efficiency of the treatment. Areas of tangled weeds and grass can be cleared easily by spraying and then burning; in fact many garden problems are now much easier to solve.

The revolution, however, is not one of weed control but one of cultivation and tillage operations. For centuries we have believed that digging was necessary to aerate the soil, and to facilitate drainage and bury weeds. Now the weeds can be so readily killed, the question has been asked, 'Is digging (or ploughing) for aeration and draining really necessary?' One cannot be dogmatic on this, for evidence is still coming in, but all the pointers indicate that digging is not nearly so necessary as has been thought. Perfectly good crops of perennial fruits, such as raspberries, have been obtained for five years in succession, during which time there was no cultivation at all, the only treatment the soil received being chemical weeding with paraquat.

Selective Weedkillers in Lawns

Historically, selective weedkillers have been used since 1895 when solutions of copper sulphate were used to destroy charlock in cereal crops. In 1901 Bolley recommended the use of ferrous instead of copper sulphate and this is still a usual component of lawn sands. Latterly, ammonium sulphate has been widely used as a selective weedkiller in lawns, and it was held that the acid condition thereby produced benefited fine grasses and retarded or killed weeds. It has since been shown that the differential killing effect of ammonium sulphate is not due to altered soil acidity but to a direct effect in the plant.

An important advance was the discovery of the 2-4 D group of substances in 1940 which showed a highly selective effect, killing many broad leaved weeds but leaving grasses (and cereals) unharmed. The action of these substances was so striking that the possibility of chemical weed control was immediately apparent.

Despite great success, there are still many problems in selective weeding. For example, not all broad leaved weeds are equally susceptible to these chemicals, and whereas daisies and dandelions are easily dealt with, creeping buttercup, clover, and creeping bugle are very difficult, and even repeated applications may not be completely successful.

There has also been developed a wide range of substances some of which are more effective against certain weeds than others. For example, 2-4 D kills daisies, but for buttercups one requires MCPA and for clover mecaprop. Also there is a real need for a substance which will kill grasses but leave broad leaved plants unaffected, for only then will the selective weeding of borders and vegetable beds become possible.

The use of selective weedkillers has created an interesting biological evolutionary situation which is rapidly assuming practical significance. It is now easy to kill weeds which are very dissimilar from grass, and so a selective advantage is being conferred, not only on the grass, but also on those weeds which are resistant to the weedkillers. As this process of selection continues we ought to see an increase in those weeds which are resistant. This situation has already been reached in cereal crops where the old weeds such as poppies and charlock have almost gone but there has been an increase in the types of grass which mimic cereals in resistance to the standard weedkillers.

Thus, in lawns, as we kill off daisies, dandelions, plantains, etc., we can expect an increase in coarse grasses and in difficult weeds such as creeping buttercup, and it may be that in the end we shall be left with only the coarse grass weeds whose physiology is so similar to that of the lawn grasses that selective killing is virtually impossible.

Windbreaks and Insects

Of recent years considerable research has been done on the efficiency of windbreaks of different heights and construction and the concomitant effects on the distribution of insects. Technically the work is simple but it reveals many interesting facts which deserve discussion.

When a solid obstacle is placed at right-angles to the direction of the wind, there is a build-up of pressure against the object and the air is forced up over the barrier. This, of course, produces an area of decreased pressure on the leeward side of the barrier and consequently a considerable amount of turbulence immediately on the sheltered side of the obstacle.

This can do considerable damage to crops.

If, however, the obstacle is not solid but is permeable, e.g., a lath fence with a 50% air space and 50% wooden strip, then this build-up of pressure and turbulence is much reduced and a more gentle and even flow of air is produced. The height of the barrier may be called '1h' and distances from the barrier may then be measured in terms of 'h', e.g., if the barrier is 4 ft high, then h = 4 ft, and a distance of 20 ft will be expressed as 5h.

Using a lath fence of 48% permeability, there was a reduction of about 50% in wind force at a distance of 4h on the leeward side of the fence and of 30% at 6h. Translated into actual measurements a fence 4 ft high of 3 in laths set 3 in apart would reduce the wind speed by 30% up to 24 ft away from the fence, and a beneficial effect could still be seen at 10h.

In a series of experiments using fences 4 ft high made of different materials and with differing degrees of permeability, the most satisfactory results were obtained with coir netting, followed by horizontal laths, vertical laths, iron sheeting, polythene net, double-run ½ in wire netting and a single-run wire netting.

Where a microclimate is produced, as in these experiments, one can expect a differential distribution of insects dependent, for example, on their size, or their ability to fly in winds of differing strengths. Thus at a 50% permeable barrier there is a noticeable reduction in wind strength immediately on the windward side and, as described above, a 50% reduction at 4h in the lee of the barrier, and in these relatively still areas one finds an increased number of flying insects. This increase is partly brought about by a decrease in the energy of the wind, for a rather similar distribution occurs if small discs of paper are liberated into the wind. But the fact that there are consistent differences in the distribution of different sorts of insects implies that insect behaviour also has a consistent influence. So a benefit to the crop as a result of protection from wind damage could be offset by a greater amount of damage done by insects. In one experiment on lettuce root aphis the infection near (3h) the barrier was approximately 70%, while in the open field it was only 15-20%.

Britain is a windy country, and information of this type can help to reduce damage and to aid in planting and spraying programmes.

Don't Splash it, Soak it

There is no doubt that Britain has an international reputation for being a rainy country. We recognize this by going to Italy or the Mediterranean in order 'to get the sun'. This reputation is only moderately well deserved, but we do get a fair amount of rain spread evenly throughout the year so that one can never count on having a completely dry month or even fortnight. Nevertheless, there is a shortage of water in Britain and this shortage is becoming one of our greatest national problems.

In Spain the rain falls mainly in the plains but in Britain it falls nearly everywhere, and then one of three things happens to it. The water may first of all be soaked up and absorbed by the soil particles and held very strongly indeed. This water is of considerable importance to the soil but of not very much importance to the plant since it cannot tap this source. For this reason if a soil dries out it should not be watered sparingly but very liberally in order that more than absorbed water shall be present and the plant may get some.

Secondly, water may also go into the spaces between soil particles. This water is held in rather the same way as in a nylon shirt, and this 'capillary' water is easily removed by even gentle forces, and is available to plants and constitutes much of their water supply.

The third way in which the water is dissipated in soil is as drainage water. This can be looked on as excess water draining through the soil down to the rivers and eventually out to sea or into reservoirs. Plants can use this water, but it is only temporarily available and cannot be looked on as a constant source of supply.

A good soil therefore should have plenty of spaces between the soil particles sufficiently small to hold the water as if it were in blotting paper, but not too large to let the water run through as it were through a pipe. This is where humus is important, for it can not only absorb water but it can alter the texture of the soil, so that a soil which is rich in humus is almost certainly a soil containing a good supply of water readily available to the plant. A soil that is only humus is not a good soil. It is too wet, and too acid, and if you want a perfect example of one you have just to look at a peat bog or a heather moor. At the opposite extreme is a sandy beach where some plants can grow but it is too dry and difficult for others.

Between these extremes is the ideal soil with a good supply of humus and, at the same time, a considerable quantity of mineral material such as sand. As humus is slowly exhausted from the soil it is advisable to try to replace some each year, and it should be obvious that this is especially important in dry areas of the country or in sandy soils. It is by using humus, compost, or farmyard manure, that one can begin to make the desert blossom like the rose.

Viruses and Virus Diseases

Viruses are probably the most insidious of all the troubles which beset plants. For many years they were recognized only by the symptoms which they produced, but since the discovery of the electron microscope they have been seen and their structure analysed. A virus particle proves to be composed of two parts, namely, a protein and a small amount of the basic 'life-material' Deoxyribonucleic Acid (DNA).

Such a simple structure clearly does not permit of any complex chemical reactions, and it becomes meaningless to talk of viruses feeding or even reproducing. When a virus particle enters a plant cell the virus DNA directs the metabolism of the cell away from the normal metabolism of

310

the plant to the production of virus particles. Thus it is the plant which directly increases the number of virus particles, and it is therefore easy to see that the host plant and the parasitic virus must live very intimately together. The result of virus infection is that the plant becomes unthrifty and may display external symptoms, often as leaf mottles (mosaic) or as leaf roll and yellows.

It is sometimes possible to cure plants of virus attack by a heat treatment which will destroy the virus particle but leave the plant unharmed. The degree of intimacy between plant and virus, however, is so great that there is only a very narrow margin of safety, and too little heat leaves the virus unaffected while too high a temperature will also kill the plant.

Another safer but more difficult technique depends on the fact that the virus particles do not invade the actual growing tip of the plant, and by delicate surgery it is possible to excise the microscopic apex, grow it under sterile aseptic conditions in a culture bottle, and from it rear a healthy virus-free plant which can be multiplied under suitable conditions by cuttings or other forms of vegetative propagation.

In the field viruses are mainly spread by insects feeding on a diseased plant and then carrying the infection to a healthy plant, and in an area where there is abundant insect life the spread of virus can be rapid. This leads to two points, namely, the importance of removing or 'roguing' any infected plant immediately it is spotted, and, secondly, the reduction of the numbers and spread of virus-carrying aphids.

This is one of the values of the new aphicides, such as menazon, which are highly selective in their action. It is also the reason why seed potatoes are grown in the cooler, windier, and wetter parts of Britain. Under these conditions aphids multiply slowly, their movements are very limited, and it is quite possible to rogue infected plants from a field, confident in the knowledge that the virus has been confined to one plant and other plants will remain virus free.

These diseases are especially widespread in plants which are not propagated by seed; and growers of dahlias, strawberries, raspberries, chrysanthemums, and so on should watch their crops carefully, ready to remove any infected plants.

Humus and Compost

Humus is a word which every gardener uses with conviction but little understanding. If one tries to define it a difficulty immediately arises for it is not a single or a simple substance, like table salt. It is a complex of substances, most of them as yet unanalysed; moreover, it does not have the same substances everywhere, for in different soils there are different complexes, all called humus.

The closest we approximate to it is to describe humus as a lignoprotein formed as a result of the decomposition of organic matter by bacterial and fungal action. Note that it is not simply the result of decomposition, but is formed from such products plus certain materials such as lignin which cannot be broken down easily, the residues of bacterial cells, and so on.

Despite its variability humus plays many roles in soil for it holds and releases slowly such plant nutrients as nitrogen, phosphorus, potash, and even CO_2. (There is always more CO_2 near the ground than in the open air, and plants can benefit from this.) Humus also helps to prevent plant food leaching away, and its presence influences the colour, texture, water holding capacity, and aeration of soil.

Although there are artificial substances whose structure and function closely approximate to that of humus in soils, most gardeners try to increase the humus content and therefore the fertility of their soil by making compost. Compost is really waste plant materials whose decay is much accelerated by creating conditions in the compost heap which are conducive to bacterial action. If the details of bacterial action are considered then the factors which must prevail in a compost heap become clear. Bacteria act by multiplying in numbers and using the vegetable material as a source of food. But in vegetable matter there is not sufficient nitrogen to

312

allow the maximum growth in number of bacterial cells, and so there is always a need for an auxiliary source of nitrogen.

For example, dry oak leaves contain 0.47% of available nitrogen, i.e. there are 0.47 lb of available N_2 per 100 lb of oak leaves. In order to break down and utilize this quantity of leaf material, bacteria require 0.98 lb of N_2. Thus for every 100 lb of dry oak leaves, 0.98-0.47 lb of nitrogen must be added, i.e., 0.51 lb of N_2 or 2½ lb of sulphate of ammonia. This nitrogen is usually supplied to wet leaves in a compost heap as calcium cyanamide or ammonium sulphate, at about ½ oz a sq yd of 6-in thick layer, but poultry manure at about 3 oz a sq yd will also add the nitrogen necessary. This additional nitrogen is often sold as a starter or accelerator, and a number of rather esoteric claims are made for specific proprietary substances. In general, however, close examination reveals little if any gain in using these in preference to sulphate of ammonia.

In the early stages of decomposition a plentiful supply of oxygen and of water is essential, and care must be taken to avoid producing a sodden and airless condition. Bacteria are also inhibited by an acid medium and, to avoid this effect, many gardeners sprinkle the heap with lime or super-phosphate at ½ oz a sq yd.

There is no doubt that all materials would compost slowly if simply left alone, but under an intensive cropping system, as in a vegetable garden or allotment, there is considerable gain in being able to supplement the natural soil processes by the regular addition of well composted plant remains.

The Problem of Soil Sickness

Soil 'sickness' is a general term used to cover a variety of different conditions which have some factors in common. These are the growth of the same type of plant continuously for a number of years in the same bed, and a gradual diminution of the vigour and size of the crop. Thus soils can be said to be potato sick, rose sick, flax sick, etc.

At one time it was considered that a lack of nutrients was

313

the prime cause of soil sickness, but many experiments showed that, although feeding improved the crop, normal growth was not maintained and the deterioration continued. In a few cases the crop has been shown to be improved by applications of straw but in many cases which have been carefully analysed the sickness has been associated with a great increase in the number of specific organisms in the soil. Thus potato sick soil has been traced to the potato rool eelworm *Heterodera rostochiensis* and flax sickness to *Fusarium lini*, tomato sickness to species of *Phytophthora*, etc., but in a few cases the situation has proved to be so complex that no simple explanation will suffice.

In all cases, however, a very dramatic improvement can be obtained by partial sterilization of the affected soil. This process can be carried out physically by heat, or chemically by using one of a range of substances. By its very nature, heat sterilization can only be performed with limited areas and volumes of soil; otherwise it becomes too costly for the economic value of the crop. It is clear, therefore, that chemical soil sterilization is the method of choice for gardeners.

Many substances have been used under different descriptions as soil fumigants, soil antiseptics, soil sterilizers, and all have a limited measure of success. Nevertheless, all chemical soil treatments suffer from a number of disadvantages which reduce their efficiency. For example, when liquids such as the coal tar or creosote substances are applied to the soil surface they are absorbed by the top 2 in of soil and very little, if any, penetrates to 6-9 in. But many of the organisms producing soil sickness are at that depth, so the sterilization is very local and, therefore, temporary.

Deeper penetration may be obtained by applying greater quantities of the disinfectant but then one meets the problems of cost and of toxicity to the plants; in fact some of our best soil sterilizants based on the thiocarbamates require a period of about four months before it is safe to plant in treated soil. The question of build-up in the soil must also be guarded against.

314

Heavier-than-air gases such as carbon disulphide have been used with some success, the gas being liberated from granules of material buried and dug into the soil. Injection techniques are possible and are used but they are costly and cumbersome.

Partial sterilization initially reduces the number of soil organisms and may eradicate harmful ones. There follows a period when the number of soil bacteria rises to very great heights. Then, depending on the method of sterilization, there is a gradual return to the original soil population. Simultaneously, there is a considerable increase in the amount of available nitrogen in the soil, and it is good policy to apply potash fertilizers after soil sterilization.